3,000

3,000

Baseball's Elite Clubs for Hits and Strikeouts

Douglas J. Jordan

McFarland & Company, Inc., Publishers
Jefferson, North Carolina

LIBRARY OF CONGRESS CATALOGUING-IN-PUBLICATION DATA

Names: Jordan, Douglas J., 1959– author.
Title: 3,000 : baseball's elite clubs for hits and strikeouts / Douglas J. Jordan.
Other titles: Three thousand
Description: Jefferson, North Carolina : McFarland & Company, Inc. Publishers, 2024. | Includes bibliographical references and index.
Identifiers: LCCN 2024044944 | ISBN 9781476696287 (paperback : acid free paper) ∞
ISBN 9781476654614 (ebook)
Subjects: LCSH: Baseball players—United States—Biography. | Baseball players—United States—Statistics. | Batting (Baseball)—Statistics. | Pitching (Baseball)—Statistics.
Classification: LCC GV865.A1 J669 2024 | DDC 796.357092/273—dc23/eng/20241023
LC record available at https://lccn.loc.gov/2024044944

BRITISH LIBRARY CATALOGUING DATA ARE AVAILABLE

ISBN (print) 978-1-4766-9628-7
ISBN (ebook) 978-1-4766-5461-4

© 2024 Douglas J. Jordan. All rights reserved

No part of this book may be reproduced or transmitted in any form or by any means, electronic or mechanical, including photocopying or recording, or by any information storage and retrieval system, without permission in writing from the publisher.

Front cover images: (clockwise, from top left) Honus Wagner (Cleveland Public Library); Hank Aaron (National Baseball Hall of Fame Library, Cooperstown, New York); Derek Jeter (UC International); Max Scherzer (Jeffrey Hayes); Nolan Ryan (UCLA Library); Walter Johnson (Library of Congress)

Printed in the United States of America

McFarland & Company, Inc., Publishers
Box 611, Jefferson, North Carolina 28640
www.mcfarlandpub.com

For Samwise,
John Carter, and Tommy,
the best furry friends
I've ever had

Acknowledgments

Many thanks to my wife Ann and my friend Dixon Wragg. Their careful proofreading of the manuscript was extremely helpful. It was a big ask. Their comments significantly improved the final product, and I greatly appreciate the effort it took to provide them. Any errors that remain are mine.

I also have to thank my editor at McFarland, Gary Mitchem, for all of his help. He patiently answered all my queries and was instrumental in guiding me through the publication process.

Table of Contents

Acknowledgments vi
Preface 1
Introduction 5

Part I—Analysis of Players with 3,000 Hits 7

1. A First Look at the Hitters 8
2. Awards 13
3. How Frequently Does a Player Reach 3,000 Hits? 18
4. A Closer Look at the Hitters 25
5. Handedness 28
6. Age 31
7. Franchises and Teams 37
8. Type of Hit 49
9. The Pitchers 56
10. The Stadiums 64
11. Birthplaces and Birthdays 75
12. Age and Game Number of 3,000th Hit 85
13. Close, but No Cigar 99
14. Who's Next to 3,000 Hits? 107

Part II—Analysis of Pitchers with 3,000 Strikeouts 115

15. Who Are the Pitchers? 117

Table of Contents

16. How Frequently Does a Player Reach 3,000 Strikeouts?	120
17. Age	153
18. Franchises and Teams	156
19. The 3,000th Strikeout Hitters	163
20. The Stadiums	168
21. Birthdays and Birthplaces	176
22. Age and Game Number at 3,000th Strikeout	183
23. Close, but No Cigar	188
24. Who's Next to 3,000 Strikeouts?	196
Chapter Notes	207
Bibliography	215
Index	217

Preface

I've been a baseball fan since I was young. The game is closely intertwined with the major events of my life. The details are described in my story "The Constants," which appeared in the baseball periodical *Nine: A Journal of Baseball History and Culture* in 2020, so I won't repeat them here. But like many people, I followed the game but didn't really make an effort to study it closely or grasp its history. This hit home for me one day when I realized I didn't have any idea how many doubles constituted an excellent season. I learned that the single-season record for doubles is 67. It was set by Earl Webb in 1931. An examination of the doubles record list showed that any total in the mid to upper 50s is excellent.

This started me on the road to being a serious baseball fan. The first thing that required was no study of data from other sports. If I was going to make an effort to look up, and try to retain, statistics, it would be only baseball-related information (with the exception of Stephen Curry's amazing, and unbreakable, in my opinion, record of 402 three-point field goals in 2015–16; more about unbreakable baseball records later). So I set out to memorize all the World Series matchups, all the men with 500 or more home runs, all the pitchers with 300 wins, and all the men with more than 3,000 hits. I tried to learn all the major single-season and career records.

How did I go about remembering this information? By using the memory palace technique. The technique involves mentally inserting images of the players to be memorized in a familiar location (the house you grew up in, for example). You then mentally walk through the location to recall the players in order. This method works very well to memorize lists. Where did I find time to do this? I'm a runner, and I would bring the data I was working with on runs with me. I would mentally review new information while driving to and from work. And, of course, I have to periodically go over the information or I forget it.

My newfound focus as a serious baseball fan also prompted me to

Preface

act on a longstanding notion that I should join the Society for American Baseball Research (SABR). For a few years after I joined, my primary contact with the organization was the *Baseball Research Journal* (*BRJ*) which comes semi-annually in the spring and the fall. I enjoyed reading the articles and thought it would be very cool to someday get an article in that journal. But I wasn't sure what topic to write about or how to conduct the baseball-oriented research. Watching the World Series in 2013 prompted me to investigate the historic probabilities of teams coming from behind to win the Series (the Red Sox trailed two games to one before winning three straight) and resulted in my first *BRJ* article in 2014.

Over time I became more familiar with SABR research efforts. I found out about two ongoing research programs conducted by SABR: the Biography Project and the Games Project. These two streams of research do exactly what the names imply. Members of SABR write biographies about people in the world of baseball and also write stories about games that are particularly notable. Somewhere along the line I noticed that Jay Buhner did not have a SABR biography. Living in Seattle in the mid–1990s, I watched Buhner, Ken Griffey, Jr., and Randy Johnson lead the Mariners on a stirring pennant chase and memorable victory over the Yankees in the American League Division Series in 1995. With that in mind, I decided to write my first biography about Buhner.

I wrote my first Games Project story about a game I attended in 1993. Hindsight showed that the game had historic significance. When Nolan Ryan came to the Rangers in 1989 I lived in Fort Worth, Texas. Knowing that this legendary pitcher was near the end of his career, I went to see him pitch as often as I could. That resulted in me having the great fortune to watch Ryan collect his 5,000th strikeout during his first year with the Rangers. After I moved to the Northwest in 1991, I continued my personal mission of watching Ryan pitch whenever the Rangers came to Seattle. That's how I came to be at the 1993 game and why I was able to witness the last pitch of Ryan's 27-year career on September 22. A description of that game became my first Games Project article.

That earlier work provided the intellectual foundation for this book. Looking at the Games Project research, I noticed that there is a milestones section and that one of the milestones listed was games in which players collected their 3,000th hit. After reading some of those stories, and knowing how many players were in the group, I realized that about half the 3,000th hit games were missing. The lacunae included not only the game where Willie Mays collected his historic hit but also

Preface

those of the five most recent additions. Given the historical significance of a player collecting 3,000 hits, I was surprised that all the games were not there and thought that was a problem that needed to be remedied. I decided that I would complete the collection and spent about a year writing the stories and shepherding them through the SABR review process.

As part of my research efforts, I read the most recent book about this group of players, *The 3,000 Hit Club: Stories of Baseball's Greatest Hitters*, by Fred McMane and Stuart Shea. Their 2012 book contains short biographies and anecdotes about the men who had reached the 3,000-hit milestone up to that time. The book is interesting and contains a great deal of information about each of the players individually. But my writing of the games stories had shown me that there are often connections between the players with 3,000 hits, and the games in which they had collected their 3,000th hit, that are not obvious. I found these connections interesting and wondered what else might be revealed by further research.

That's the genesis of this book. Rather than looking at the players individually, the focus of the book is an examination of the players as a group and the connections between them. The results of that research are found in Part I of the book.

The investigation into players with 3,000 hits naturally led me to wonder about pitchers with 3,000 strikeouts. Are there more pitchers with 3,000 strikeouts than players with 3,000 hits? Are there similar connections between the pitchers as a group as there are between the hitters as a group? Answering these questions led to a similar examination of pitchers with 3,000 strikeouts as was conducted for players with 3,000 hits. The results for the pitchers are found in Part II. I hope you find the information in the book as interesting as I do.

Introduction

Our lives are filled with numbers. Every day we deal with phone numbers, addresses, costs, stock prices, temperatures, days of the month, years, and numerous other numerical data points. But all numbers are not created equal. Some are much more important to us than others. Turning 30 or 50 has much more psychological impact than turning 29 or 49. Something that costs $9.99 seems less expensive to us than something that costs $10.00. One million dollars is thought to be a lot of money by most people. The tendency to put more psychological weight on a round number is formally referred to as round number bias.

Baseball is also number-centric. The very fabric of the game is described numerically. Hits are singles, doubles, or triples. An umpire keeps the count of balls and strikes. With three strikes a batter is out, and three outs end the inning. We keep track of the number of hits, home runs, RBIs, walks, etc., that each batter achieves during a season and a career. We know how many wins, losses, strikeouts, and walks a pitcher earns seasonally and career-wise. These types of statistics are referred to as counting statistics. In addition, there are numbers that are calculated based on the underlying data. These are referred to as rate statistics. The simplest of these is batting average (hits per at-bat). On-base percentage, slugging percentage, and wins above replacement are more complicated examples of rate statistics.

Round number bias is prevalent in baseball too. Well-recognized seasonal marks for hitters include 200 hits, 100 RBIs, 100 runs scored, and 50 home runs. A .300 batting average is highly coveted. Pitching standards have changed dramatically over time, but 20 wins, 200 strikeouts, and 200 innings pitched are excellent season totals for pitchers in today's game. Many career standards are also associated with round numbers. Sluggers who clobber 500 homers in a career are highly respected. Scoring 2,000 runs or hitting 2,000 RBIs marks an excellent career. On the mound, 300 career wins for pitcher is almost a

Introduction

guaranteed ticket to Cooperstown. And although it's not as well known, 300 saves mark a great career for a reliever.

Another significant round number is 3,000. Let's think about what it takes to get there. The math is simple. Twenty times 150 is 3,000. So is 200 times 15. In baseball terms, this arithmetic means a player must average 150 events per year for 20 years, or he must have 200 events per year for 15 years. More specifically, a pitcher must average 200 strikeouts a year for 15 years to reach 3,000 strikeouts. A hitter must average 150 hits a year for 20 years to accumulate 3,000 hits. Each aspect of this equation is difficult to achieve. Most players don't reach 15 years in their careers, let alone 20 years. And although it's not unusual for a player to get 150 hits in a single season, to do it for 20 years is much more difficult.

This makes the achievement of 3,000 hits worthy of celebration. That's part of the point of this book: to celebrate the men who have achieved such a noteworthy milestone. The media does this today. Players who reach 3,000 hits are national news. But with that news usually comes a simple statement along the lines of "He was the XXth player to reach 3,000 hits." For example, Tyler Kepner's *New York Times* story on April 23, 2022, about Miguel Cabrera's 3,000th hit carried the headline "A 'Catalyst' from the Start, Miguel Cabrera Reaches 3,000 Hits." In addition to an interview with Cabrera's first major league manager, Jack McKeon, Kepner noted, "On Saturday, with a single against the Colorado Rockies at Comerica Park, he became the 33rd player in major league history with 3,000."

These unadorned facts are necessary, but not sufficient. In addition to celebrating those men who had the skill and endurance to reach the milestone—whether 3,000 hits or 3,000 strikeouts—we shall explore the connections between these players and other aspects of their achievements that are noteworthy. The goal is to better understand this group of men and to increase our awareness of how truly difficult it is to be a member of this club. With that awareness will come a deeper appreciation of the men who have achieved the feat.

Finally, there are a lot of baseball-related statistics included in the analysis that follows. There is information about individual players, teams, seasons, records, and other assorted baseball-related statistics throughout the book. The primary source for most of that data was the Baseball-Reference.com website. Notes are used to indicate when data and / or information was obtained from other sources.

PART I
Analysis of Players with 3,000 Hits

1

A First Look at the Hitters

Exploring the connections between these players means examining topics such as the age of the players when they struck their 3,000th hit, the franchises that have (and have not) celebrated a 3,000th hit, and the pitchers who surrendered the hits. These and other topics related to the group of 3,000-hit players will be examined in detail. But we have to begin the investigation somewhere. Therefore, a simple list of the 33 players and the dates they achieved their 3,000th hits (including their major awards) will be the starting point. This list, provided by the National Baseball Hall of Fame and Museum in Cooperstown, New York, is shown in Table 1. The Awards data is not from the Hall of Fame list.

Table 1:
Players with 3,000 Hits in Chronological Order

	Player	Date of 3,000th Hit	Awards			
			ROY	MVP	AS	No GG*
1.	Cap Anson	Unknown				No GG
2.	Honus Wagner	June 9, 1914				No GG
3.	Nap Lajoie	September 27, 1914 (first game)				No GG
4.	Ty Cobb	August 19, 1921 (second game)		MVP		No GG
5.	Tris Speaker	May 17, 1925		MVP		No GG
6.	Eddie Collins	June 3, 1925		MVP		No GG
7.	Paul Waner	June 19, 1942		MVP	4x AS	No GG

1. A First Look at the Hitters

	Player	Date of 3,000th Hit	Awards			
			ROY	MVP	AS	No GG*
8.	Stan Musial	May 13, 1958		3x MVP	24x AS	No GG
9.	Hank Aaron	May 17, 1970 (second game)		MVP	25x AS	
10.	Willie Mays	July 18, 1970	ROY	2x MVP	24x AS	
11.	Roberto Clemente	September 30, 1972		MVP	15x AS	
12.	Al Kaline	September 24, 1974			18x AS	
13.	Pete Rose	May 5, 1978	ROY	MVP	17x AS	
14.	Lou Brock	August 13, 1979			6x AS	No GG
15.	Carl Yastrzemski	September 12, 1979		MVP	18x AS	
16.	Rod Carew	August 4, 1985	ROY	MVP	18x AS	No GG
17.	Robin Yount	September 9, 1992		2x MVP	3x AS	
18.	George Brett	September 30, 1992		MVP	13x AS	
19.	Dave Winfield	September 16, 1993			12x AS	
20.	Eddie Murray	June 30, 1995	ROY		8x AS	
21.	Paul Molitor	September 16, 1996			7x AS	No GG
22.	Tony Gwynn	August 6, 1999			15x AS	
23.	Wade Boggs	August 7, 1999			12x AS	
24.	Cal Ripken, Jr.	April 15, 2000	ROY	2x MVP	19x AS	
25.	Rickey Henderson	October 7, 2001		MVP	10x AS	
26.	Rafael Palmeiro	July 15, 2005			4x AS	
27.	Craig Biggio	June 28, 2007			7x AS	
28.	Derek Jeter	July 9, 2011	ROY		14x AS	
29.	Álex Rodríguez	June 19, 2015		3x MVP	14x AS	
30.	Ichiro Suzuki	August 7, 2016	ROY	MVP	10x AS	
31.	Adrián Beltré	July 30, 2017			4x AS	

Part I—Analysis of Players with 3,000 Hits

	Player	Date of 3,000th Hit	ROY	MVP	AS	No GG*
32.	Albert Pujols	May 4, 2018	ROY	3x MVP	11x AS	
33.	Miguel Cabrera	April 23, 2022 (first game)		2x MVP	12x AS	No GG

*Player did NOT win a Gold Glove Award. An empty space means the player won at least one Gold Glove Award.

Since most of the data in Table 1 came from the Hall of Fame, it's reasonable to start this investigation by asking if collecting 3,000 career hits is an automatic ticket to Cooperstown. Hall of Famer Joe Torre, who managed the Yankees from 1996 to 2007, and finished his major league career with 2,342 hits, thinks it is. He argued, "When you get your 3,000th hit, by the time you get back to your locker, they should already have your ticket for the Hall of Fame waiting for you."[1] But what does the actual history say?

Thirty of the players in Table 1 are Hall of Fame eligible as of this writing. All but three of them are enshrined in the Hall of Fame. The three who aren't are Pete Rose, Rafael Palmeiro, and Álex Rodríguez. Rose admitted he gambled on baseball, and Palmeiro and Rodríguez have been associated with performance-enhancing drugs. This is not the appropriate venue for a detailed discussion of the Hall of Fame case for or against these three players, other than to note that without the outside issues, all three players would almost certainly be in the Hall of Fame. The three players in Table 1 not eligible for Cooperstown as of this writing, because they haven't been retired for five years—Ichiro Suzuki, Albert Pujols, and Miguel Cabrera—are virtual locks to be voted into Cooperstown. So the answer to the initial question is yes, 3,000 hits will get a player into Cooperstown, unless the player engaged in an off-the-field activity so egregious that Hall of Fame voters won't overlook it in spite of the player's great career numbers.

There is a lot we can learn just from the information in Table 1, but we should start with the obvious question from the top of the list. Why is the date of Cap Anson's 3,000th hit listed as unknown? Anson was one of the stars of the early years of professional baseball. His 27-year career (which is tied with Nolan Ryan for the longest ever) started in 1871 in the National Association. That introduces the first problem with Anson's hit totals: experts disagree about whether or not the

1. A First Look at the Hitters

National Association was a major league. This makes the 423 hits Anson collected in that league between 1871 and 1875 a source of controversy.[2]

Rule changes are another source of confusion. The National League had a rule in 1887 that bases on balls would count as a hit. Anson had 60 walks that year. Some sources count those walks as hits since that was the rule at the time; others do not. There is also some evidence that Anson's stature in the game may have caused his hit totals to be inflated. Finally, it doesn't help that nobody at the time, inside or outside of baseball, cared about him reaching the 3,000-hit milestone. The end result is that Anson's career-hit total and the date of his 3,000th hit are both uncertain. This is why the date of his 3,000th hit is listed as unknown. It's also the reason that Anson is not included in most of the statistical analyses that follow. Anson's absence explains why many of the results are based on 32, rather than 33, men with 3,000 hits.

Baseball card portrait of Cap Anson in 1887. Anson was the first ballplayer to collect 3,000 hits but the exact date of his 3,000th hit is unknown (Library of Congress).

It would make sense to move down the list and discuss each of the

Part I—Analysis of Players with 3,000 Hits

players in turn. That's what Fred McMane and Stuart Shea did in their 2012 book, *The 3,000 Hit Club: Stories of Baseball's Greatest Hitters*. They listed the players in order of total career hits rather than chronological order, but the idea is the same. The procedure they used was to relate an anecdote about the player, and follow that with a short biography. That procedure will not be repeated here since they've already done it. Instead, we're going to look at these players as a group to learn what we can about them. Interesting and pertinent biographical details about various players will be mentioned and discussed as appropriate, but this investigation will not provide complete biographical information about the players.

2

AWARDS

In addition to the date of each player's 3,000th hit, Table 1 also contains some of the awards the players won during their careers. Not surprisingly, this group of outstanding players won a lot of awards. The four awards that will be discussed are Rookie of the Year (ROY), Most Valuable Player (MVP), All-Star selections, and Gold Glove (GG) Awards. We will not be discussing each award for each player. Rather, the discussion will focus on a sub-group of these players who won, or did not win, each award.

The first question is why didn't any player from Anson to Aaron win a ROY Award? That seems surprising. But the answer is simple. The first ROY Award wasn't given until 1947, so any player who debuted before then could not have won the award. Jackie Robinson won the inaugural award in 1947. Al Dark won in 1948, and starting in 1949 there was one award for each league. Eight of the 25 players with 3,000 hits who debuted after 1947 have won a ROY Award. That's roughly one-third of the eligible players, which means that about two-thirds of the eligible players in Table 1 didn't win a ROY Award. To put it another way, you don't necessarily need to have an outstanding rookie campaign to have an outstanding career.

Two of the eight ROY campaigns stand out. Ichiro Suzuki batted .350 with 242 hits and 56 stolen bases during his rookie year in 2001. All three of those numbers led the league and the 242 hits is the 10th highest season total ever. Ichiro also won the American League MVP Award in 2001. The only other player to win these two awards in the same year was Fred Lynn in 1975. It was an outstanding season, but Suzuki wasn't a typical rookie in 2001. He was a superstar in Japan with nine years of professional baseball experience before he made his MLB debut. That may explain how he was able to put together such a great rookie season, but it doesn't make it any less impressive.

Part I—Analysis of Players with 3,000 Hits

Albert Pujols wasn't drafted by St. Louis until the 13th round of the 1999 draft. He played in the Cardinals' minor-league system in 2000 and made his big-league debut in 2001. And like Suzuki, he made an impressive entrance. Pujols collected 194 hits, pounded 37 home runs, scored 112 runs, and drove in 130 runs in his rookie year. His 130 RBIs are a National League rookie record and were the most by a rookie since Walt Dropo had 144 in 1950. Pujols wasn't a flash in the pan. His first decade is arguably the best 10-year period at the start of a career in major league history. He won three MVP Awards and came in second in four other years. He collected 1,900 hits and hit 408 home runs. A start like that helps to explain how he became fourth all-time in home runs (703) and 10th all-time (3,384) in hits.

The Baseball Writers' Association of America began voting for an MVP in each league in 1931. The history of the award before that time is complicated, but Baseball-Reference.com recognizes MVP Awards back to 1911, when Ty Cobb and Frank Schulte won the award. That's why Cobb is the first MVP Award winner in Table 1. It means that 30 of the 33 players with 3,000 career hits could possibly have won an MVP Award over the course of their careers. Table 1 shows that 11 of those 30 players, roughly one-third of them, never won the award. But that's not to say those 11 players never had an MVP-worthy season. A couple of examples will suffice to make the point.

Al Kaline is the first player in the group who could have won the award but didn't. That bare fact hides a lot of nuance concerning Kaline and the MVP Award. He came in second in the MVP voting twice, in 1955 and 1963, losing out to Yogi Berra the first time, and Elston Howard the second. Both of those men played for the marquee Yankees in the center of the baseball universe at the time, New York. Kaline toiled in the relative backwater of Detroit, which likely cost him votes.

It's slightly disingenuous to apply modern sabermetric statistics after the fact to assess past decisions. But doing so in this case will show how easily Kaline could have won an MVP Award. In 1955, Kaline had a Wins Above Replacement (WAR) figure of 8.2, compared to 4.5 for Berra. The WAR figures were closer in 1963 (5.4 for Kaline versus 5.2 for Howard) but in both cases Kaline's WAR was higher than that of the man who won the award. Those two seasons were clearly MVP worthy even if Kaline didn't win the award.

Table 1 also shows that Derek Jeter never won an MVP Award. This is surprising, given that he played in New York and was the face of a Yankee dynasty. But his story is similar to Kaline's. In 2006, he batted

2. Awards

.343 with 214 hits and 118 runs scored, but came in second to Justin Morneau in the MVP Award voting. Why did that happen? It's likely because Morneau had 34 home runs, compared to the 14 long balls that Jeter hit. But like Kaline, Jeter had a higher WAR figure for the season than Morneau (5.6 for Jeter versus 4.3 for Morneau). Jeter is another case where a player in Table 1 could have won an MVP Award but didn't.

What about the two-thirds of the players in Table 1 who did win an MVP Award? By definition, an MVP season is one of the greatest seasons ever, but are there any MVP campaigns in the table that really stand out? Yes, there are, but let's first talk in general about one of the players who took home two MVP Awards during his career, Willie Mays. Who is the only player with at least 3,000 hits, 300 home runs, 300 stolen bases, and a .300 career-batting average? Willie Mays. Who was the first player to record a season with at least 50 home runs and 20 stolen bases? The answer, Mays in 1955. The feat has been repeated just three times since then. Who is one of only four players with at least 20 doubles, triples, home runs, and stolen bases in the same season? The answer, Mays in 1957. There are more of these types of statistics for Mays. He produced this offense while also being one of the best center fielders of all time. The rare combination of stellar offense and defense is why he's recognized as one of the greatest players ever.[1]

Mays won his first MVP Award in 1954 and his second in 1965. During the 10 seasons between the two awards, he finished below sixth in the MVP voting just once, and had two second place finishes. His 1965 season was arguably the best of Mays' career and is one of the outstanding MVP seasons in Table 1. Mays batted .317 with 177 hits, 118 runs scored, and 112 RBIs. He led the league in home runs (52, his career high), on-base percentage (.398), and slugging percentage (.645). Will Leitch ranks that season as the sixth-best MVP season in history.[2]

Two years later, Carl Yastrzemski put together one of the greatest seasons any player has ever had. Yastrzemski's 1967 season was remarkable. He led the league in almost every offensive category. The short list of what Yaz didn't lead the league in that year makes the point more dramatically than the long list of what he did lead in. He did not lead in doubles (he was three off the pace with 31), triples, stolen bases, or bases on balls. He led in every other category, winning the triple crown with 44 home runs, 121 RBIs, and a .326 batting average. This tremendous season resulted in a unanimous MVP vote and a 12.4 WAR. How good is that? It's the highest WAR figure for any MVP season, including ones that aren't in Table 1. In fact, just one player in history had better

Part I—Analysis of Players with 3,000 Hits

seasons in terms of WAR than Yaz in 1967. That would be Babe Ruth in 1921, '23, and '27. Yaz's season is even more impressive considering it took place at the height of pitcher domination during the late 1960s.

How is it possible that Honus Wagner and Ty Cobb were never selected to an All-Star Game? That's because they, like every player before Paul Waner in Table 1, finished their careers before the first All-Star Game was played at Comiskey Park in Chicago in 1933. Given the stature of the players in Table 1, it's not terribly surprising that all of the other players in the table played in at least three All-Star Games.

Stan Musial (22-year career), Hank Aaron (23-year career), and Willie Mays (23-year career) lead with 24, 25, and 24 All-Star Game appearances, respectively. But the numbers in the previous sentence don't make sense. As great as these three players were, how could they have more All-Star appearances than years in their careers? To those of us who started paying attention to baseball after the early 1960s (which is most fans today), the answer is surprising. Baseball actually played two All-Star Games each season in the four years from 1959 to 1962. Musial, Aaron, and Mays played in both games all four years, and hence were able to play in more All-Star Games than years in their careers. The reason that two games were played during those years is money. Part of the funding for the players' pension plan came from the annual All-Star Game, and having two games instead of one would raise more money for the plan. Andrew Harner does a nice job telling the complete story at HowTheyPlay.com.[3]

The Gold Glove Awards began in 1957. As with the other awards, that explains why no player before Henry Aaron in Table 1 won a Gold Glove. However, since almost every player in the table since Stan Musial has won at least one Gold Glove, the Gold Glove column in the table is structured to emphasize the four players in the table who did not win a Gold Glove during their careers. It's easier to remember the four names that are the exception rather than all the names of the players who did win at least one Gold Glove Award.

But let's start by discussing a few of the excellent defenders in Table 1 who won multiple Gold Gloves. The two players in the table who won the most Gold Gloves were Roberto Clemente and Willie Mays. Both men were well known for their defense, so it's not surprising they each won the award a dozen times. Ichiro Suzuki was also recognized as an excellent defender, and he took home 10 Gold Gloves. Who is the only other player in the table with double-digit Gold Glove Awards? The surprising answer is Al Kaline. He and Suzuki are tied with 10 awards each.

2. Awards

Although Kaline's defensive abilities are not widely remembered today, he was an excellent right fielder who worked very hard on his defense and was always in the proper position to throw after making a catch.[4]

The skills needed to play baseball are not evenly distributed among players. Some players are great defensively but weak offensively. A good example of this type of player is Mark Belanger. The Orioles shortstop was an outstanding defender who won eight Gold Glove Awards. But he was a weak hitter, batting .228 lifetime. The opposite can also be true. There are strong hitters who don't play defense well. The four players in Table 1 who never won a Gold Glove—Lou Brock, Rod Carew, Paul Molitor, and Miguel Cabrera—are good examples of this type of player.

Brock and Cabrera are the quintessential archetypes. Brock is best remembered for his base-stealing ability. He led the league in steals eight times, and set the single-season steals record (118 in 1974) and career-steals record (938). (Rickey Henderson later broke both records.) Brock was also an excellent hitter, batting .292 lifetime with four seasons of at least 200 hits. But his defense was weak. He made 193 errors in his career and had a career defensive WAR of -16.8. Cabrera is similar. He batted .306 lifetime, but he made 153 errors and had a defensive WAR of -21.4. To put those numbers in perspective, Henderson (who was considered an average defender and won one Gold Glove during his 25-year career) made 141 errors with a -2.3 defensive WAR.

3

◂║║▸ ◂║║▸ ◂║║▸

How Frequently Does a Player Reach 3,000 Hits?

Table 1 shows the dates that players reached 3,000 hits. However, that information is easier to understand graphically, rather than as a list. The data are shown in Graph 1.

Graph 1 can be interpreted as follows. The first data point represents Honus Wagner. He was the second player to reach the 3,000-hit milestone in 1914. Tris Speaker was fifth in 1925 and Willie Mays was 10th in 1970. Miguel Cabrera was 33rd in 2022.

The visual display of the data in Table 1 shows how the achievement of the 3,000-hit plateau has occurred through time. Horizontal spacing of the data points represents the distance in time between players who achieved 3,000 hits. Data points that are closely spaced vertically mean a player reached the milestone close on the heels of the previous player to reach 3,000 hits.

The first thing to notice about Graph 1 is that there are many more data points on the right side of the graph than on the left side. This means that the rate of accumulation of 3,000th hits has increased over time. Just seven players collected their milestone hits in the 56 years from 1914 (when Honus Wagner and Nap Lajoie reached the plateau) through 1969. But over the next 53 years, from 1970 (when Henry Aaron and Willie Mays reached the milestone) through 2022, a total of 25 men collected their 3,000th hit. It's likely that this is simply a result of more men having the chance to get there due to expansion during the latter period. After the American League was established in 1901, there were 16 teams in major league baseball until 1960. In 1969 there were 24 teams, and there have been 30 teams since 1998. Expansion has given more men the opportunity to collect 3,000 hits.

Another interesting feature in Graph 1 is the six pairs of data

3. How Frequently Does a Player Reach 3,000 Hits?

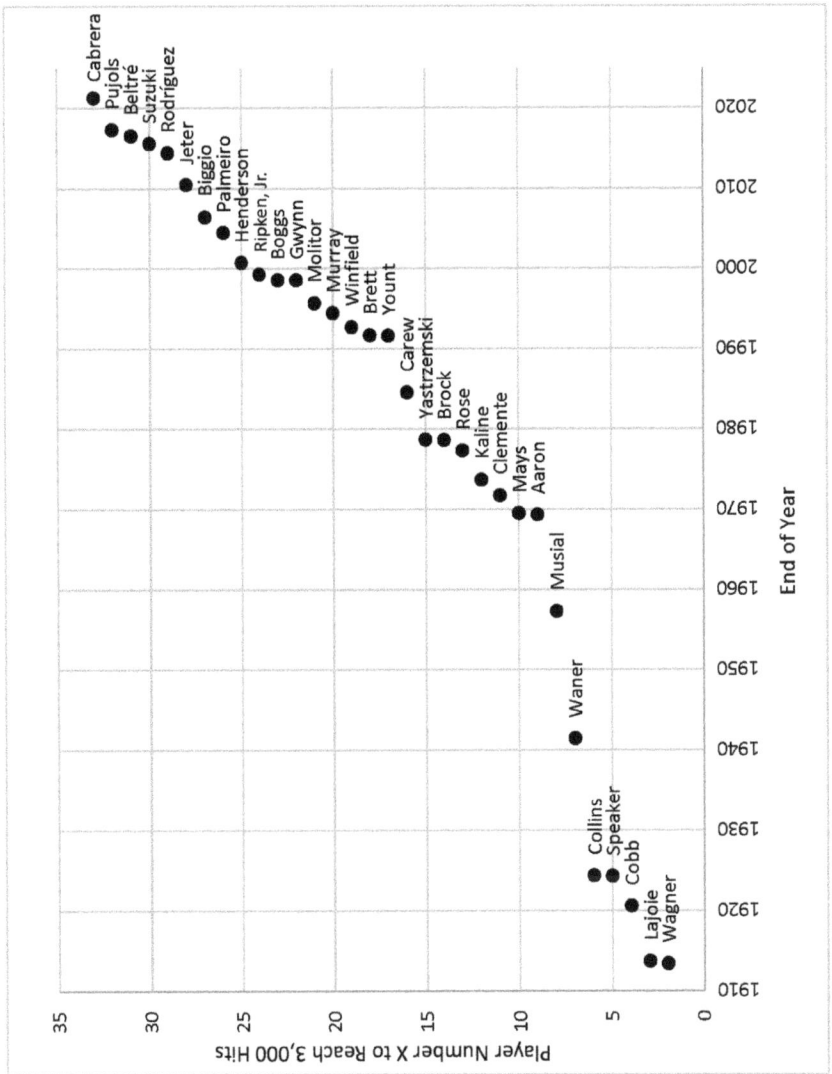

Graph 1: Players with 3,000 Hits Graphed in Chronological Order

points with close vertical spacing. This means that there have been six years where two men collected their 3,000th hit in the same year. Two of those pairs were mentioned in the previous paragraph. The four other instances were 1925 (Tris Speaker and Eddie Collins), 1979 (Lou Brock and Carl Yastrzemski), 1992 (Robin Yount and George Brett), and Tony

Part I—Analysis of Players with 3,000 Hits

Gwynn and Wade Boggs in 1999. So 12 out of 33 (about 36 percent) of the milestone hits have come in the same year. Some of these pairs will be discussed in more detail below.

Two of the data points that stand out in Graph 1 are Paul Waner and Stan Musial. They are isolated because they are the only two players to reach 3,000 hits between Eddie Collins in 1925 and Henry Aaron in 1970. Waner reached the milestone 17 years after Collins. Musial was 16 years after Waner, and it was another dozen years between Musial and "Hammerin' Hank." In spite of the flurry of men reaching 3,000 hits from 2015 to 2018, history shows there can be long dry spells between achievements.

That said, it's also true that some unusual circumstances contributed to the dry spell between 1925 and 1970. Babe Ruth was 127 hits shy of 3,000 when he retired in 1935. He probably would have reached the milestone if he hadn't spent the first six years of his career mostly as a (very good!) pitcher. Lou Gehrig was 279 hits short of 3,000 hits when his 17-year career was tragically cut short in 1939 by the disease that now bears his name. Two or three more productive seasons and he likely would have reached 3,000 hits. Ted Williams lost three full years to World War II, and most of two other seasons to the Korean War, before finishing his career 346 hits below 3,000 in 1960. His time in the service probably kept him from reaching 3,000 hits and 600 home runs (he finished with 521 long balls).

It's an interesting coincidence that two of the giants of the game, Aaron and Mays, reached the milestone just two months apart in 1970. And it's surprising that Aaron got there first because he started his career in 1954, three years after Mays broke in. But the mystery is easily explained by Mays' time in the Army. He lost most of 1952 and all of 1953 to military service. The two great hitters initiated a decade where a total of seven players achieved the milestone. The 1970s are tied with the 1990s for the decade with the most players, seven, reaching 3,000 hits.

One of the hitters who reached the plateau in the 1970s, Roberto Clemente, famously achieved his 3,000th hit in the last regular season at-bat of his career in 1972, so he finished with exactly 3,000 hits. Clemente's achievement of the milestone was significant because in addition to being the 11th player to collect 3,000 hits, he was the first player who wasn't born in the continental United States (he's from Puerto Rico) to reach the plateau. Clemente's life was tragically cut short in a plane crash three months after the 1972 season ended while he was taking relief supplies to Nicaragua after an earthquake.

3. How Frequently Does a Player Reach 3,000 Hits?

(From left) Roberto Clemente, Willie Mays and Henry Aaron, date unknown. These three all-time greats were the 11th, 10th, and 9th men to reach 3,000 hits, respectively (National Baseball Hall of Fame and Museum, Cooperstown, N.Y.).

But his achievement highlighted the emergence of Caribbean and Latin American players as a force in the game. Their emergence was a direct result of the manpower shortage during World War II which left major and minor league teams scrambling to find players, during the war. U.S.–born players were susceptible to being drafted but foreign-born players were not. This made the Caribbean a rich source of potential baseball talent. The Washington Senators had a scout in the region, Joe Cambria, who was especially adept at finding talented youngsters from the area.[1] The Senators, and later the Minnesota Twins after the franchise left Washington following the 1960 season, benefited greatly from Cambria's efforts in the Caribbean. Tony Oliva and Zoilo Versalles (both from Cuba) helped the Twins win the pennant in 1965.

Another data point that stands out in Graph 1 is Rod Carew. Carew was the only player to reach 3,000 hits during the 13 years between

Part I—Analysis of Players with 3,000 Hits

Carl Yastrzemski in 1979 and Robin Yount in 1992, and he was the only player to reach the plateau during the 1980s. In an interesting round-number coincidence, Carew reached 3,000 hits on the same day in 1985 that Tom Seaver earned his 300th win. In addition, Carew and Seaver both started their major league careers in 1967.

The left-handed batting Carew was one of the best pure hitters the game has ever seen. Asked about facing Carew from the mound, Hall of Fame pitcher Catfish Hunter replied, "He has no weakness as a hitter. Pitch him inside, outside, high, low, fast stuff, breaking balls—anything you throw he can handle. He swings with the pitch; that is why he's so great, He has no holes."[2] Carew won the Rookie of the Year Award in 1967. That year marked the first of his 18 consecutive All-Star selections. He made a run at batting .400 in 1977, finishing the year with 239 hits (tied with Wee Willie Keeler for the 16th highest season total), a .388 batting average, and the Most Valuable Player Award. The Panamanian-born Carew was the second foreign-born player, and 16th player overall, to reach the milestone. He was also the first player from an expansion franchise, the California Angels, to join the group.

Echoing the 1970s, the 1990s saw seven players reach the 3,000-hit plateau. That included two pairs of players who reached the milestone within days of each other. Early in the decade, George Brett collected his 3,000th hit exactly three weeks after Robin Yount in September 1992. The two players had remarkably similar career arcs, so it's not surprising they achieved the milestone at close to the same time. Brett got a five-hit head start on Yount by playing 13 games at the end of the 1973 season, but both players started playing regularly in 1974. They both spent their entire careers with one team in the American League. Not including the few games Brett played in 1973, both players had 20-year careers. Yount had one season with more than 200 hits (210 in 1982) and won two MVP Awards (1982 and 1989), while Brett had two seasons with more than 200 hits (215 in 1976 and 212 in 1979) and won one MVP Award in 1980. Brett came close to a second MVP Award in 1976, finishing second to Thurman Munson in the voting. Both players finished their careers in 1993, Yount with 3,142 hits and Brett with 3,154 hits. It seems fitting that they reached the 3,000-hit milestone at roughly the same time and that both of them gave their Hall of Fame induction speech the same year (1999).

The last year of the decade also saw a pair of hitters reach the 3,000-hit plateau together. But Tony Gwynn beat Wade Boggs to the

3. How Frequently Does a Player Reach 3,000 Hits?

mark by just a single day in 1999. Like Brett and Yount, Gwynn and Boggs had very similar career arcs. Both players started their big-league careers in 1982, and had career batting averages well over .300 (Gwynn at .338 to Boggs' .328). Both earned multiple batting titles and Silver Slugger Awards without winning an MPV Award. Gwynn's eight batting titles are tied with Honus Wagner for most in National League history (Ty Cobb leads with 12 batting titles in the American League) while Boggs won five titles. Boggs earned more Silver Slugger Awards, eight to Gwynn's seven, but Gwynn had 15 All-Star selections to Boggs' dozen. Boggs ended his career in 1999 with 3,010 hits in 18 years. Gwynn played two more years to finish with 3,141 hits over a 20-year career.

Although Rickey Henderson's data point does not visually stand out in Graph 1, there are some interesting coincidences associated with his achievement of major hitting milestones. Henderson took 909 games to attain the 1,000 hit milestone, and he reached that milestone on 9/9/1985. He reached the 2,000-hit plateau on the last day of the 1992 season, and the 3,000-hit plateau on the last day of the 2001 season. Henderson, who suited up for nine franchises during his impressive 25-year career, played for San Diego in 2001. That was Tony Gwynn's final season, so Henderson's 3,000th hit occurred in Gwynn's last game.

The 2010s featured five players collecting their 3,000th hit, and the only instance where four players reached the 3,000-hit milestone in four consecutive years. Yankee icon Derek Jeter started the decade off in style in 2011, when he slammed a home run over the left field wall in Yankee Stadium to attain the 3,000-hit milestone. Given the long, storied history of the Yankees, it's surprising that Jeter was the first player to reach the plateau as a Yankee, and the first to get the historic hit in Yankee Stadium.

However, Jeter's unique status didn't last very long. Álex Rodríguez joined him in 2015 when he hammered a home run to right field in the Bronx for his 3,000th safety. The pair are the only duo to reach the milestone by hitting consecutive home runs, and the only two players from the same team to reach the milestone consecutively.

A-Rod's achievement initiated four consecutive seasons where a player joined the 3,000-Hit Club. Ichiro Suzuki, Adrián Beltré, and Albert Pujols collected their 3,000th hits over the following three seasons. All three of these outstanding hitters, and Miguel Cabrera who was the next player to reach 3,000 safeties in 2022, were born outside

Part I—Analysis of Players with 3,000 Hits

the continental U.S. Since it takes roughly 20 years for most players to attain the plateau, it's clear that major league baseball had successfully recruited outstanding players from outside the country starting at about the turn of the century. Beltré and Pujols were the first non–U.S. players from the same country (they are both from the Dominican Republic) to join the 3,000-Hit Club consecutively.

4.

A Closer Look at the Hitters

The information in Table 1 and Graph 1, although interesting, is relatively superficial. We don't learn anything about these players except who they are, when they achieved the 3,000-hit milestone, and awards they won. But of course, there are lots of other questions we can ask about these men. How many of them were left-handed batters? How old were they when they reached the milestone and what team did they play for? How many games did it take for each of them to reach 3,000 hits? Table 2 contains data that allows us to answer these, and several other questions.

Table 2: Additional Data About Players in the 3,000-Hit Club

	Player	Bats	Age	Team	Hit	Game #	Pitcher	Opposing Tm.	H/A	Career Hits
1.	Cap Anson	R	45	Colts	uk	unk	unk	unk	Unk	3,011(?)
2.	Honus Wagner	R	40	Pirates	2B	2,332	Erskine Mayer	Philadelphia (N)	Away	3,430
3.	Nap Lajoie	R	40	Naps	2B	2,224	Marty McHale	N.Y. (A)	Home	3,252
4.	Ty Cobb	L	34	Tigers	1B	2,135	Elmer Myers	Boston (A)	Home	4,189
5.	Tris Speaker	L	37	Indians	1B	2,341	Tom Zachary	Washington	Home	3,514
6.	Eddie Collins	L	38	White Sox	1B	2,505	Rip Collins	Detroit	Away	3,314
7.	Paul Waner	L	39	Braves	1B	2,314	Rip Sewell	Pittsburgh	Home	3,152

Part I—Analysis of Players with 3,000 Hits

Player	Bats	Age	Team	Hit	Game #	Pitcher	Opposing Tm.	H/A	Career Hits
8. Stan Musial	L	37	Cardinals	2B	2,301	Moe Drabowsky	Chicago (N)	Away	3,630
9. Hank Aaron	R	36	Braves	1B	2,460	Wayne Simpson	Cincinnati	Away	3,771
10. Willie Mays	R	39	Giants	1B	2,639	Mike Wegener	Montréal	Home	3,293
11. Roberto Clemente	R	38	Pirates	2B	2,433	Jon Matlack	N.Y. (N)	Home	3,000
12. Al Kaline	R	39	Tigers	2B	2,825	Dave McNally	Baltimore	Away	3,007
13. Pete Rose	B	37	Reds	1B	2,370	Steve Rogers	Montréal	Home	4,256
14. Lou Brock	L	40	Cardinals	1B	2,629	Dennis Lamp	Chicago (N)	Home	3,023
15. Carl Yastrzemski	L	40	Red Sox	1B	2,848	Jim Beattie	N.Y. (A)	Home	3,419
16. Rod Carew	L	39	Angels	1B	2,417	Frank Viola	Minnesota	Home	3,053
17. Robin Yount	R	36	Brewers	1B	2,708	José Mesa	Cleveland	Home	3,142
18. George Brett	L	39	Royals	1B	2,559	Tim Fortugno	California	Away	3,154
19. Dave Winfield	R	41	Twins	1B	2,840	Dennis Eckersley	Oakland	Home	3,110
20. Eddie Murray	B	39	Indians	1B	2,764	Mike Trombley	Minnesota	Away	3,255
21. Paul Molitor	R	40	Twins	3B	2,411	José Rosado	Kansas City	Away	3,319
22. Tony Gwynn	L	39	Padres	1B	2,284	Dan Smith	Montréal	Away	3,141
23. Wade Boggs	L	41	Rays	HR	2,430	Chris Haney	Cleveland	Home	3,010
24. Cal Ripken, Jr.	R	39	Orioles	1B	2,800	Hector Carrasco	Minnesota	Away	3,184
25. Rickey Henderson	R	42	Padres	2B	2,979	John Thomson	Colorado	Home	3,055
26. Rafael Palmeiro	L	40	Orioles	2B	2,809	Joel Piñeiro	Seattle	Away	3,020
27. Craig Biggio	R	41	Astros	1B	2,781	Aaron Cook	Colorado	Home	3,060

4. A Closer Look at the Hitters

Player	Bats	Age	Team	Hit	Game #	Pitcher	Opposing Tm.	H/A	Career Hits
28. Derek Jeter	R	37	Yankees	HR	2,362	David Price	Tampa Bay	Home	3,465
29. Álex Rodríguez	R	39	Yankees	HR	2,631	Justin Verlander	Detroit	Home	3,115
30. Ichiro Suzuki	L	42	Marlins	3B	2,452	Chris Rusin	Colorado	Away	3,089
31. Adrián Beltré	R	38	Rangers	2B	2,771	Wade Miley	Baltimore	Home	3,166
32. Albert Pujols	R	38	Angels	1B	2,607	Mike Leake	Seattle	Away	3,332
33. Miguel Cabrera	R	39	Tigers	1B	2,600	Antonio Senzatela	Colorado	Home	3,066

5

Handedness

It's estimated that roughly 10 percent of the human population is left-handed. Why that percentage isn't higher (or lower) is an interesting question that won't be addressed here. But what is relevant to this discussion is how does the fraction of "lefties" in baseball compare to the general population? You probably won't be surprised to learn that there are many more left-handed players in the world of baseball than in the rest of the population. According to Baseball-Reference.com's Stathead, in August 2022 there were 1,797 active players in major league baseball. There were 515 left-handed batters within that active player population. That means that roughly 29 percent of active players hit lefty. Similar analysis for pitchers shows that about 26 percent of active pitchers are southpaws. These numbers are in accordance with other sources that find that between 25 and 35 percent of baseball players are left-handed.[1,2]

The question is, why is the proportion of left-handed players in baseball so much higher than the population as a whole? From an offensive perspective, the answer is that there are significant advantages to hitting from the left side. The first advantage is that the batter is one step closer to first base. Statistical analysis by Jordan Young showed that for batters with similar speed, the left-handed batter gets to first base an average of 0.1 second faster. Some left-handers can get to first base 0.5 second faster.[3] This can easily be the difference between being safe or out. The shorter time to first also puts more pressure on the defense, and makes it more likely that a fielder will make an error.

A second advantage is that a left-handed batter has a better view of the ball coming out of a right-handed pitcher's hand than a right-handed batter. This is important because most pitchers, roughly three-quarters of the total, are righties. Many pitches from a right-handed pitcher

5. Handedness

to a right-handed batter initially appear to the batter to be coming directly toward him. A left-handed batter views the same pitches across his body which makes the pitches easier to hit. Breaking pitches from right-handed pitchers break away from right-handed batters, but break toward left-handed batters. These pitches are also easier for a left-handed batter to handle.

Left-handed batters also have an advantage when there is a runner on first base. When the first baseman holds the runner by playing close to the base, there is a hole in the defense between first and second base. A left-handed batter can more easily pull a groundball through the opening than a right-handed batter can shoot the ball to the opposite field. Another advantage is that the momentum from the follow-through of a left-handed batter's swing is toward first base, versus toward third base for a righty.

These advantages are not a secret, and result in roughly 40 percent of major league plate appearances occurring from the left side.[4] Given this overrepresentation of left-handed batters, one explanation for the higher proportion of southpaw pitchers is simply to counter the high proportion of lefty at-bats. However, this theory does not survive close scrutiny. Guy Molyneux and Phil Birnbaum show that southpaws actually enjoy a smaller platoon advantage than right-handed pitchers, which means that this cannot explain why there are so many left-handed pitchers.[5] Molyneux and Birnbaum argue that the southpaw's advantage is simply unfamiliarity. From Little League to the majors, right-handed batters face far fewer left-handed pitchers than right-handed pitchers, which results in a big advantage for southpaw pitchers. This results in southpaws being overrepresented in the big leagues. The southpaw advantage is found in other confrontational sports as well. Left-handed players are overrepresented in boxing, fencing, tennis, and volleyball also.

Given the advantages that left-handed hitters enjoy, it's not surprising to find many of them on the list of players who accumulated 3,000 hits in their careers. Of the 33 men on the list, 18 (about 55 percent) batted right-handed, 13 (about 39 percent) batted left-handed, and two were switch-hitters. This means that almost 40 percent of the men who produced the most hits in major league history were left-handed batters. The preponderance of left-handed hitters is even more pronounced at the top of the list of hitters with the most career hits. The top third of players on that list are shown in Table 3.

Part I—Analysis of Players with 3,000 Hits

Table 3:
Top Third of Players with 3,000 Hits, in Order of Career Hits

	Player	Bats	Hits
1.	Pete Rose	B	4,256
2.	Ty Cobb	L	4,189
3.	Hank Aaron	R	3,771
4.	Stan Musial	L	3,630
5.	Tris Speaker	L	3,514
6.	Derek Jeter	R	3,465
7.	Honus Wagner	R	3,430
8.	Carl Yastrzemski	L	3,419
9.	Albert Pujols	R	3,359
10.	Paul Molitor	R	3,319
11.	Eddie Collins	L	3,314

A switch hitter, Pete Rose, tops the list, and the left-handed batting Ty Cobb is second. The only right-handed hitter in the top five is Hank Aaron. Looking at the top third as a group, five of the 11 hitters bat right-handed, and five bat left-handed. In the rarefied air of the top 11 men with the most hits in history, half of them bat left-handed. Given that only about 10 percent of the overall population is left-handed, these results dramatically demonstrate the significant advantages that left-handed batters enjoy over right-handed batters.

6

AGE

Three thousand is a big number. To accumulate 3,000 hits a player must average 150 hits per year for 20 years or 200 hits per year for 15 years. Assuming the player starts his major league career at about 20 years old, this means that even the best hitters will not get to 3,000 hits until they are in their mid to late 30s or later. The data bears out this rudimentary analysis. Age-oriented results for the 32 men with 3,000 hits are shown in Graph 2. Cap Anson is not included in the age analysis because it's not known when he got his historic hit.

The average age of players when they collected their 3,000th hit was 38 years, 10 months old. Almost one-third (10/32) of the players with 3,000 hits were 39 years old when they got their historic hit. The second most common age is 40 years old. Six players reached the milestone at that age. So half of the players in the club (16/32) were 39 or 40 years old when they got to 3,000 hits. Another eight players were 37 or 38 years old at the time of their 3,000th hit, which means that the majority of players (24/32, 75 percent) were between 37 and 40 years old when they reached the milestone.

As with many data sets, the outlying data points are often the most interesting. At the far left of Graph 2, Ty Cobb stands by himself. At age 34, Cobb was not just the youngest player to reach 3,000 hits, but he was also *two* years younger than any other player when he reached the plateau. How did he get there so fast? First, he started his career at 18 years old, with 149 hits before he turned 20. Then, starting with his third year in 1907, Cobb averaged a very impressive 194 hits per year for 15 years until 1921. This time period included eight years when he led the American League in hits, and seven years with more than 200 hits. The 248 hits he achieved in 1911 at age 24 is the eighth highest total all-time. Being so young when he reached 3,000 hits, Cobb was able to play for seven more seasons to accumulate his career total of 4,189 hits.

Part I—Analysis of Players with 3,000 Hits

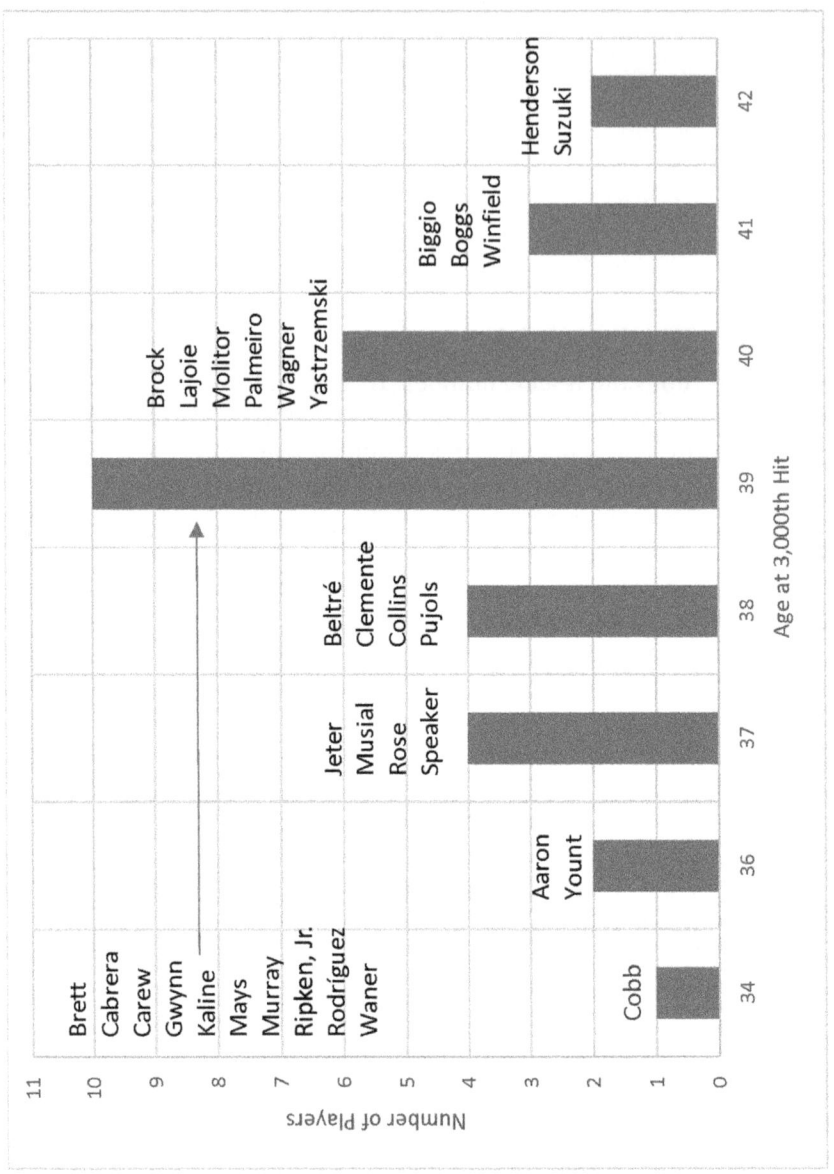

Graph 2: Players with 3,000 Hits Graphed by Age at 3,000th Hit

Cobb ended his career in 1928 with the Philadelphia Athletics. Two of his teammates on the A's were Tris Speaker and Eddie Collins. Speaker and Collins had joined Cobb in the 3,000-Hit Club in 1925,

6. Age

Ty Cobb in front of the Detroit Tigers dugout in 1913. Note the mitt on his left hand and the size of the bats in the lower right. Cobb collected his 3,000th hit off Elmer Myers in 1921 (Library of Congress).

so Athletics manager Connie Mack had the pleasure of having three of the greatest hitters of all time on his squad in 1928. The team won 98 games, but finished 2½ games behind the Yankees in the American League. After Cobb retired following that season, Collins (who was also over 40 years old) had the second-highest career hits total of any active player. His 3,314 hits at the time trailed Cobb's record by 875 hits. Contemporary observers assumed Cobb's hit record would never be broken. Never is a long time, and history shows those observers were wrong, but Cobb's record did stand for 57 years until Pete Rose broke it in 1985.

At the other end of the age spectrum are Rickey Henderson and Ichiro Suzuki, both of whom collected their 3,000th hits at age 42. But before discussing how their pursuit of 3,000 hits was unique, we will make a short digression to address how each of these players has a different record that I believe will never be broken.

The first unbreakable record is Henderson's 1,406 career stolen bases. Lou Brock, second on the steals list with 938, is more steals behind Henderson (468) than the active leader in steals, Elvis Andrus (as of 2023), has for his career (347). It would take 20 years of 70

Part I—Analysis of Players with 3,000 Hits

stolen bases per year to reach 1,400. Even though Ronald Acuña, had an unprecedented 40 home run and 70 stolen base season in 2023, it's not likely he will be able to steal 70 bases enough times to catch Henderson. And without elaboration, Henderson's 130 steals in 1982 is also in the never-to-be-broken category.

Suzuki's untouchable record is the 262 hits he recorded in 2004. I'm sure you're thinking, how can I argue that a record that was set only about 20 years ago will never be broken? Here's the logic. The single season hits record that Suzuki broke was set at 257 by George Sisler in 1920. Sisler's record had stood for 84 years before Ichiro broke it. Other than Suzuki, the closest any modern (the last 50 years) player has come to Sisler was the 240 hits that Wade Boggs collected in 1985, and the 240 hits that Darin Erstad accumulated in 2000. Those are impressive hit totals, but an additional 23 hits is a tall order. In addition to his 262-hit effort, Suzuki also had 242 hits in 2001, so he has two of the top 10 seasons for hits. He and Sisler are the only players with two seasons in the top 10 (Sisler had 246 hits in 1922).

In order to challenge the hits record, a player has to play in virtually every game of the season, make a very high number of plate appearances, and hit for high average. High average by itself will not get it done. For example, even with the 56-game hitting streak in 1941 and a .357 batting average that year, Joe DiMaggio had 193 hits that season. Ted Williams had 185 hits that same year when he batted .406. DiMaggio and Williams career best hit totals are 215 and 194, respectively.

What were Suzuki's numbers for 2004? He played in all but one of the Mariners games (161), led the league in plate appearances (762) and batting average (.372), and struck out just 63 times. His 762 plate appearances are eighth on the all-time list, which is topped by Jimmy Rollins' 778 appearances in 2007. Suzuki had four games where he got five hits, six games where he got four hits, 24 games where he got three hits, 46 games where he got two hits, 54 games with a single hit, and he failed to get a hit in only 27 games that season. In spite of having such a tremendous season, Suzuki had 251 hits after playing in the same number of games as Sisler (154) and reached that total only because he had a five-hit game and a four-hit game a few games earlier. In subsequent games he got 1, 2, 1, 1, 3 (October 1, 2004, the day he broke the record), 1, and 2 hits to get to his total of 262. He got at least one hit in the last 13 games of the season, getting a total of 26 hits in those 13 games. If Suzuki had gotten 20 hits in those last 13 games he would not

6. Age

have broken the record. It's highly unlikely that anyone will break Suzuki's record of 262 hits in a season.

Returning to the main theme, Rickey Henderson's achievement of the 3,000-hit milestone at 42 years old was a testament to his love of the game, and his perseverance. He started his big league career at 20 years old in 1979, and he never exceeded the 179 hits he collected in 1980. In sharp contrast to Cobb, Henderson averaged a modest 141 hits per year in the 15-year period starting in 1980, and he finished the 1994 season with 2,216 hits. In spite of a number of mediocre seasons after 1994, Henderson never stopped believing he could compete in the big leagues, and he found team after team that was willing to take a chance on the former MVP. At the end of the 2001 season, Henderson was 42 years old and was approaching the 3,000-hit milestone with the Padres in San Diego. He joined teammate Tony Gwynn in the 3,000-Hit Club on the last day of the season. The game also marked the end of Gwynn's illustrious career.

There's a good reason why Ichiro Suzuki was so old (in baseball terms) when he achieved the 3,000-hit milestone. It's because he didn't start his American major league career until he was 27 years old. And there's a good reason he started at such a relatively advanced age. It's because he had a stellar nine-year career in Japan before he came to the U.S. During his Japanese baseball career, Suzuki won an unprecedented seven consecutive batting titles, seven consecutive Gold Glove awards, and three consecutive MVP awards. He became the first position player from Nippon Professional Baseball to join the major leagues in 2001. Proving many doubters wrong, his excellent hitting continued in the U.S. against major league pitching, as Suzuki began his big-league career with an unprecedented 10 straight 200-hit seasons (another record that's not likely to be broken). He averaged an amazing 224 hits per year for those 10 years.

It took Suzuki just 696 games to reach 1,000 hits, and only 10 more games than that, 706, to get to 2,000. These are impressively few numbers of games to accumulate 1,000 hits. It's rare to get 1,000 hits in under 700 games. Chuck Klein holds the 20th Century record for fastest to 1,000 hits at 683 games and Nap Lajoie managed the feat in 653 games, but Lajoie started his career in 1896. For comparison, Ty Cobb, Tony Gwynn, and Wade Boggs took 762, 783, and 747 games, respectively, to reach 1,000 hits. The slowest player to 1,000 hits, who still made it into the 3,000-Hit Club, was Adrián Beltré. He took 1,020 games to accumulate 1,000 hits. Given how late he started, it's very impressive that Suzuki was able to collect 3,000 big league hits in his career.

Part I—Analysis of Players with 3,000 Hits

Beltré's 1,020 games to 1,000 hits raises a question that is worth another short digression. Have there been any players who collected 1,000 hits in exactly 1,000 games? The answer is yes, eight players have managed that feat. In reverse chronological order of when they reached their 1,000th hit, those players are Erick Aybar, Eric Chavez, Will Cordero, Alan Trammell, Johnny Callison, Joe Gordon, Gus Suhr, and Red Smith. Trammell and Gordon are in the Hall of Fame. Gordon is not widely remembered now, but he was a key member of four Yankee teams that won World Series titles between 1938 and 1943, and he won another ring with the Indians in 1948. He also won the American League MVP Award in 1942. Trammell played shortstop for the 1984 Detroit Tigers squad that started the season with an impressive 35 wins against just five losses. Trammell's .314 batting average was fifth best in the American League that year.

7

Franchises and Teams

The next question is the distribution of 3,000th hits by franchise and team. In other words, which teams were the players on when they collected their 3,000th hit? How many teams have been able to celebrate multiple 3,000th hits? How many have never had that special opportunity? The results are shown in Table 4.

**Table 4:
Players with 3,000 Hits
by Franchise and Team**

	1903 Franchise	Expansion Franchise	City	Team Name	No. 3,000 Hit Players	Player(s)
1.			Baltimore	Orioles	2	Palmeiro, Ripken
2.	x		Boston (A)	Red Sox	1	Yastrzemski
3.	x		Boston (N), Atlanta	Braves	2	Waner, Aaron
4.		x	California, L.A.	Angels	2	Carew, Pujols
5.	x		Chicago (A)	White Sox	1	Collins
6.	x		Chicago (N)	Colts	1	Anson
7.	x		Cincinnati	Reds	1	Rose
8.	x		Cleveland	Naps, Indians	3	Lajoie, Speaker, Murray
9.	x		Detroit	Tigers	3	Cobb, Kaline, Cabrera
10.		x	Houston	Astros	1	Biggio

Part I—Analysis of Players with 3,000 Hits

	1903 Franchise	Expansion Franchise	City	Team Name	No. 3,000 Hit Players	Player(s)
11.		x	Kansas City	Royals	1	Brett
12.		x	Miami	Marlins	1	Suzuki
13.		x	Milwaukee	Brewers	1	Yount
14.			Minnesota	Twins	2	Molitor, Winfield
15.	x		New York (A)	Yankees	2	Jeter, Rodríguez
16.	x		Pittsburgh	Pirates	2	Wagner, Clemente
17.		x	San Diego	Padres	2	Henderson, Gwynn
18.			San Francisco	Giants	1	Mays
19.	x		St. Louis	Cardinals	2	Brock, Musial
20.		x	Tampa Bay	Devil Rays	1	Boggs
21.		x	Texas	Rangers	1	Beltré
Total	10	8			33	

Table 4 shows that 21 different teams have celebrated a 3,000th hit, and that just two of those teams have had three players reach their 3,000th hit while playing for the team. With the addition of Miguel Cabrera in 2022, the Detroit Tigers reached three 3,000th hit celebrations. After Cabrera recorded the hit, the *Vintage Detroit* website carried a headline, "Tigers Are Only Team with Three 3,000-Hit Club Members." In the story that followed, Dan Holmes wrote, "Detroit is the only franchise to have three players get a 3,000th hit in their uniform."[1] But Table 4 shows that Cleveland also had three players get their 3,000th hit with the team. Is Table 4 correct, or is *Vintage Detroit*?

To answer the question, we must understand the distinction between franchise and team. Legally, franchise refers to the contractual right granted by Major League Baseball to own and operate a major league team in a specific location. The Brooklyn Dodgers and the Los Angeles Dodgers are the same franchise, even though the team moved from one coast to the other. The same is true of the Washington Senators

7. Franchises and Teams

and the Minnesota Twins. The Washington franchise moved to Minneapolis before the 1961 season. It was the same franchise even though the name changed to Twins in honor of the Twin Cities, Minneapolis and St. Paul. This is just one example of a name change that accompanied a franchise relocation. It's a common practice. Fans often refer to the team by the moniker rather than the franchise identification.

One further clarification about the name Senators is necessary. The Washington franchise actually went by the name Nationals from 1905 to 1956. That's part of the reason the current Washington Nationals team chose that name when the Expos moved to the capital in 2005. But to avoid confusion with today's Nationals franchise, the Washington team from 1901 to 1960 will always be referred to as the Senators in this book. Even though that's not strictly correct, it's likely most fans think of the Washington team from that time period by that name.

The *Vintage Detroit* story conflates the concepts of team and franchise. The headline about the Tigers team being the only one with three 3,000th hit players is correct if the standard being used is team name. The Cleveland *Indians* had only two players, Tris Speaker and Eddie Murray, get their 3,000th hit as a Cleveland Indian. When Nap Lajoie got his 3,000th hit in 1914, the team was known as the Cleveland Naps. Lajoie was such a popular player when he got to Cleveland in 1902, that the team name was changed from Blues to Napoleons in his honor in 1903. The name was shortened to Naps in 1906. He's the only active player to ever have had a team named after him. When Lajoie left after the 1914 season, the team was then referred to as the Indians. However, if the question is which *franchise* had the most players collect their 3,000th hit with the franchise, both the Cleveland and the Detroit franchises are tied with three.

Table 4 shows that eight teams have had two 3,000th hit celebrations: the Orioles, Braves, Angels, Twins, Yankees, Pirates, Padres, and Cardinals. The Braves and the Angels are special cases. The first of the two Braves to reach 3,000 hits was Paul Waner. He collected his 3,000th hit as a Boston Brave in 1942. But the franchise moved to Milwaukee in 1953, and moved again to Atlanta in 1966. So when Hank Aaron reached 3,000 hits, he did so as a member of the Atlanta Braves. Waner and Aaron played for the same franchise, with the same name, but in different cities when they collected their historic hit. In the case of the Angels, what changed between Rod Carew's and Albert Pujols' 3,000th hits was the name of the franchise. When Carew collected his 3,000th hit in 1985, the franchise was known as the California Angels.

Part I—Analysis of Players with 3,000 Hits

Nap Lajoie wearing Philadelphia Athletics uniform in 1915. In 1901, Lajoie won the first triple crown in American League history when he batted .426, drove in 125 runs, and hit 14 homers (Library of Congress).

The franchise name has changed several times since then, and when Albert Pujols reached 3,000 hits in 2018, it was known as the Los Angeles Angels. In this case, it's the same franchise with a different franchise name, but in the same location.

These 16 players, combined with the six from Cleveland and Detroit, mean that in order to get to 33 players, 11 teams have each had one 3,000th hit celebration. One of the special cases among these 11 teams is the Chicago franchise in the National League. We know this team as the Cubs, but line six in Table 4 says that the name of the Chicago (N) team that Cap Anson played for when he collected his 3,000th hit was the Colts. The mystery is easily explained. When the National League was formed in 1876, the Chicago franchise was known as the White Stockings. The team changed names to the Colts in 1890, and then to the Orphans in 1898, before becoming the Cubs in 1903. Anson played for the National League Chicago franchise for the first 22 years of its existence, from 1876 to 1897. That means that the last eight years of his career, from age 38 to 45, Anson played for the team when it was

7. Franchises and Teams

called the Colts. Even though we don't know exactly when Anson collected his 3,000th hit, it's safe to assume his historic hit came while he was a Colt.

Another special case in the single 3,000th hit celebration camp is Tampa Bay. Wade Boggs reached the milestone while playing for the Devil Rays in 1999. This was unusual for two reasons. First, the franchise had only been established in 1998, so the team had the milestone celebration in just the second year of its existence. This was highly unusual because there are franchises that have been existence for over 100 years that have never celebrated a 3,000th-hit milestone. The second reason this was uncommon is that Boggs got the historic hit while playing for his hometown team. Although Boggs was born in Omaha, Nebraska, his family moved to Tampa when his father retired from the military in 1967. The then 9-year-old Boggs went on to star in both football and baseball at Henry B. Plant High School in Tampa before he graduated in 1976 and was drafted by the Red Sox.[2] Over two decades later, at Tropicana Field in St. Petersburg, Boggs drove a pitch from Indians pitcher Chris Haney over the right field wall for the 3,000th hit of his career. He was the 23rd player in baseball history to record his 3,000th hit, and the first to do so with a home run.

We can also examine the team data from the standpoint of when the franchises were established. This book isn't meant to be a complete history of baseball, so we will simply make a distinction between the eight franchises in each league that were extant in 1903 (the year of the first official World Series) and expansion franchises that were established in 1961 or later. For purposes of this discussion, the important thing to recognize is that the baseball world was stable, meaning there was no franchise movement, nor were any new franchises added, between 1903 and 1952. Every team that existed in 1903 had a half century of history in which to have a player reach the 3,000-hit milestone.

Table 4 shows that 10 of the 16 franchises in existence in 1903 have had a 3,000th-hit celebration. The most striking thing about these 10 franchises is how long some of them had to wait for that celebration. The Yankees are the biggest surprise. In spite of the team's long lineage of great players: Ruth, Gehrig, DiMaggio, Mantle, Mattingly, etc., the team had to wait until 2011 before it celebrated Derek Jeter's 3,000th hit. Why did it take so long? None of the earlier Yankee greats had the longevity to get to 3,000 hits. The particulars vary by player. Ruth and Gehrig have already been discussed. DiMaggio finished with 2,214 hits. Joltin' Joe didn't get to 3,000 because he played for a relatively short

Part I—Analysis of Players with 3,000 Hits

13 years, having lost three years to military service. The Mick had an 18-year career, but he was hobbled by injuries during the latter portion and finished with 2,415 hits. Donnie Baseball's career was too short at 14 years for him to have a shot at 3,000 hits. He finished with 2,153 safeties.

The other two 1903 teams that stand out in this regard are the Reds and the Red Sox. Neither team celebrated a player with 3,000 hits until the late 1970s. Pete Rose got his 3,000th hit as a Red in 1978, and Carl Yastrzemski collected his with the Red Sox in 1979. Except for the already discussed Ted Williams, neither franchise had another player with a realistic chance at 3,000 hits until those two players got there. Rose went to the Phillies in 1979, the year after he reached 3,000 hits. But he came back to the Reds late in the 1984 season, so when he broke Ty Cobb's career hit record (4,189 or 4,191 hits, depending on the source) in 1985, he wore a Reds uniform. In between, Rose collected his 4,000th hit as a member of the Montréal Expos.

There's an interesting coincidence associated with Rose's historic 3,000th hit. He collected that hit on May 5, 1978. With two more hits on May 6, Rose was sitting on a .327 batting average for the season. But he went 32-for-145 (.221 batting average) from May 7 until June 13, which drove his batting average for the season down to .267 entering play on June 14, when he collected two hits. Why do we care about these particular five weeks of that season? Because Rose got a hit in all 44 games from June 14 to July 31 to tie him with Willie Keeler for the second-longest hit streak of all time. Of course, Joe DiMaggio holds the record at 56 games. It's interesting that the hitting streak occurred in the same year that Rose reached 3,000 hits, and it's interesting that Rose was in a slump when the streak started. Rose was batting .316 at the end of the streak, and he finished the season with 198 hits and a .302 batting average.

That leaves six teams in existence since 1903 without a player achieving 3,000 hits. For these six teams, the distinction between team name and franchise makes a difference. That's because three of the teams did have a 3,000th-hit celebration, if we look at the franchise level. Those three teams are the St. Louis Browns, Washington Senators, and New York Giants. But the Browns, Senators, and N.Y. Giants never celebrated a 3,000th hit, although they played for at least 50 years under those team names.

However, these three franchises have each had a 3,000th-hit player. The St. Louis Browns franchise moved to Baltimore in 1954 and became

7. Franchises and Teams

the Baltimore Orioles. Cal Ripken, Jr., collected his 3,000th hit with them in 2000 and Rafael Palmeiro reached the milestone in 2005. Like the Yankees, the franchise went roughly a century without a 3,000th-hit celebration. The Washington franchise moved to Minnesota in 1961 and became the Twins. Dave Winfield (in 1993) and Paul Molitor (in 1996) collected their 3,000th hits while playing for the Twins. But once again, it was almost a century in the making.

The third of the three franchises is the N.Y. Giants. In what are arguably the most well-known franchise relocations in baseball history, the Giants moved to San Francisco (and the Dodgers to Los Angeles), in 1958. A dozen years later, in 1970, Willie Mays collected his 3,000th hit in Candlestick Park while playing for the San Francisco Giants. It's somewhat surprising that the N.Y. Giants had never seen a celebration. The team was a perennial contender under manager John McGraw during McGraw's tenure from 1903 to 1931. Over the years, the team featured stellar hitters such as Frankie Frisch, Larry Doyle, Monte Irvin, Bill Terry, and Mel Ott.

Only Ott had a serious chance to collect his 3,000th hit as a N.Y. Giant. Ott spent his entire 22-year career, from 1926 to 1947, with the Giants. He clobbered 511 home runs so Ott is better remembered as a power hitter, but he also batted .304 lifetime and collected many hits along the way. By the end of the 1945 season, the 36-year-old Ott was sitting on 2,871 hits, just 129 hits short of the 3,000 milestone. Since Ott had collected 139 hits the previous season, it was possible he could have reached the milestone by the end of the 1946 season. It was not to be. Ott was beaned during spring training, and then suffered a knee injury in the second game of the year.[3] Although he played in 31 games in 1946, he managed just five hits for the season and finished his career with 2,876 hits. Ott coming up 124 hits short of 3,000 left the door open for Willie Mays to be the first Giant to reach that milestone.

That leaves three franchises that have been in existence since 1903 that have never celebrated a 3,000th hit. Two of those franchises coexisted for about 50 years in the same city, Philadelphia. In the American League, the Athletics (in Philadelphia, Kansas City, and Oakland) have been denied the pleasure of a 3,000th-hit celebration in spite of having a player in the 3,000th-Hit Club who is widely associated with the franchise. Rickey Henderson played for the A's for 14 years, and broke Lou Brock's career steals record (Brock had 938 stolen bases) as an Athletic. He famously held the base he stole for his 939th steal over his head to

Part I—Analysis of Players with 3,000 Hits

mark the occasion. But Henderson was wearing a Padres uniform when he joined the 3,000-Hit Club.

The name that immediately comes to mind when thinking about Philadelphia's National League franchise is Mike Schmidt. Schmidt was a tremendous player who spent his entire 18-year career with the Phillies. But as great as Schmidt was, he was more of a power hitter than a hits collector. His 548 homers are 16th on the all-time list, but he batted just .267 for his career and finished with 2,234 hits. Hence, the Phillies franchise has not had a 3,000th-hit celebration since its establishment as the Philadelphia Quakers in 1883.

The final franchise that has never celebrated a 3,000th hit is the Dodgers. This is almost as surprising as the Yankee franchise taking over a century to celebrate a 3,000th hit. The storied franchise was a force in the National League during much of the 1940s and 1950s. The Brooklyn Dodgers players during the 1950s are legendary. Names like Robinson, Snider, Hodges, Campanella, and Reese immediately come to mind, but none of those players approached 3,000 hits. In general, their careers were too short to reach the 3,000th-hit plateau.

After the franchise moved to Los Angeles in 1958, the team became more famous for its pitchers than position players. Pitchers Sandy Koufax, Don Drysdale, Fernando Valenzuela, Orel Hershiser, and Clayton Kershaw are some of the most famous Dodgers. One position player exception to this rule is Steve Garvey. Garvey played for the Dodgers for 14 years before finishing his career with the Padres. Like Mike Schmidt he had a great career, but his career hits total is 401 hits short of 3,000. And so, surprisingly, like the Phillies, the Dodgers franchise has not seen a 3,000th-hit celebration since its founding in 1884 as the Brooklyn Atlantics.

As of 2023 there were 30 franchises in major league baseball. Table 4 lists the 21 franchises that have experienced a 3,000th-hit celebration. Adding the Athletics, Phillies, and Dodgers to that list leaves six expansion franchises that have never celebrated a 3,000th hit. From oldest to newest, those teams are the Mets (1962), Nationals (franchise origin as Montréal Expos in 1969), Blue Jays and Mariners (1977), Rockies (1993), and Diamondbacks (1998). So nine out of 30, or almost one-third of franchises, have not had a player collect his 3,000th hit wearing their uniform.

The Mets are like the Los Angeles version of the Dodgers, in that many of its most famous players have been pitchers. Hurlers Tom

7. Franchises and Teams

Seaver, Jerry Koosman, Dwight Gooden, and Jacob deGrom immediately come to mind when thinking of the Mets franchise. The Mets have had some excellent position players but none of them have approached 3,000 hits. Keith Hernandez and Gary Carter were key members of the 1986 World Championship team, but both finished with a little over 2,000 hits. David Wright played his entire 14-year career with the Mets, but he was hobbled by injuries, and finished with 1,777 hits. José Reyes started and ended his career with the franchise, but his career hit total was 2,138.

The story is similar for the other five expansion franchises, so each will not be discussed in detail except to mention a few special cases. Hall of Famer Todd Helton played his entire 17-year career with the Colorado Rockies. Helton was an excellent hitter with a .316 career batting average and four seasons with 190 hits or more. And yet he finished with 2,519 hits. Helton and Edgar Martínez (discussed next), exemplify how hard it is to collect 3,000 hits, and why we rightly celebrate the players that do it. The Mariners had three great hitters grace their lineup cards. You almost can't think of the franchise without Ken Griffey, Jr., Edgar Martínez, and Ichiro Suzuki coming to mind. Griffey Jr. began and ended his career in Seattle, but he finished 219 knocks short of 3,000. He probably would have gotten to 3,000 hits but for three injury riddled seasons with Cincinnati between 2002 and 2004. Martínez played his entire 18-year career in the Northwest, but finished with 2,247 hits. Suzuki did reach 3,000 hits, just not while he was wearing a Mariner uniform.

It needs to be noted that two of the nine franchises without a 3,000th-hit celebration have had a 4,000th-hit celebration. Ty Cobb collected his 4,000th hit as a member of the Philadelphia Athletics in 1927. Cobb played for 22 years in Detroit before going to the Athletics in 1927. Ironically, Cobb collected his milestone-4,000th hit in Detroit, but he was in an Athletics uniform as a visiting player. Pete Rose reached the 4,000-hit plateau in 1984 as a member of the Montréal Expos with a double off Jerry Koosman. Rose spent just part of one year out of a 24-year career with the Expos, but that's when he collected the milestone hit.

Since we've talked about which franchises and teams have seen a player produce a 3,000th hit, it is appropriate to discuss which franchises and teams have given one up. The data is shown in Table 5.

Part I—Analysis of Players with 3,000 Hits

Table 5:
Franchises and Teams That Have Given Up a 3,000th Hit

	1903 Franchise	Expansion Franchise	City	Team Name	No. 3,000th Hits Allowed	Player(s) Hit Allowed To
1.			Baltimore	Orioles	2	Kaline, Beltré
2.	x		Boston (A)	Red Sox	1	Cobb
3.		x	California	Angels	1	Brett
4.	x		Chicago (N)	Cubs	2	Musial, Brock
5.	x		Cincinnati	Reds	1	Aaron
6.	x		Cleveland	Indians	2	Yount, Boggs
7.		x	Colorado	Rockies	4	Henderson, Biggio, Suzuki, Cabrera
8.	x		Detroit	Tigers	2	Collins, Rodríguez
9.		x	Kansas City	Royals	1	Molitor
10.			Minnesota	Twins	3	Carew, Murray, Ripken Jr.
11.		x	Montréal	Expos	3	Mays, Rose, Gwynn
12.	x		N.Y. (A)	Yankees	2	Lajoie, Yastrzemski
13.		x	N.Y. (N)	Mets	1	Clemente
14.			Oakland	Athletics	1	Winfield
15.	x		Philadelphia (N)	Phillies	1	Wagner
16.	x		Pittsburgh	Pirates	1	Waner
17.		x	Seattle	Mariners	2	Palmeiro, Pujols
18.		x	Tampa Bay	Rays	1	Jeter
19.	x		Washington (A)	Senators	1	Speaker
Total	9	7			32	

Table 5 shows that 19 teams have yielded a 3,000th hit. It might be expected that one of the long-lived teams would have given up the most 3,000th-milestone hits, but an expansion franchise holds

7. Franchises and Teams

the distinction of being the opponent for most of these historic safeties.

The Colorado Rockies, established relatively recently in 1993, have given up four of the milestone hits. Rickey Henderson, Craig Biggio, Ichiro Suzuki, and Miguel Cabrera are the four batters who stroked their 3,000th hit against the Rockies. Fans in Colorado got to see just one of the milestone hits, as Ichiro's triple off the right field wall in 2016 was the only one of these four knocks to take place in Denver. The Montréal Expos and Minnesota Twins are tied for second, at three each, in the most 3,000th hits allowed competition. Again, it's surprising that Montréal gave up so many, since the team played in Montréal for a relatively short 36 years. Hitters who victimized the Expos in this manner were Willie Mays, Pete Rose, and Tony Gwynn. And just like Coloradans, Canadians witnessed only one of the three hits, as Tony Gwynn singled for his milestone hit at Olympic Stadium in Montréal in 1999. The Twins gave up the milestone hit to Rod Carew, Eddie Murray, and Cal Ripken, Jr. Murray's and Ripken's hits came at the Metrodome in Minnesota.

Six other teams have given up two 3,000th milestone hits. These teams are the Baltimore Orioles, Chicago Cubs, Cleveland Indians, Detroit Tigers, N.Y. Yankees, and Seattle Mariners. What's interesting about the pairs of players who got the historic hit against these teams are the large differences in times between the hits for some of the teams. For example, the Indians, a franchise with roots back to 1901, gave up its first 3,000th hit to Robin Yount in 1992. Just seven years later, Wade Boggs collected his 3,000th hit against the Indians in 1999. The Tigers gave up 3,000th hits to Eddie Collins and Álex Rodríguez. In contrast to the short time between historic safeties for the Indians, there was a 90-year gap between hits for the Tigers. The time between hits given up for the other four teams is between these extremes.

Of course, the listing of teams in Table 5 that have given up a historic 3,000th hit raises the question of which teams have not given up one of these hits. In discussing such teams that were extant in 1903, the distinction between franchise and team once again becomes important. As teams, the Philadelphia Athletics and the St. Louis Browns never gave up a 3,000th hit. But as franchises, they have. The Oakland version of the Athletics allowed Dave Winfield to collect his 3,000th hit in 1993, and the Baltimore version of the Browns (the Orioles) gave up the 3,000th hits of Al Kaline and Adrián Beltré.

But there are five other teams that were around in 1903 that have

47

Part I—Analysis of Players with 3,000 Hits

not yielded a hit as a team or a franchise: the Boston Braves, Brooklyn Superbas (later the Dodgers), Chicago White Sox, N.Y. Giants, and St. Louis Cardinals. There are seven expansion franchises that have not given up a 3,000th hit: the Arizona Diamondbacks, Houston Astros, Miami Marlins, Milwaukee Brewers, San Diego Padres, Toronto Blue Jays, and Texas Rangers.

It appears that something doesn't add up properly in this analysis. Table 5 says there are 19 franchises that have given up a 3,000th hit, and the previous paragraph says there are five plus seven other franchises that have never given one up. Nineteen plus five plus seven is 31. There are only 30 MLB franchises. Something is wrong. The solution to the mystery is in Table 5. The Washington Senators yielded the 3,000th hit of Tris Speaker in 1925. The Minnesota Twins gave up three such hits to Rod Carew, Eddie Murray, and Cal Ripken, Jr. But the Twins are the same franchise as the Senators, so from a franchise standpoint, that franchise is double counted in Table 5. Eighteen plus 12 does add up to the required 30 franchises.

It's also interesting to compare Tables 4 and 5. Exactly one dozen teams appear in both tables, or to put it another way, 12 teams have had a player collect, and have yielded, a 3,000th hit. Those teams are Baltimore, Boston (A), California, Chicago (N), Cincinnati, Cleveland, Detroit, Kansas City, Minnesota, N.Y. (A), Pittsburgh, and Tampa Bay. That's of some interest, but how many teams do not appear in either table? Just three. The two expansion teams are Arizona and Toronto. It's not surprising that Arizona is there because the franchise only came into existence in 1998. Toronto has been around roughly 20 more years than Arizona, so Toronto too, is not surprising.

But what is surprising is that a marquee team that's been in existence for over a century has never had a player collect his 3,000th hit in its uniform, nor has it yielded a 3,000th hit to an opposing player. That franchise is the Brooklyn / Los Angeles Dodgers. The Dodgers are the only team that's been around since 1903 that doesn't appear in either table. Interestingly, the Dodgers National League counterpart during their time in New York, the Giants, would also not appear on either table if not for Willie Mays collecting his 3,000th hit as a San Francisco Giant.

8

TYPE OF HIT

It's also interesting to look at the type of hit each of these great players collected for their 3,000th hit. The data for each individual player is shown in Table 2. The data for the group is shown in Table 6. Cap Anson is not included so the total is 32 instead of 33 players.

Table 6:
3,000th Hits by Type of Hit

Hit Type	Players	Number	Percent	2022 Data	2022 Percent	Historical Percent*
Home Run	Boggs, Jeter, Rodríguez	3	9%	5215	10%	8%
Triple	Molitor, Suzuki	2	6%	643	1%	3%
Double	Wagner, Lajoie, Musial, Kaline, Rose, Henderson, Palmeiro, Pujols	8	25%	7940	15%	17%
Single	All others	19	59%	39,675	74%	72%
Total		32	100%†	53,473	100%	100%

*The historical percent is from the founding of the National League in 1876 to 2022.[1]
†Doesn't total 100% due to rounding.

Before discussing the data in Table 6, we need to recognize that there is some uncertainty associated with Honus Wagner's and Nap Lajoie's career hit totals. For example, Baseball-Reference.com shows that Wagner's career hit total was 3,420, while Major League Baseball shows Wagner with 3,430 career hits. As with Cap Anson's numbers, the source of the uncertainty is ambiguity in baseball statistical data before 1903. In 1914, the year both Wagner and Lajoie collected their 3,000th hits, the *Spalding Guides* were considered the authoritative source for baseball statistics. This is the source of the MLB data

Part I—Analysis of Players with 3,000 Hits

for Wagner. However, the pre–1903 statistics in the 1969 edition of the Macmillan *Baseball Encyclopedia* sometimes differ from the *Spalding Guides*. Baseball-Reference.com (as well as Retrosheet) uses the Macmillan *Baseball Encyclopedia* for their early data rather than using the *Spalding Guides*. This is why the Wagner and Lajoie hit totals differ from source to source.

It follows that if the hit totals differ, then the date of each player's 3,000th hit will differ, and the hit that constituted the milestone hit could differ as well. In Wagner's case, the press at the time, using the *Spalding Guide* data, celebrated Wagner's 3,000th hit on June 9, 1914, and reported that it was a double.[2] However, under the Macmillan data, that was Wagner's 2,990th hit, and he reached 3,000 hits about three weeks later on June 28 with a single. So, was Wagner's 3,000th hit a double or a single? A case can be made for either. Since the Hall of Fame data in Table 1 says that Wagner collected his 3,000th hit on June 9, 1914, we will assume that his 3,000th hit was a double as the press at the time reported, and use that in the Table 6 discussion. In Lajoie's case, the hit totals differ by just one hit for the different sources. Lajoie hit consecutive doubles in the game on September 27, 1914, so one of them was his 3,000th hit under either source. Unlike Wagner, Lajoie's 3,000th hit was definitely a double.

The first player to collect his 3,000th hit with a home run was Wade Boggs in 1999. It's somewhat surprising that it took that long for any player to get the milestone hit by going deep, given that sluggers like Musial, Aaron, Mays, and Kaline had the opportunity before Boggs. But it's even more surprising that Boggs did it first because he was definitely not a power hitter. His milestone hit was just the second home run he'd hit that season. Boggs put just 118 balls over the fence in his entire 18-year career, and about 20 percent of that total, 24, came in one year, 1987. He was a very unlikely candidate to be the first player to have his 3,000th hit be a home run. With that in mind, it's somewhat ironic that both Musial and Aaron hit a home run for their 3,001st safeties.

The second player to have his 3,000th hit be a home run was Derek Jeter. Jeter had a flair for the dramatic throughout his career. He won the Rookie of the Year Award and the World Series in 1996. His backhand toss to get Jason Giambi at the plate in the 2001 ALDS is now simply referred to as "The Flip." He became known as "Mr. November" for his walk-off home run after midnight to win Game 4 of the 2001 World Series for the Yankees. His headlong dive into the stands to catch a foul

8. Type of Hit

(From left) An unknown player, Honus Wagner and Ty Cobb in 1909. Wagner's Pirates defeated Cobb's Tigers in the 1909 World Series. Wagner collected his 3,000th hit off Erskine Mayer in 1914 (Library of Congress).

Part I—Analysis of Players with 3,000 Hits

ball in 2004 is known as "The Dive." So, it's not terribly surprising that Jeter also reached the 3,000-hit plateau in dramatic fashion.

Going into the July 9, 2011, game at Yankee Stadium, the 37-year-old Jeter had hit just two home runs all season. Both long balls came in the same game at Texas on May 8. He hadn't hit a home run at Yankee Stadium in almost a year, his last homer in the Bronx being on July 22, 2010. Jeter needed two knocks to get to 3,000 hits on July 9, and it wasn't a sure thing. He had gone 1-for-5 in the previous game, and David Price, who would win the Cy Young Award the following season, was on the mound for Tampa Bay.

Naturally, because it was Derek Jeter, none of the history mattered that day. Jeter singled in his first at-bat, and then pulled the eighth pitch he saw in his second at-bat over the left field wall for his 3,000th hit. And of course, Jeter being Jeter, that wasn't sufficiently impressive. He got three more hits in the game to go 5-for-5, and he threw in a stolen base for good measure. Jeter became the first Yankee to reach the 3,000-hit plateau, and the first player in any uniform to get the historic hit in Yankee Stadium.

Álex Rodríguez famously agreed to move to third base when he joined the Yankees in 2004. That change in position (Rodríguez had played shortstop during his time with the Texas Rangers) was necessary because Derek Jeter was manning shortstop in the Bronx. The two men were teammates for 10 years. Rodríguez was on the Yankee team when Jeter collected his 3,000th hit, but he was not in the lineup during Jeter's historic game due to a knee injury.

A little less than four years after Jeter's 3,000th hit, and the season after Jeter retired, Rodríguez faced his own date with destiny. He met that destiny in Jeterian style. Sitting on 2,999 hits in the first inning of a game against Detroit, Rodríguez confronted Justin Verlander in his pursuit of history. Verlander, four years after his first Cy-Young-Award-winning season, had retired the first two batters, and faced A-Rod with the bases empty.

His first pitch to Rodríguez caught too much of the plate, and the slugger drove the ball the opposite way over the right-center field wall. With that long ball, Rodríguez joined the 3,000-Hit Club, and became the third player to do so with a home run. He was also just the second player to wear a Yankee uniform when he collected the historic hit. And since no other player reached the milestone between the two Yankees, the pair became the first players from the same team to hit consecutive 3,000th hits, and the first two players to have their 3,000th hits be

8. Type of Hit

consecutive home runs. But Rodríguez couldn't match the rest of Jeter's historic day. He went hitless the rest of the game and finished 1-for-4, compared to 5-for-5 for Jeter. Rodríguez was, however, the first number one overall draft pick to reach the 3,000-hit plateau.

Modern fans are accustomed to many more home runs being hit than triples. For example, during the 2022 season, the home run / triple ratio was 5215 / 643, or a little more than eight home runs for every triple. It may surprise some fans that this has not always been the case in baseball. In 1920 the ratio was 721/1460 or about 0.5. To put it another way, there were about twice as many triples as home runs. By 1930 the ratio was 1786/1613 or about 1.1, meaning there were roughly the same number of home runs as triples. After 1930 the ratio became what we expect in today's game, more home runs than triples.

The brief discussion of the ratio of home runs to triples has bearing on the expectation of the number of 3,000th hits that were home runs compared to the number that were triples. The modern ratio suggests many more home runs than triples in the 3,000th hit universe. But in actuality, three players connected with a long ball for their 3,000th hit, and two players got there with a triple. This (two triples in 32 hits) is mildly surprising given the relative rarity of triples in today's game, but the result is most likely due to the small sample size, and the fact that this particular group of players consists of some of the best hitters to ever wield a bat.

That said, it took almost as long for a player to get his 3,000th hit with a triple as it did for a player (Boggs in 1999) to reach the milestone with a home run. Paul Molitor's triple on September 16, 1996, was the first 3,000th hit that went for three bases. However, Molitor's three-bagger was not as unexpected as Boggs' home run. Molitor had already hit seven triples that year, including a game in July with two triples, and two triples in September prior to the game on the 16th. Facing an 0-and-2 count, the Ignitor sent a long fly ball to right-center field that fell between the two outfielders, and he sped around second before diving safely into third.

None of the next eight players to reach 3,000 hits after Molitor did so with a triple. But 17 years later Ichiro Suzuki joined him on the short list of players who tripled for their 3,000th hit. In addition to the fact that the historic safety was a triple, a fascinating aspect of Ichiro's milestone hit is where it occurred. For most of the 2016 season the Marlins had used Ichiro primarily as a late-inning defensive replacement. This trend continued during a six-game road trip to Chicago and Colorado

Part I—Analysis of Players with 3,000 Hits

at the beginning of August. When Ichiro collected his 2,999th hit on the fifth game of the trip, the Marlins could have elected not to play him in the Sunday finale. This would have given Ichiro the opportunity to reach the milestone at home in Miami, with the expected attendance boost, during the Monday home game on August 8. This type of thinking is likely why 19 of the 32 3,000th hits (about 59 percent) occurred at home. But the Marlins' old-school manager, Don Mattingly, was having none of that. Mattingly had Ichiro start the finale in Denver on August 7, and Ichiro reached the milestone with a standup triple off the right field wall in his fourth at-bat of the day.

Table 6 shows that eight players doubled for their 3,000th hit. There are a couple of interesting aspects to the doubles list shown in the table. First, exactly 25 percent of all 3,000th hits were doubles. This is much higher than the 15 percent of hits that were doubles in 2022, and also higher than the 17 percent of major league hits since 1876 that were doubles.[3] Again, this is most likely due to the great hitters in this small sample. There could have been nine players on the doubles list in Table 6 except that Craig Biggio was thrown out at second trying to stretch his 3,000th hit from a single to a double. The video shows that Biggio was out easily at second. He made a poor decision to try for two bases because the ball didn't make it to the wall. Biggio is the only player who reached the milestone on a play where he was retired.

The second interesting aspect to the doubles list is that five of the eight players on the doubles list in Table 6 are in the top 10 in career doubles. Listed in the order shown in Table 6; Wagner is 10th in career doubles, Lajoie is 8th, Musial is 3rd, Rose is 2nd, and Pujols is 5th. In addition, 16 of the top 17 players with the most career doubles are also in the 3,000-Hit Club. The fact that players with the most career hits also have the most career doubles isn't unexpected, but the dominance of the 3,000-hit group at the top of the doubles list is mildly surprising. The only player of the top 17 who is not in the Club is David Ortiz. Ortiz finished with 632 doubles (12th on the all-time doubles list) but he was a little under 2,500 hits for his career. Why did Big Papi hit so many doubles? The 14 years that Ortiz spent playing his home games for Boston in Fenway Park with its short right-field line and short wall in right field (which allowed for more ground-rule doubles) significantly boosted his career doubles total.

Table 6 also shows the percentages of 3,000th hits that went for home runs, triples, doubles, and singles (the integers don't add to 100 percent due to rounding) compared to those same percentages for the

8. Type of Hit

2022 season and the historic percentages. Given the historically high rate that home runs are hit in today's game, it's a little surprising that the 2022 percentage of home runs is roughly the same as the percentage of home runs in the 3,000th-hit group. But three homers between 1999 and 2015 for the 3,000-Hit Club group evened these percentages up. And given the talent of the hitters in the 3,000-Hit Club, it's also not surprising that that group has a higher percentage of triples and doubles than occurred in 2022. More triples and doubles for the 3,000th-hit group mean fewer singles for the group. The data bears this out. In 2022, 74 percent of all hits were singles, but only 59 percent of the 3,000th-hit group were singles. It's interesting to note that there are higher percentages of home runs and singles in today's game compared to the historical data. Of course, that means fewer doubles and triples today.

9

THE PITCHERS

Table 2 also includes the names of the pitchers who gave up each of the 3,000th hits. Before discussing some of the pitchers as individuals, in conjunction with the earlier discussion of the higher than expected percentage of left-handed players in baseball, we will examine the handedness of the pitchers who surrendered 3,000th hits as a group, and the resulting right-on-right, right-on-left, etc., pitcher versus hitter confrontations. Twenty-two out of the 32 pitchers (about 69 percent) who surrendered a 3,000th hit were right-handed. Thus, there were 10 southpaws (about 31 percent) in the group. Given the small sample size, this percentage of left-handed pitchers is consistent with the earlier statement that roughly 26 percent of all pitchers are lefty.

The 3,000th hit pitcher versus hitter confrontation results are shown in Table 7.

Table 7:
3,000th Hits by Pitcher
Versus Hitter Confrontation

		Pitcher Throws	
		R	L
Batter Hits	R	12	5
	L	8	5

There is a problem with the numbers shown in Table 7 that must be addressed before discussing the results. The issue is that the numbers in the table total to 30, not the expected 32. The reason for this is that Pete Rose and Eddie Murray were switch hitters. They always enjoyed the opposite hand advantage. Both of them actually faced a right-handed pitcher and batted from the left side when they reached the 3,000th-hit

9. The Pitchers

plateau. This means the number eight in Table 7 technically should be a 10. This accounts for the difference between 32 and 30.

However, it would be slightly disingenuous to show Table 7 with a 10 in place of the eight, and no explanation. We are trying to better understand the nature of the pitcher versus hitter confrontation for this group of players. If every hitter were a switch hitter, we wouldn't learn anything from Table 7 because all of the numbers would be in the lower left or upper right corners of the table. That wouldn't be very informative. The table is more instructive without the two switch hitters being included in the results.

Neglecting the two righties who faced switch hitters leaves 20 right-handed pitchers who surrendered a 3,000th hit. A dozen of those pitchers faced a right-handed hitter, and eight of them faced left-handed hitters. That means that 12 of the 30 milestone hits (exactly 40 percent) came in the form of a right-handed batter facing a right-handed pitcher. In the other eight cases (8/30 is about 27 percent) a left-handed batter faced a righty pitcher. These numbers aren't surprising since over half (roughly 54 percent) of the batters in the 3,000-Hit Club hit righty, and about 40 percent hit lefty (the other six percent are switch hitters).

Examining the left-handed pitcher results shown in Table 7, five out of 30 milestone hits (about 17 percent) came during a southpaw pitcher versus righty matchup, and another five (again, about 17 percent) came from a southpaw versus lefty batter matchup. It's a little surprising that five of the 13 3,000th-hits by left-handed batters came against left-handed pitchers. Left-handed batters have a notoriously difficult time hitting against left-handed pitchers. There is data to support the notion.

A 2016 study found that lefty hitters had a .787 on-base plus slugging (OPS) percentage against right-handed pitchers, and a .698 OPS against left-handed pitchers.[1] For right-handed hitters, the OPS percentage against left-handed pitchers was .781 compared to .723 for righty hitters versus righty pitchers. In other words, not only do left-handed batters do significantly worse against southpaws than right-handed pitchers; in addition, the decline against same-handed pitchers for left-handed batters is worse than it is for right-handed batters.

Do these general conclusions apply to the great hitters under study here? The five left-handed hitters who reached the 3,000-hit plateau with a hit off a southpaw pitcher were Tris Speaker, Rod Carew, George Brett, Wade Boggs, and Ichiro Suzuki. Table 8 shows the career batting average splits for these players against both right-and-left handed pitchers.

Part I—Analysis of Players with 3,000 Hits

Table 8:
Career Batting Average Splits
for Selected Left-Handed Hitters

	Speaker	Carew	Brett	Boggs	Suzuki
vs. RHP	0.349	0.336	0.318	0.341	0.304
vs. LHP	0.338	0.31	0.28	0.297	0.329
RHP–LHP	0.011	0.026	0.038	0.044	-0.025

The data in Table 8 reveals that even the best left-handed hitters have difficulty with left-handed pitchers. Four of the five players have a higher batting average against righty pitchers, and in three of those cases the decline in batting average is significant. Wade Boggs lost 44 points off his batting average against lefties, and George Brett suffered a 38-point decline. In contrast, Tris Speaker was just 11 points worse against southpaws, and it's very surprising that Ichiro Suzuki actually batted better against left handers than he did against right handers. Setting Suzuki aside as an outlier, why do we see these results? It's likely that unfamiliarity is the culprit. Left-handed batters simply don't face left-handed pitching as much as they face right-handed pitching. As an aside, it's interesting to note that Brett did something none of the other great hitters in this study accomplished. He collected at least three hits in six consecutive games during May 1976. Brett is the only hitter to accomplish that feat since Jimmy Johnston in 1923.

In terms of the data in Table 7, all of this means that it's a little surprising that five of the 3,000th hits came from a lefty-on-lefty situation. However, even though left-handed batters do not do as well against southpaws in general, in the case of great hitters, not as well is still pretty good. Brett's career average against lefties is .280, and the other four hitters are near or above .300 for their careers versus southpaws. With that in mind, it's not too surprising that five of the milestone hits came in a left-on-left situation.

Returning to the data in Table 2, there are a few interesting tidbits just in the names of the pitchers. In the sole example of this in the data, the name of the pitcher who gave up Eddie Collins' 3,000th hit in 1925 was Rip Collins (no relation). Seventeen years later, in another singular example, a different pitcher with the nickname Rip, Rip Sewell, served up the next 3,000th hit to Paul Waner. This is the only example of pitchers with the same first name giving up consecutive 3,000th hits. Sewell has another claim to fame in addition to serving up the pitch to Waner.

9. The Pitchers

Tris Speaker posing with bat in 1911. Speaker was teammates with Ty Cobb and Eddie Collins on the 1928 Philadelphia Athletics. Collins and Speaker collected their 3,000th hits less than three weeks apart in 1925 (Library of Congress).

He is also recognized as the first player to use the eephus, or extremely slow, lob pitch. Many people thought it was impossible to hit the offering over the fence.[2] In the 1946 All-Star Game he famously threw it to Ted Williams who belted it for a home run.

None of the 32 pitchers who surrendered a 3,000th hit had the same surname. But three of them had the same first name. Mike Wegener, Mike Trombley, and Mike Leake gave up the 3,000th hits to Willie Mays, Eddie Murray, and Albert Pujols, respectively. The second most common given name to surrender 3,000th hits is John, of which there were two. Jon Matlack gave up the 3,000th hit to Roberto Clemente in 1972, and John Thomson surrendered Rickey Henderson's on the last day of the 2001 season.

Graph 2 shows the distribution of the ages at which hitters collected their 3,000th hit. The average age for the hitters was 39 years

Part I—Analysis of Players with 3,000 Hits

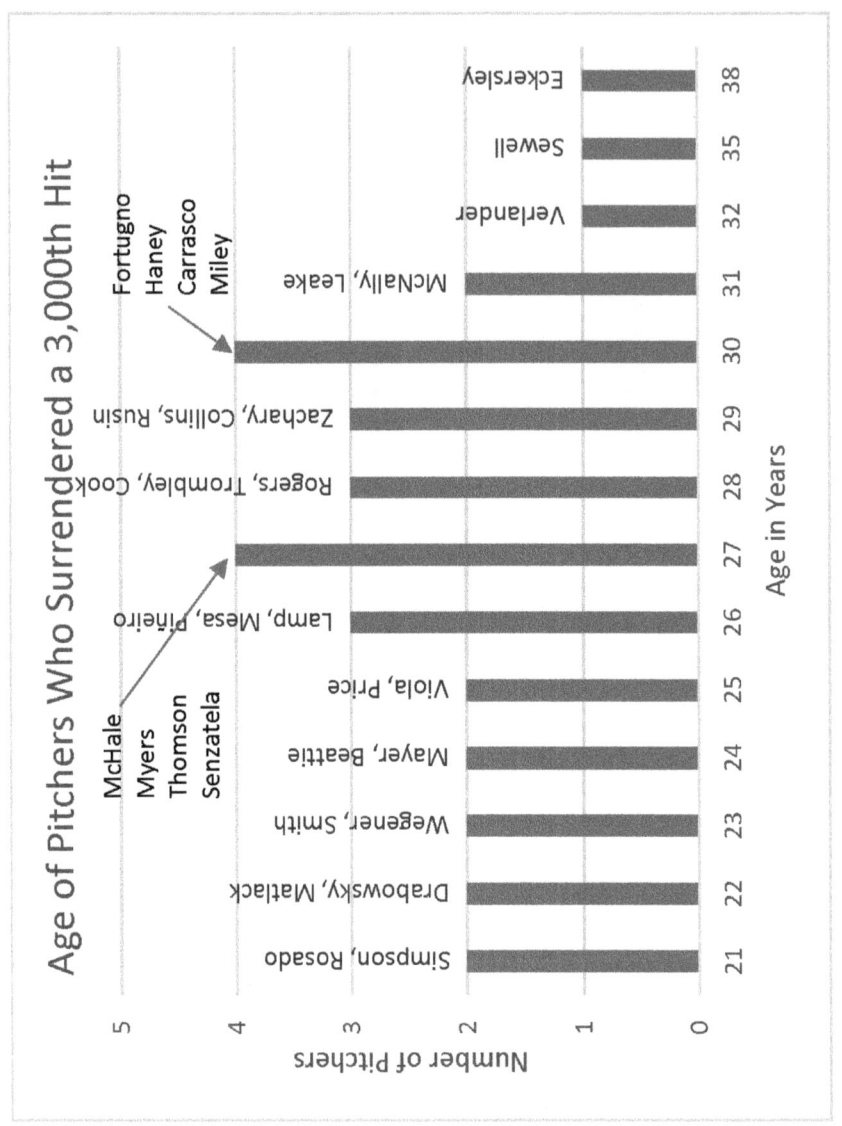

Graph 3: Pitchers Who Surrendered 3,000th Hits, Graphed by Age When Surrendered

old. That raises the same question for the pitchers who gave up those hits. What is the distribution of ages for those pitchers? The results are shown in Graph 3.

9. The Pitchers

It's not surprising that the distribution of the ages of pitchers who surrendered 3,000th hits is much wider than the hitter age distribution shown in Graph 2. Pitchers of any age can give up a hit, but it takes a long career as a hitter to reach 3,000 hits. Therefore, it's also not surprising that the average age of the pitchers who surrendered a 3,000th hit was about 27, compared to an average of about 39 for the hitters. As with the hitter distribution in Graph 2 the outlying data points are the most interesting. In Graph 3, this means looking at the youngest and oldest pitchers.

There were two 21-year-olds who surrendered a 3,000th hit. Wayne Simpson gave up the milestone single to Hank Aaron in 1970, and José Rosado surrendered Paul Molitor's milestone triple in 1996. Both Simpson and Rosado were in the first year of their careers when the opportunity to be part of history presented itself to them.

Although Simpson was making just the eighth start of his career for the Cincinnati Reds, he had begun that career in sensational fashion, with two complete game shutouts in his first three games, a 5–1 record, and a 2.05 ERA entering his start against the Braves with Aaron. In spite of the great start to the season, Simpson must have been nervous facing 36-year-old Hank Aaron with history on the line. Aaron was in the 17th year of his stellar 23-year career, and was third on the career home run list with 569 (behind only Ruth and Mays) when he stepped in the box before Simpson. The slugger reached the 3,000-hit milestone during his at-bat against the rookie in the first inning, and then took Simpson deep to add to his home run total in the third. After the game Simpson remarked, "If he hits like that now, how'd he hit 10 years ago?"[3]

Rosado was in a similar situation. Although the 40-year-old Molitor didn't enjoy the iconic stature that Aaron had at the time of his 3,000th hit, he was still a highly respected veteran who was intimidating when he stepped in the box. Molitor's historic hit took place in September, so Rosado, who had been called up in June, had a little more experience than Simpson. His effort against the Twins was the 14th start of his career. He went into the game with a 6–5 record and a 2.67 ERA. Molitor singled in the first inning for his 2,999th hit, and then reached the 3,000-hit plateau with a triple in the fifth. Giving up this hit wasn't the only notable event in Rosado's career. He was an All-Star the following year, and was the winning pitcher (with a blown save) in the 1997 All-Star Game. How did Rosado manage a blown save and a win? He entered the All-Star game in the top of the seventh inning with the American League-leading 1–0, but allowed a home run that tied

Part I—Analysis of Players with 3,000 Hits

the game and saddled Rosado with a blown save. Sandy Alomar's two-RBI homer in the bottom of the inning were the last runs scored in the game, so Rosado got the win. His short five-year career ended in 2000.

Three years to the day before the young Rosado would give up Molitor's historic hit on September 16, 1996, a pitcher at the other end of his career had given up a similar hit. When Dave Winfield singled for his 3,000th hit on September 16, 1993, the man on the mound was eventual Hall of Famer Dennis Eckersley. The 38-year-old Eckersley, who had won the Cy Young Award and the MVP Award the previous season, was in the 19th year of his career. He entered the game on September 16 in the bottom of the ninth inning with the A's holding a two-run lead over Winfield's Twins. But Eckersley did not have his great stuff in this game. In addition to the historic hit by Winfield, Eckersley allowed three other hits in the inning, and two runs scored to tie the game. The Twins eventually won in the 13th inning.

This wasn't the only famous (or infamous, to an Oakland A's fan) hit that Eckersley allowed to a batter. Most baseball fans have probably seen the video, and heard Vin Scully's historic call, of Kirk Gibson's walk-off home run (surrendered by Eckersley) during Game 1 of the 1988 World Series. In fact, Eckersley is widely credited with coining the phrase "walk-off," as the pitcher walks off the mound after allowing a game winning hit. But what happens in the national spotlight of the World Series becomes lore, for better or worse. Just as Bill Buckner could never live down the error he made in Game 6 of the 1986 World Series, the Gibson homer is arguably what Eckersley is most famous for.

But this is terribly unfair to these two players, and any other player in a similar situation. Eckersley had a stellar *24-year* career. His first 12 years (1975–86) he was almost exclusively a starting pitcher. During this period he had a record of 151–128, with an ERA of 3.67 and 100 complete games. The following 12 years he was primarily used as a relief pitcher. He registered 387 saves, and a 2.96 ERA in this time frame. Over his entire career he appeared in 1,071 games. It's very likely that Eckersley will be the last pitcher to throw 100 complete games and appear in over 1,000 games, given the rarity of complete games in modern baseball.[4] One bad pitch under World Series klieg lights should not eclipse the accomplishments of a long and noteworthy career.

The other name that stands out from the right side of Graph 3 is Verlander. Justin Verlander was 32 years old when he delivered the pitch that Álex Rodríguez sent over the wall for his 3,000th hit in 2015. Before surrendering that knock, he'd won the Rookie of the Year Award

9. The Pitchers

in 2006, and the Cy Young Award, along with the Most Valuable Player Award, in 2011. That's a pretty good pitching resume by itself, and for many pitchers, that would have been the end of any hardware collected. But unlike most other pitchers, Verlander improved as he aged. At 36 years old in 2019, he went 21–6 with a 2.58 ERA, and won his second Cy Young Award. He topped that performance three seasons later. As a 39-year-old in 2022, he went 18–4 with a 1.75 ERA, for which he was rewarded for that performance with a third Cy Young Award. Only three men have won that award at an older age. Those pitchers are Roger Clemens (42 in 2004), Gaylord Perry (40 in 1978), and Early Winn (39 in 1959).

In addition to Eckersley and Verlander, two other pitchers shown in Table 2 have won a Cy Young Award. In 1985, when he surrendered Rod Carew's 3,000th hit, Frank Viola was a 25-year-old in his fourth year in the big leagues, who was clearly still learning the craft of pitching. Evidence that the learning process was working came in the form of a 2.90 ERA in 1987. In 1988, Viola went 24–7 with a 2.64 ERA on his way to 27 out of 28 first-place votes for the Cy Young Award. Dennis Eckersley got the one other first place vote that year.

Sixteen years later in 2011, another 25-year-old in his fourth year in the majors, David Price, surrendered the home run that put Derek Jeter into the 3,000-hit Club. Price went 12–13 that year, but he turned things around in 2012. That stellar season included a 20–5 record with a 2.56 ERA and a Cy Young Award. However, in contrast to Viola who won the award almost unanimously, Price won the award in a very close vote. He edged out one of the other pitchers on the Table 2 list, Justin Verlander, by a mere four vote points.

Another pitcher in Table 2 who deserves to be mentioned is José Mesa. In 1992, Robin Yount hit a single to right field off Mesa to reach the 3,000-hit plateau. Like Viola and Price, Mesa was in the fourth year of his career and was the starting pitcher when he surrendered the historic hit. But like Eckersley who also began his career as a starter, Mesa transitioned to a relief role and became an excellent closer. In 1995, he led all of baseball with 46 saves, and came in second in the Cy Young Award voting. He finished his 19-year career with 321 saves. As of year-end 2023, he was tied for 21st on the all-time career saves list with Aroldis Chapman.

10

The Stadiums

Another topic related to this exploration of 3,000th hits is the stadiums where these hits took place. The 32 (once again ignoring Cap Anson because we don't know when he reached 3,000 hits) safeties under discussion were struck in 25 different stadiums. These venues are listed in alphabetical order in Table 9.

Table 9:
Stadiums Where 3,000th Hits Took Place

Stadium	3,000th Hits	Player(s)	When Stadium Closed*
1. Anaheim Stadium, Anaheim	2	Carew, Brett	
2. Baker Bowl, Philadelphia	1	Wagner	1938
3. Braves Field, Boston	1	Waner	1952
4. Busch Memorial Stadium, St. Louis	1	Brock	2005
5. Candlestick Park, San Francisco	1	Mays	1999
6. Comerica Park, Detroit	1	Cabrera	
7. Coors Field, Denver	1	Suzuki	
8. County Stadium, Milwaukee	1	Yount	2000
9. Crosley Field, Cincinnati	1	Aaron	1970
10. Fenway Park, Boston	1	Yastrzemski	
11. Globe Life Park, Arlington	1	Beltré	2019
12. Hubert H. Humphrey Metrodome, Minneapolis	3	Winfield, Murray, Ripken Jr.	2009

64

10. The Stadiums

	Stadium	3,000th Hits	Player(s)	When Stadium Closed*
13.	Kauffman Stadium, Kansas City	1	Molitor	
14.	League Park, Cleveland	2	Lajoie, Speaker	1946
15.	Memorial Stadium, Baltimore	1	Kaline	1991
16.	Minute Maid Park, Houston	1	Biggio	
17.	Navin Field, Detroit	2	Cobb, Collins	1999
18.	Olympic Stadium, Montréal	1	Gwynn	2004
19.	Qualcomm Stadium, San Diego	1	Henderson	2003
20.	Riverfront Stadium, Cincinnati	1	Rose	2002
21.	Safeco Field, Seattle	2	Palmeiro, Pujols	
22.	Three Rivers Stadium, Pittsburgh	1	Clemente	2000
23.	Tropicana Field, Tampa Bay	1	Boggs	
24.	Wrigley Field, Chicago	1	Musial	
25.	Yankee Stadium, N.Y.	2	Jeter, Rodríguez	

*When the stadium closed for baseball. Some venues continued to be used for other events.

The location of the first of the known 3,000th hits has an interesting twist. According to the Hall of Fame (which is the source for Table 9), Honus Wagner struck his 3,000th hit at the Baker Bowl in Philadelphia. However, as discussed earlier, if we look at the alternative count of Wagner's hits provided by Baseball-Reference.com and Retrosheet, Wagner got his 3,000th hit on June 28, 1914, at Redland Field in Cincinnati. Redland Field, better known as Crosley Field, opened in 1912.[1] The Reds finished fourth (of eight) in the National League in 1912 and seventh in 1913. This means that Wagner's hit in 1914 was the first event of historical significance to take place in the ballpark under the alternate count.

The twist is that the last major historical event to take place at Crosley Field was also a 3,000th hit. Crosley Field was scheduled to close after the 1969 season. However, when Riverfront Stadium was not ready in time for the 1970 season, the Reds were forced to play home games during the first half of the 1970 campaign at Crosley Field. This is why Henry Aaron's 3,000th hit on May 17, 1970, took place at Crosley Field,

Part I—Analysis of Players with 3,000 Hits

rather than Riverfront Stadium. The last game the Reds played at Crosley Field took place a little over a month later, on June 24. If Riverfront Stadium had opened on time, that venue would have seen the 3,000th hit of both Aaron and Pete Rose. Instead, under Wagner's alternative hit accounting, Wagner's and Aaron's 3,000th hits were significant historical events at the beginning and end of Crosley Field's existence. In between these two milestones, Crosley Field hosted the first night game in major league history on May 24, 1935.

Regardless of whether Wagner's milestone hit took place at Baker Bowl or Crosley Field, the venue no longer exits. These two stadiums closed in 1938 and 1970, respectively. In fact, an interested observer can visit just 10 of the 25 ballparks where a 3,000th hit took place. Most of the other venues have been torn down. All 15 of these defunct stadiums have interesting histories, but we'll just discuss a few.

Two of the three players that struck their 3,000th hit in the 1920s did so at Navin Field in Detroit. Both Ty Cobb (in 1921) and Eddie Collins (in 1925) joined the 3,000-Hit Club there. The ballpark opened in 1912 so it was roughly a decade old when these two historic hits took place.

The right-field bleachers at the Baker Bowl in Philadelphia in 1915. The venue hosted Honus Wagner's 3,000th hit in 1914 and Babe Ruth's last plate appearance in 1935. It was the home field for the Philadelphia Phillies from 1895 to 1938 (Library of Congress).

10. The Stadiums

The interesting aspect of the park is how long fans were able to watch a game in the venue where Cobb's and Collins' hits took place. Navin Field, also called Briggs Stadium, is better known to late 20th-century fans as Tiger Stadium. The stadium got a series of facelifts in the late 1970s and early 1980s that extended its life to the end of the century, but it closed its doors to baseball after the 1999 season. For nearly three quarters of a century after Eddie Collins joined the 3,000-Hit Club in 1925, fans could watch a game in the historic venue.

The Baker Bowl, home to the Philadelphia Phillies from 1895 to 1938, unwittingly hosted a significant event three years before it closed. Most baseball fans know that Babe Ruth played for the Yankees. However, many fans may not be aware that Ruth finished his career with the Boston Braves. Ruth wanted to manage, but it was clear to him that that wasn't going to happen with the Yankees. He was led to believe that he would get to manage with the Braves after he retired, so he went to Boston for the 1935 season.[2] However, except for a couple of flashes of brilliance, the aging Ruth played poorly for the Braves, and by the end of May he decided it was time to retire. His last plate appearance took place at the Baker Bowl on May 30, 1935. Unfortunately for Ruth, the Braves never really intended to allow him to manage the club. That was just a ploy to get him to play in order to put more fans in the seats.

The name Braves has an interesting history. Modern fans think of the franchise as the Atlanta Braves. But before the team moved to Atlanta in 1966, it played in Milwaukee for 13 years, where it won a World Series in 1957. Prior to Milwaukee, the franchise was in Boston. The Boston franchise had a number of names prior to James Gaffney's purchase of the team in 1912. Gaffney was a member of the Tammany Hall political organization, which had an Indian on their logo. That association led the press to refer to Gaffney's team as the Boston Braves.[3] When Gaffney's new stadium for the team (located about a mile west of Fenway Park) was completed in 1915, it was called Braves Field. Paul Waner, who spent most of his career in Pittsburgh before moving to the Braves in 1941, singled off of his Pirate teammate from 1938 to 1940, Rip Sewell, at Braves Field to become the seventh member of the 3,000-Hit Club in 1942. Braves Field closed after the 1952 season because the franchise moved to Milwaukee.

The third and the fifth of the 3,000th hits were struck at League Park in Cleveland. Napoleon Lajoie's double at League Park in 1914 was his 3,000th hit and made him the third player to reach the plateau. Nine

Part I—Analysis of Players with 3,000 Hits

years later, Tris Speaker became the fifth player with 3,000 hits with a single at League Park.

In addition to these two events, League Park hosted other events of historical significance. The venue had been built in 1891 as the home for the National League's Cleveland Spiders. Cy Young played for the Spiders from 1890 to 1898, and led the team to a Temple Cup victory (the championship series at the time) in 1895.

However, poor attendance in 1898 caused the team's owner to transfer the Spider's best players, including Cy Young, to the St. Louis Browns after the 1898 season.[4] As a result, League Park hosted the worst team in major league history. The 1899 Spiders compiled an all-time worst record (with a minimum of 120 games) of 20–134, for a .130 winning percentage. Attendance was so low (the Spiders drew about 6,000 fans for the whole season) that other teams refused to come to Cleveland because they couldn't cover travel costs with their portion of the gate receipts. This forced the Spiders to play the last 36 games of the season on the road. The team lost all but one of those 36 road games. Not surprisingly, the Spiders were one of four teams removed from the National League when the league contracted from 12 teams to eight in 1900.

Cleveland and League Park were without major league baseball for just one season. The American League placed the Cleveland Blues in League Park in 1901. The team name changed to Bronchos in 1902, and Naps (named after the popular player Napoleon Lajoie) in 1903. Lajoie recorded his 3,000th hit at League Park as a Cleveland Nap in 1914. When he left after that season, the team became the Cleveland Indians. Tris Speaker collected his 3,000th hit at League Park as a Cleveland Indian in 1925. League Park hosted another event of historical significance between these two hits, the 1920 World Series.

The 1920 World Series pitted two teams that had never won a modern World Series since the initiation of the Fall Classic in 1903. The Brooklyn Robins represented the National League, while the Indians represented the American League. The terrible tragedy of Ray Chapman's death cast a pall over the event. Chapman was Cleveland's shortstop for most of the 1920 season. He was struck in the head by a pitch from Carl Mays on August 16, and he died the next day.[5] Chapman remains the only player to die after being hit by a pitch.

As was customary at the time, Chapman was not wearing a batting helmet when he was hit in the head by Mays' pitch a century ago. Modern sensibilities suggest that his tragic death would lead to an

10. The Stadiums

immediate call for something to be done to prevent it from happening again, an obvious solution being some form of head protection. Take a minute to consider when you think batting helmets became required in major league baseball. The answer may surprise you.

How long did it take after Chapman's death for batting helmets to be required in the big leagues? The answer: half a century! Major league baseball did not require hitters to wear a batting helmet until 1971.[6] Why did it take so long? The surprising answer is that the players, and their coaches, opposed it. Joe McCarthy, who managed the Yankees from 1931 to 1946 with seven championships over that period said, "No man on my team will ever wear one. I don't think any wants to. Wearing protection like that is an indication the batter is plate-shy. And plate-shy batters don't make any winning teams!" Tommy Henrich, who spent 11 years with the Yankees from 1937 to 1950 opined, "Injuries to batters on pitched balls are purely accidents and accidents will happen. [Mickey] Cochrane and Chapman were struck because they were careless."[7]

To be fair, the danger to batters was known, and baseball did require a batting helmet or a plastic cap insert in the 1950s. Most players chose the insert. In addition, there were numerous individual and team efforts at instituting a batting helmet in the 1940s–1960s. Ear flaps on batting helmets became required in 1983. However, veterans were grandfathered in such that they weren't required to adhere to the 1971 or 1983 rules. The last player to bat with an insert instead of a helmet was Red Sox catcher, Bob Montgomery in 1979. The last player to bat without an ear flap on his batting helmet was Tim Raines in 2001.[8]

Baseball experimented with a nine-game World Series four times (1903 and 1919–21), and three of those four Series went eight games. The 1920 Series was the exception, concluding with an Indian victory in the seventh game at League Park. The Series had opened with three games at Ebbets Field in Brooklyn before moving to Cleveland for four games. After splitting the first four games of the Series, the Indians won the final three games at League Park to take the crown.

Game Five provided highlights that are worthy of note. Indians right fielder, Elmer Smith, hit the first grand slam in World Series history in the first inning. In another offensive first, Cleveland pitcher Jim Bagby hit the first home run by a pitcher during a World Series in the seventh inning. Both of these feats have been replicated in subsequent Series. In between these two blasts came a feat that has never been equaled in the Fall Classic. Indian second baseman, Bill Wambsganss, turned the only unassisted triple play in World Series history in the fifth

Part I—Analysis of Players with 3,000 Hits

inning. With men on first and second, a hard line drive came right to Wambsganss. He stepped on second for a force out, and then tagged out the runner from first (who was running with a hit-and-run on) to complete the triple play. Over a span of 11 years, League Park witnessed two 3,000th hits, a World Series unassisted triple play, and a home team World Series victory.

The Hubert H. Humphrey Metrodome was the home of the Minnesota Twins from 1982 until 2009. The notoriously loud stadium helped the Twins win the World Series in 1987 and 1991. It was so loud there during the 1987 Series that broadcaster Al Michaels alleged that the Twins piped in artificial crowd noise. The team denied the accusation.[9] In addition to these two events, the Metrodome also has the distinction of hosting more 3,000th hits than any other stadium (three), and of being one of just two venues where consecutive 3,000th hits took place. The other venue with consecutive 3,000th hits is Yankee Stadium where Derek Jeter (2011) and Álex Rodríguez (2015) reached the milestone.

The first of the three historic hits at the Metrodome took place in 1993 when Dave Winfield singled off Dennis Eckersley. That safety was noteworthy for a number of reasons. In addition to Eckersley being the oldest pitcher to surrender a 3,000th hit, Winfield's safety was the first 3,000th hit to be struck in an indoor stadium. Winfield, who was born in St. Paul and went to high school and college locally, also became the first player to reach the 3,000-hit plateau while playing for his hometown team. He was the second man in the 3,000-Hit Club (after Al Kaline) who never played in the minors.

Less than two years later, the Metrodome was the site where the next member of the Club, Eddie Murray, got his historic hit. Murray's single off Mike Trombley in 1995 marked the first time that consecutive 3,000th hits had been struck in the same venue. Five years later, Cal Ripken, Jr., became the third player to join the club with a hit at the Metrodome when he singled off Hector Carrasco in 2000. Ripken's milestone hit came on Tax Day. He's the only player to collect his 3,000th hit in April.

The Metrodome came close to being the site of a third consecutive 3,000th hit and a fourth historic 3,000th hit. In September of 1996, Paul Molitor was playing for the Twins and approaching the 3,000-hit plateau. After a game at the Metrodome on September 14, Molitor was sitting on 2,998 hits with the final game of a nine-game homestand coming up on the 15th. The Twins were going to embark on a road trip starting on the 16th, so if Molitor didn't get two hits on the 15th, he would likely reach the milestone on the road.

10. The Stadiums

Two hits in a game is no cinch, even for hitters of Molitor's caliber, but he had gotten two hits on the 14th, two hits on the 13th, and three hits on the 11th, so it was entirely possible that he would get the hits he needed to reach the milestone in front of the hometown fans on the 15th. But it was not to be. Molitor was hit by a pitch in the bottom of the first inning, and he then grounded out to short three times to finish the game without a safety. Of course, he got three hits the next day at Kauffman Stadium in Kansas City to put him into the 3,000-Hit Club. The second of those hits was a triple, which made Molitor the first man to hit a triple for his 3,000th hit.

There are several interesting coincidences associated with Molitor's achievement of the 3,000-hit milestone. He joined Dave Winfield as the second native of St. Paul, Minnesota, to join the 3,000-Hit Club. This made them the first two players from the same hometown to join the Club. Both players reached the milestone while playing for their hometown team, the Twins, and Molitor's 3,000th hit came three years to the day after Winfield reached the plateau on September 16, 1993.

Now we turn to the 10 venues that are still open where a 3,000th hit took place. Many fans attending games at these stadiums may not realize this aspect of the history of the venue. Technically, the oldest of these stadiums is Fenway Park in Boston, which opened in 1912. However, from a 2020s perspective, the fact that Wrigley Field in Chicago opened two years later is immaterial. Both venues deserve the recognition they get for being hallowed ground in the world of baseball.

Even though Fenway is older, Wrigley was the first of these two iconic parks to host a 3,000th hit. In 1958 Stan Musial doubled off Moe Drabowsky at Wrigley to become the eighth player to reach 3,000 hits. Those are the raw facts, but the story behind these details is more interesting. As was customary during that time period, Musial's Cardinals had a long homestand from May 2–18, 1958, where the team played 16 games over the fortnight, with a two-day road trip to Chicago on May 12 and 13 to play the Cubs, sandwiched between games in St. Louis on the 11th and 14th.

The Cardinals played a doubleheader on May 11. The hot-hitting Musial, who was batting .480 going into the twin bill, collected five hits over the two games on the 11th to increase his career hit total to 2,998. As fate would have it, the next two games were in Chicago, so it seemed likely that Musial would reach the milestone there instead of in front of the home fans in St. Louis. That prospect seemed almost certain when Musial doubled in the first inning on May 12 leaving him just one safety

Part I—Analysis of Players with 3,000 Hits

short of the milestone. But, in his other four at-bats during the game, Stan the Man walked, and grounded out three times, which meant he was sitting on 2,999 hits going into the last of the two contests in Chicago on May 13.

The Cardinals' manager, Fred Hutchinson, wanted Musial to collect the milestone hit in St. Louis (where the Cardinals would be playing the next day), so Hutchinson did not put Musial in the starting lineup for the May 13 game.[10] The Cardinals trailed 3–1 going into the top of the sixth inning of the contest on the 13th. The leadoff hitter for the Cardinals that inning doubled, but a ground out brought pitcher Sam Jones to the plate with one out and a man on second. With right-handed Drabowsky on the mound, the situation called for a left-handed pinch hitter. Hutchinson called on Musial to be that pinch hitter. When Musial doubled to drive in a run, he became the only man to reach his 3,000th hit as a pinch hitter.

Portrait of Stan Musial, date unknown. In an interesting coincidence, Musial had the same number of hits, 1,815, at home and on the road. He collected his 3,000th hit off Moe Drabowsky in 1958 (National Baseball Hall of Fame and Museum, Cooperstown, N.Y.).

The 37-year-old Musial was immediately replaced by a pinch runner, and the Cardinals went on to win the game 5–3.

That's how Wrigley Field became the site of a 3,000th hit. Any number of slightly different circumstances likely would have resulted in Musial reaching the milestone at Busch Stadium I in St. Louis. That stadium had been known as Sportsman's Park until brewer Anheuser-Busch bought the Cardinals in 1953. No matter the name, Busch Stadium I could easily have been the venue for a 3,000th hit, and then it would have been 20 of 32 (about 63 percent) 3,000th hits being struck at home.

10. The Stadiums

It seems appropriate that Carl Yastrzemski was the player who collected his 3,000th hit at Fenway Park. Few players are more closely associated with the Red Sox than Yaz, who spent the entirety of his outstanding 23-year career in Boston. He singled to right field off Jim Beattie of the Yankees on September 12, 1979, to reach the milestone. But as with Musial's historic hit, the story behind Yaz's milestone safety is more interesting than the simple facts.

The Red Sox opened a seven-game homestand against Baltimore and New York on September 7. Yastrzemski collected three hits in the opening game of that homestand on the 7th to increase his career hit total to 2,998. That seemed to ensure he would reach the milestone in Boston. Another hit in the contest on September 9 put him within one hit of the coveted plateau. But Yaz came up empty in the next two contests, causing the press and the public to get a little nervous. The *Boston Globe* reported, "For this old soldier, the Yaz watch is hell."[11] Early events in the game on the 12th seemed to confirm that notion.

Yastrzemski walked in the first inning and flied out in the third. The Red Sox took a seven-run lead into the sixth inning, which meant that the home team was not likely to bat in the ninth. When Yaz grounded out in the home half of the sixth, it meant he would not get another at-bat in the game without the Red Sox putting another runner on base. Dwight Evans came to the rescue with a two-out single in the seventh. Yastrzemski would get one more at-bat in the eighth. He came up with two outs, and the Red Sox leading by six. This was his last chance in this game, and the next game was the last of the homestand. It suddenly seemed much more likely he would collect the historic hit on the road. But the fates were kind to Yaz and the Boston faithful. His groundball past Willie Randolph at second ended the suspense, and put Yastrzemski into the 3,000-Hit Club.

Your humble scribe finds the spelling of Yastrzemski's name interesting. If you don't already know how to spell that name, from the pronunciation it sounds like it should be something like Y-a-z-t-r-e-m-s-k-y. His nickname, Yaz, helps to reinforce this misspelling notion. The pronunciation definitely does *not* sound like the name starts with Y-a-s. Nor does it sound like the next three letters are t-r-z. All of which means you can't go by the pronunciation when spelling his name. You just have to remember that it is Y-a-s instead of Y-a-z, and that the next three letters are t-r-z. The rest makes sense. Of course, you can argue this kind of thing is very common in English, and that it's not unusual.

Part I—Analysis of Players with 3,000 Hits

That argument is reasonable, but it still seems counterintuitive that the name starts with Y-a-s instead of Y-a-z.

Any discussion of past and present baseball stadiums would not be complete without mentioning Yankee Stadium. What's surprising in the context of this examination of 3,000th hits, is how long that historic venue existed without hosting a 3,000th-hit milestone. The original Yankee Stadium, accurately referred to as "The House That Ruth Built," opened in 1923. The stadium was extensively renovated in the 1970s, and the Yankees played there until 2008. The team played at Shea Stadium while the renovations took place, so Yankee Stadium hosted baseball for 84 seasons. But the venue never saw a 3,000th hit in spite of hosting baseball for such a long time, as well as being the home field for baseball luminaries such as Babe Ruth, Lou Gehrig, Joe DiMaggio, Mickey Mantle, and Reggie Jackson.

The new Yankee Stadium, a completely different edifice, was built across the street from the site of the original stadium, and opened for the 2009 season. Just two years later, the almost brand-new building witnessed Derek Jeter's historic home run for his 3,000th hit in 2011. And a mere four years after that, Álex Rodríguez became the second player to join the 3,000-Hit Club with a home run in 2015. It's mildly ironic that the original Yankee Stadium did not host a 3,000th hit in over 80 years of existence, but the new building of the same name saw two of the historic hits in its first seven years.

11

BIRTHPLACES AND BIRTHDAYS

Another question related to these 33 special players is, where are they from? There are a couple of ways this question could be answered. The answer could refer to the player's place of birth, but it could also refer to where the player spent his childhood, or where he went to high school or college. Which of these locations is best depends on the purpose behind the question. If the purpose is to understand the formative experiences that enabled a player to reach the major leagues, then where he spent his childhood, or played high school ball, is probably the best way to answer the question. But for the purpose of this investigation, the goal is simply to see where the players are from in terms of distribution around the country (or outside the country), and to see if there are any interesting patterns to the distribution. Therefore, this investigation will use place of birth to define where the players are from.

The story that baseball was invented by Abner Doubleday at Cooperstown in 1839 is a myth. Many of the rules of the game as we know it today were set down by Alexander Cartwright and other members of the New York Knickerbocker Club, around 1850. The game became very popular in the New York City area before the Civil War. This little bit of history suggests that the early players of the game would be from the New York and eastern seaboard area of the country. It further suggests that the first few players to reach 3,000 hits would be from that part of the country, and that as the game spread, so would the distribution of the birthplaces of our special set of 33 players.

Those assumptions about the spread of the game (and 3,000-hit players' birthplaces) are incorrect. The game was played by soldiers on both sides during the Civil War. When those soldiers returned to their hometowns, baseball experienced a post–Civil War boom nationwide.

Part I—Analysis of Players with 3,000 Hits

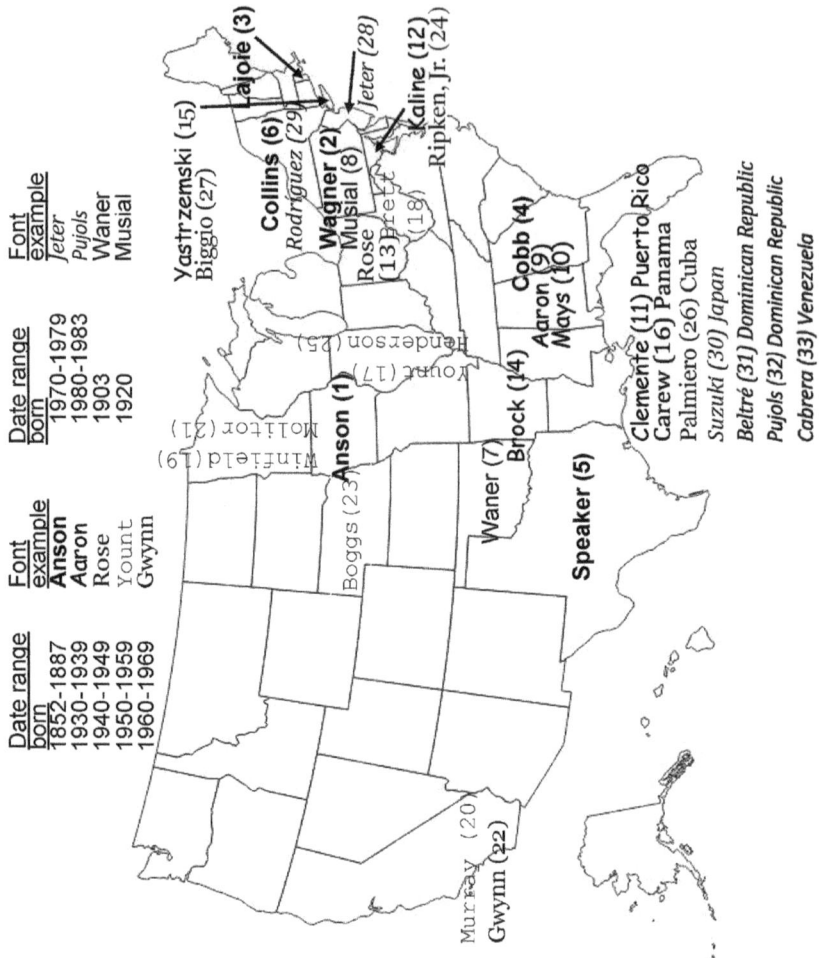

Figure 1: Birth Locations and Date Range Born for 3,000-Hit Club Members

That boom explains why the first players to eventually reach 3,000 hits were not all from the eastern seaboard. Figure 1 shows the birthplaces of these players in terms of the states where they were born. It also shows the shows the distribution of the births through time by the decade the player was born. It should be noted that the location of the names within a state is not significant. With the exceptions of Eddie Murray and Tony Gwynn (who were born in Los Angeles) there is no intention in Figure 1 to indicate town of birth by name location within a state.

Figure 1 shows that the 26 members of the 3,000-Hit Club born in

11. Birthplaces and Birthdays

the continental United States came from 16 different states. Only one state west of Texas, California, had a member of the Club born there. Six states were home to two club members, those states being Alabama, California, Illinois, Maryland, Minnesota, and Pennsylvania. The only state with more than two club members was New York, where four members of the Club were born. Two of those four native New Yorkers were born about 50 miles apart on eastern Long Island.

The other seven members of the Club were not born in the continental United States. Four of them were from the Caribbean area: Puerto Rico, Cuba, and two from the Dominican Republic. Two more were from Central America (Panama and Venezuela) with the last of the seven being from Japan. The growth of baseball internationally is demonstrated by the fact that five of the last eight men who reached 3,000 hits were not born in the continental U.S.

The first six players to reach the 3,000-hit milestone were born before 1900, and they were from all over the country. The post–Civil War boom in baseball reached Cap Anson's hometown of Marshalltown, Iowa, as the young Anson (born in 1852) reached his teenage years. The boy loved the game, and somewhere in the midst of his 27-year career (which ended in 1897, and is tied for the longest-ever major league career) he reached 3,000 hits. Who is the only other player in baseball history to have a 27-year career? The answer: Nolan Ryan. Ryan played roughly a century after Anson, and threw his last pitch in 1993. It's incredible that any pitcher could throw in the major leagues for that long. Your author was lucky enough to be at the game when Ryan threw his last pitch. An account of the contest can be found at the Society for American Baseball Research website.[1] It's worth noting that Ryan's career would have spanned 28 years, except that he missed the 1967 season due to an arm injury and time in the Army Reserve.

The other five players to reach the 3,000-hit milestone who were born before 1900 were from different sections of the country. Three of them were born in the Northeast. Honus Wagner (born 1874) was from western Pennsylvania, Eddie Collins (born 1887) was from upstate New York, and Napoleon Lajoie (born 1874) was from Rhode Island. Ty Cobb (born 1886) was a Georgia native, and Tris Speaker (born 1888) hailed from central Texas. Wagner was about seven months older than Lajoie, and in an interesting coincidence he collected his 3,000th hit about three months before Lajoie did in 1914. Speaker, who was 11 months younger than Collins, collected his 3,000th hit about two weeks before

Part I—Analysis of Players with 3,000 Hits

Collins in 1925. We will see this kind of close relationship between birthdays and 3,000th hits again.

Paul Waner (born 1903) was the first man born in the 20th century to reach the 3,000-hit plateau. Waner, from Oklahoma, was the only man born between 1889 and 1919 to get to 3,000 hits. Stan Musial (born 1920) was the only man born from 1904 to 1930 to join the Club. But what's more interesting about Musial is his birthplace. Stan the Man was from Donora, Pennsylvania, a small town only 30 miles east of Chartiers, Pennsylvania, and 30 miles south of Pittsburgh. Why is that significant? Because Honus Wagner was from Chartiers. This means that western Pennsylvania, just a few miles south of Pittsburgh, produced two of the best hitters in history.

Musial is not the only excellent player from Donora. Buddy Griffey played at Donora High School with Musial. Buddy's surname is familiar for a reason. He was father to Ken Griffey, Sr., and grandfather to Hall of Famer Ken Griffey, Jr.[2] Griffey Sr. and Griffey Jr. were both born in Donora. In addition, Beaver Falls, Pennsylvania, where quarterback Joe Namath was born in 1943 is about 40 miles north of Pittsburgh. Maybe there's something in the water in that area.

Although only two players in the Club were born between 1903 and 1929, six members were born in the 1930s. The first of these was Willie Mays, in 1931. Three years later, in 1934, Hank Aaron, Roberto Clemente, and Al Kaline entered the world. This is the only instance of three players with 3,000 hits having been born the same year. It's interesting that two of the most iconic players in baseball history, Aaron and Mays, are both from Alabama, given that that state isn't usually regarded as a hotbed of baseball prospects. But perhaps that perception is incorrect, since Satchel Paige and Willie McCovey were also from Alabama. And although Aaron was born three years after Mays, he collected his 3,000th hit two months before Mays did. This happened because the Say Hey Kid spent time in the service.

Clemente was the first member of the 3,000-Hit Club born outside the continental United States. He was a native of Puerto Rico. Thirty-eight years after 1934, Clemente became the 11th man to reach 3,000 career hits. The third member of the 1934 trio, Al Kaline, hailed from Baltimore. Although he was born just four months after Clemente, Kaline reached the milestone about two years after the Puerto Rican. There are good reasons for that. Kaline missed about 500 games over the course of his career due to injuries.[3] In fact, in spite of the fact that Kaline wanted to play until he reached 3,000 hits, injuries could have prevented him from reaching

11. Birthplaces and Birthdays

Al Kaline (left) with Mickey Mantle in 1968. Kaline was the first man with 3,000 hits who never played in the minors and the first of four men to collect their 3,000th hit in the same city where they were born (National Baseball Hall of Fame and Museum, Cooperstown, N.Y.).

Part I—Analysis of Players with 3,000 Hits

the milestone. He was able to continue his pursuit of 3,000 hits because the American League instituted the designated hitter in 1973. Mr. Tiger played in 91 games and collected just 79 hits in 1973. This left him 138 hits short of 3,000. If he'd had to play the field, he might not have collected many hits in 1974. But as the designated hitter, Kaline was able to play in 147 games and collect 146 hits in 1974. He finished the year with 3,007 career hits and retired after the season.

When Kaline doubled for his 3,000th hit at Memorial Stadium in Baltimore on September 24, 1974, he became the first of four men to collect their 3,000th hit in the same city where they were born. The other three were Pete Rose (Cincinnati), Dave Winfield (Minneapolis-St. Paul), and Álex Rodríguez (New York City). In the close-but-no-cigar category, are Derek Jeter and Honus Wagner. Jeter was born in Pequannock, New Jersey, and collected his milestone hit at Yankee Stadium. It's just under 30 miles between the two locations. Wagner was born near Pittsburgh and collected his milestone hit in Philadelphia. That's in the same state, but the two cities are about 300 miles apart.

The last two members of the Club born in the 1930s were Lou Brock and Carl Yastrzemski. Yastrzemski entered the world two months after Brock, in 1939. But the two men were from different parts of the country. Brock was from Arkansas, while Yaz was the son of a potato farmer from Long Island. Given their birthdays, it's not surprising that they had similar career trajectories to the 3,000-hit plateau. Yastrzemski made his debut at the beginning of the 1961 season, while Brock debuted at the end of that season. In spite of the 154-hit head start that Yaz had over Brock by the end of their debut seasons, Brock reached 3,000 hits one month before Yaz did in 1979. That was the final season of Brock's 19-year career, while Yastrzemski played for four more years. Yaz retired after the 1983 season with 3,419 hits, good enough for ninth place on the all-time career hits list.

Brock and Yastrzemski also competed head-to-head in the 1967 World Series. Although Brock's Cardinals came out on top, both men played very well during the Series. Brock batted .414 with eight runs scored, three runs batted in, and seven stolen bases. Yaz batted .400 with four runs scored, and five runs batted in. Why wasn't Brock the MVP of the World Series with numbers like that? Because Bob Gibson threw three complete games during the Series. Gibson won all three games, and allowed a total of three runs to score, for 1.0 ERA. With a performance like that, Gibson had to be awarded the MVP trophy for the Series.

11. Birthplaces and Birthdays

The 1940s produced two eventual members of the 3,000-Hit Club, Pete Rose and Rod Carew. Even though Charlie Hustle (Rose) was born two years after Brock and Yaz in 1941, he reached 3,000 hits the year before them. Rose, who started two full seasons after Yaz in 1963, got to the milestone before the Boston outfielder / first baseman did because he produced hits like Anheuser-Busch produces beer, in great quantities. Starting with the 1965 season, Rose had at least 200 hits in all but four of the 13 seasons ending in 1977. Yaz's hit total never exceeded the 191 hits he collected in 1962. Of course, this type of hit production, combined with exceptional durability and longevity, is also what allowed Rose to overtake Ty Cobb as the career leader for hits with 4,256. Readers can draw their own conclusions about the following coincidences associated with Rose's birth. His birthday, April 14, is the same day that President Lincoln was shot in 1865, and the same day the R.M.S. *Titanic* struck an iceberg in 1912.

Figure 1 shows that Rose was born in Ohio, or to be more specific, Cincinnati. He spent his boyhood there, and he went to high school there. He also spent 19 years, out of a 24-year professional baseball career, in the Queen City. How did that happen? There are lots of promising young players who don't get drafted by the local team. Why did the Reds draft Rose? That's actually a trick question. There was no baseball draft when Rose graduated from high school in 1960. The first draft was held in 1965. Prior to that year, players would simply sign with a team, usually for a signing bonus. Rose's uncle on his mother's side, Buddy Bloebaum, had played in the minors, and was a scout for the Reds while Rose was in high school. Bloebaum used his connections with the club to make sure that the then-undersized Rose signed with the hometown team. Rose received $7,000 for signing, with the promise of $5,000 more if he made the big-league team.[4] That's how Cincinnati native Pete Rose became a member of the Cincinnati Reds.

The story of Rod Carew's birth has become legendary with his success in the major leagues. Carew was famously born on a train in Gatun, Panama, in 1945. After his mother went into labor, a physician on the train, Dr. Rodney Cline, helped with the delivery. Carew's mother was so grateful that she named the boy Rodney Cline Carew.[5] Almost 40 years later, Carew became the 16th member of the Club when he singled off Frank Viola in 1985. With that hit, he became the second man born outside the continental U.S. to reach the milestone, and the only player to do so in the 1980s.

The 1930s produced six members of the Club. But the 1950s is the

Part I—Analysis of Players with 3,000 Hits

decade when the most men with 3,000 hits were born. Seven members of the Club came out of that time period. Although Dave Winfield was the third man to join the Club of the men born in the '50s, he was the first of the seven men to be born that decade. Hailing from St. Paul, Minnesota, Winfield arrived on the scene in 1951. His birthday, October 3, was the day Bobby Thomson hit the "Shot heard 'Round the World" off Ralph Branca to give the N.Y. Giants the National League Pennant. Robin Yount and George Brett were the two hitters from that decade who joined the Club before Winfield did. Yount, from Illinois, and Brett, from West Virginia, had similar career arcs, but Yount (born 1955) was born two years later than Brett (born 1953) and four years after Winfield. Yount was able to reach 3,000 hits before Brett and Winfield because he made his major league debut at age 18. Brett made his debut at 20 years old, and Winfield debuted as a 21-year-old.

Eddie Murray and Paul Molitor entered the world in 1956. Murray, born in Los Angeles, California, was the first player in the Club from the West Coast. Molitor, though five years younger, shared the same St. Paul birthplace as Winfield. Winfield and Molitor, who grew up five blocks from each other, were the first two players from the same hometown to reach the 3,000-hit plateau.[6] The last two players from the '50s to reach 3,000 hits were both born in 1958. Wade Boggs, from Nebraska, arrived mid-year, while Rickey Henderson was born on Christmas Day in Chicago, Illinois.

The story of Henderson's arrival is as interesting as Carew's. Not only was it a special day of the year, Christmas, but the family didn't make it to the hospital on time, so Henderson was born in a car.[7] In addition, Henderson's name at birth was Rickey Nelson Henley. Mr. Henley left the family when Rickey was two years old, so Ricky acquired the surname Henderson when his mother remarried. Henderson, one of Oakland's favorite sons, grew up there because his mother moved the family to California in pursuit of a better life.[8]

The second member of the Club from Los Angeles, Tony Gwynn, arrived on the scene in 1960, four years after Eddie Murray entered the world. Murray and Gwynn are the only two men to reach 3,000 hits who were born in California. It should be noted, however, that although George Brett (born in West Virginia) and Robin Yount (born in Illinois) were not native to California, both of their families moved to suburbs of Los Angeles when the boys were very young, so they both grew up in California, even though they weren't born there. Cal Ripken also made his appearance in 1960, but he was born on the opposite coast

11. Birthplaces and Birthdays

from Gwynn, in Maryland. Although both Gwynn and Ripken were born after Rickey Henderson, both players reached the 3,000-hit plateau before Henderson did in 2001. The quartet of players born in the 1960s was filled out by Cuban Rafael Palmeiro (born 1964), and the second man in the Club to be a native of Long Island, New York, Craig Biggio (born 1965). When Palmeiro reached 3,000 hits in 2005, he became the third man not born in the continental U.S. to get to the milestone, and the first man in that category to do so since Rod Carew in 1985.

The 1970s also produced four men who eventually went on to accumulate 3,000 hits. Like Willie Mays in the '30s, and Eddie Murray in the '50s, the first man born in the decade was not the first man to reach the milestone. Ichiro Suzuki (born 1973), from Nagoya, Japan, was the first position player from Nippon Professional Baseball to make it to the major leagues in the United States. Suzuki collected his 3,000th hit in 2016. But two other men, Derek Jeter (born 1974) and Álex Rodríguez (born 1975), reached the 3,000-hit plateau before Suzuki. Jeter, born the year after Suzuki, got to 3,000 hits five years before Suzuki, and Rodríguez, born two years later, got there a year before Suzuki. The reason for these two anomalies is that Suzuki didn't start his career in the U.S. until he was 27 years old. The fourth player from the '70s who is a member of the club is Adrián Beltré (born 1979). Beltré was the first player from the Dominican Republic to collect 3,000 hits.

The final two players in the Club were born in the 1980s. Albert Pujols (born 1980) arrived in the Dominican Republic, nine months and nine days after Beltré. In another interesting coincidence, Pujols collected his 3,000th hit nine months and four days after Beltré. The two Dominicans were the first two players from a country other than the United States in the Club. The last player to reach 3,000 hits, Miguel Cabrera, was born in Venezuela in 1983. When he collected his 3,000th hit in 2022, he became the fourth consecutive player to reach the milestone who was not born in the continental U.S.

A similar analysis can be done based on where the players grew up, rather than where they were born. Using that definition, the question becomes which of the players reached the 3,000-hit milestone while playing for their hometown team. To put it another way; which of the players collected the milestone hit while playing for the team they grew up rooting for? When that happens, the achievement has special emotional significance for those players.

Over the course of the previous discussion, it was mentioned that Rose, Winfield, Molitor, and Boggs collected their 3,000th hit while

Part I—Analysis of Players with 3,000 Hits

playing for their hometown team. Two other players also collected their 3,000th hit while playing for the team they rooted for as a kid. Honus Wagner grew up in Chartiers, Pennsylvania, which is a suburb of Pittsburgh. He spent all but the first three years of his 21-year career playing for the Pirates, and reached the milestone as a Pirate in 1914. Similarly, Cal Ripken, Jr., grew up in Aberdeen, Maryland, a suburb of Baltimore. He spent his entire career playing for the Orioles, and attained his 3,000th hit as an Oriole in 2000. The only player in this group who was not born and raised in the same city is Wade Boggs. He was born in Nebraska, but raised in Tampa. Half of these six players had the honor of reaching the 3,000-hit plateau at home, in front of a hometown crowd, while playing for their hometown team. The lucky three were Pete Rose, Dave Winfield, and Wade Boggs.

12

∼ ∼ ∼

AGE AND GAME NUMBER OF 3,000TH HIT

The distribution of ages for the players with 3,000 hits has already been discussed. However, in addition to the information on the players' ages, Table 2 also contains the career game number when the player struck the milestone hit. For example, Honus Wagner reached the 3,000-hit plateau in his 2,354th game. The career game numbers are not very enlightening by themselves, but if we plot the game numbers against the age of the player when he collected his 3,000th hit, we get an interesting graph that allows us to visually compare the players on these two metrics. The data are shown in Graph 4.

Before discussing Graph 4, a comment about the ages is necessary. By convention, we say that a person is 40 years old from the day of their 40th birthday, up through the day before their 41st birthday. Of course, six months after a birthday, a person is actually one-half year older, even though we don't usually make that distinction. Sticking with Honus Wagner for our example, Table 2 shows that Wagner was 40 years old when he collected his 3,000th hit. According to convention, this is correct, but Wagner was born on February 24, 1874, and collected his milestone hit on June 9, 1914. So Wagner was actually 40 years, 3 months, and 16 days old when he reached the plateau. Converting the months and days to a fraction of a year means that Wagner was actually 40.4 years old when he got the hit. This procedure was used for all of the players. It explains why the age data points are not all on integer years in Graph 4.

The scale on the Y-axis of Graph 4 also requires some explanation. The game numbers scale goes from 2,000 to 2,162 to 2,324 etc. A more conventional scale would use 2,000 to 2,200 to 2,400 etc. Why choose the first scale when the second is easier to understand? The answer lies

Part I—Analysis of Players with 3,000 Hits

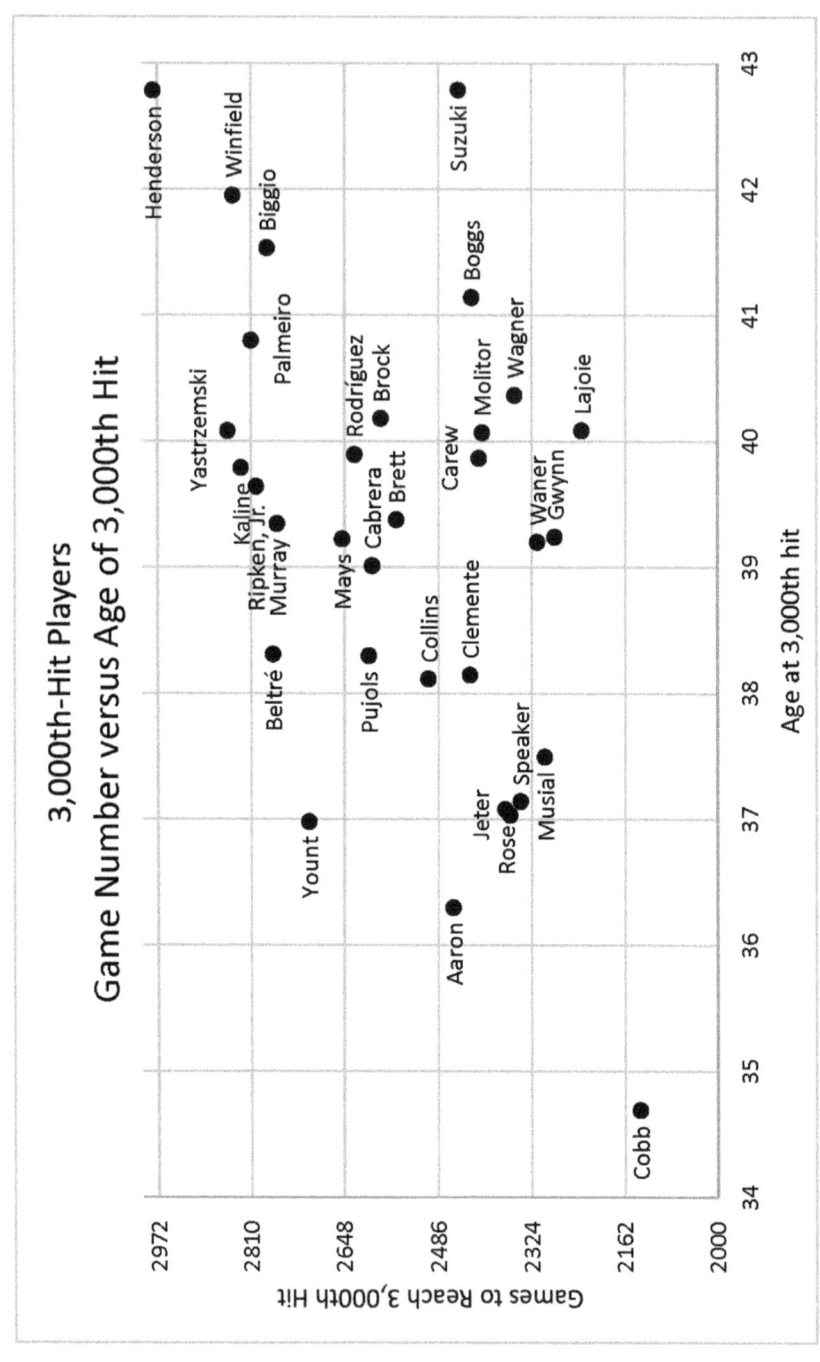

12. Age and Game Number of 3,000th Hit

in the 162 game differences in the first scale. Given that there have been 162 games in a season in both leagues since 1962, the vertical distance between lines on the Y-axis represents a single season's worth of games for most of the players in the 3,000-Hit Club. This facilitates the comparison of how many games it took each player to reach the milestone. For example, Graph 4 shows that it took Rafael Palmeiro almost exactly one more season of games to get to 3,000 hits than it took Willie Mays. Other players can be compared in a similar manner.

Now, what can we learn from Graph 4? Players in the lower left corner of the graph reached 3,000 hits at a younger age, and in fewer games, than players to the right and above them. Not surprisingly, Ty Cobb stands out in this regard. He reached the milestone at a younger age (34.7) and in fewer games (2,135) than any other player. This is what allowed him to get to 4,000 hits, and eventually conclude his career with a then-record 4,189 hits. Pete Rose is in a group of four players above and to the right of Cobb. His location on the graph (37.1 years, 2,370 games) is roughly the upper limit in terms of age and games if a player is to have any chance of reaching 4,000 hits. And even from there (reaching 3,000 hits at age 37) the chance of making it to 4,000 hits are very slim. Rose needed extraordinary longevity to make it. He played for eight more seasons *after* his age-37 season, to age 45, in order to break Cobb's record. Rose finished his career with the all-time records for games played (3,562), plate appearances (15,890), at-bats (14,053) and, of course, hits (4,256). It's likely that having Cobb's record to shoot for is part of what drove Rose during the later portion of his career. That assertion is bolstered by what Rose himself said: "I know everything about Ty Cobb except the size of his hat." He also said, "When I get the record, all it will make me is the player with the most hits. I'm also the player with the most at-bats and the most outs. I never said I was a greater player than Cobb."[1]

More typical in terms of longevity are the other players in that group in Graph 4: Jeter, Speaker, and Musial. Jeter played three more seasons after his age-37 season, and finished with 3,465 hits (sixth best all-time). Speaker also played three seasons after his age-37 season, finishing with 3,514 hits (fifth best all-time). Musial lasted five seasons after his age-37 season, and finished with 3,630 hits (fourth best all time). In another interesting statistical coincidence, Musial famously

Opposite: **Graph 4: Game Number of 3,000th Hit Graphed Against Age of Players with 3,000 Hits**

Part I—Analysis of Players with 3,000 Hits

finished with the same number of career hits at home and away: 1,815 for each.

You may have noticed that third best all-time is missing from this list. Not surprisingly, the man who reached 3,000 hits at a younger age than this group of four great hitters is in third place. Hank Aaron, who reached the 3,000-hit milestone at 36.3 years old (second youngest to Cobb), finished his outstanding career with 3,771 hits. Aaron's prowess as a hitter is demonstrated by the fact that he's third on this list behind two pure hitters, and he is second on the all-time home run list. Obviously, he could hit, and hit for power. He deserves the recognition he gets for being one of the all-time greats in the game.

The previous discussion focused on age when reaching 3,000 hits. But the number of games matters, too. Robin Yount got to 3,000 hits a week before his 37th birthday. This is slightly younger than the Jeter / Rose / Speaker trio. But Yount took about two full seasons more games to get there than these three players. As a result, Yount had a shorter career after his 3,000th hit than the trio. In fact, Yount's age-37 season was the last of his career, while the trio all played at least three seasons past age 37. Yount played in more career games (2,856) than Jeter (2,747) or Speaker (2,789), but finished well behind them in terms of career hits. Yount's final total of 3,142 career hits puts him 19th on the all-time list.

Another way to look at this is to note that Yount didn't produce hits at the same rate as the other three players in the discussion. That observation holds true for Graph 4 as a whole also. The players in the lower portion of Graph 4, those below the 2,486-game line, produced hits at a greater rate, and therefore reached 3,000 hits in fewer games, than the players in the upper part of the graph. This is true regardless of how old they were when they got to 3,000 hits. In most cases, the players who reached 3,000 hits at an older age got there later because they started later. Wade Boggs didn't make it to the big-leagues until he was 24 years old. Honus Wagner made his first big-league appearance at 23 years old. And of course, Ichiro Suzuki, who is the oldest of the group of players below 2,486 games, didn't start his major league career in the U.S. until he was 27 years old.

These three players are among the best pure hitters in baseball history. Other players like Rose, Gwynn, Carew, Boggs, and Suzuki are also widely known to be in that category. But some of the other names in the group are somewhat surprising. It's likely that most modern fans don't realize how great a hitter Wagner, Napoleon Lajoie, or Paul Waner were. Lajoie, for example, took the second fewest games after Cobb to reach

12. Age and Game Number of 3,000th Hit

3,000 hits. Waner wasn't too far behind him. The same logic applies to Stan Musial. Even though he is widely known, especially in St. Louis, as a tremendous player, it's likely that most fans don't think of him as a hitter with capabilities similar to Rose or Gwynn as well as power like Aaron.

There are nine players above and to the right of Yount in Graph 4. For most of them, it was consistency over a long career that allowed them to reach 3,000 hits, rather than great hitting by itself. If we use 190 hits in a season as the standard for an outstanding hitting campaign, the players in the lower portion of the graph collected 190 or more hits much more frequently than the players in the upper portion of the graph. For example, two players from the lower portion, Jeter and Musial, collected 190 or more hits in their careers a total of 11 and 10 times, respectively. The only players to exceed 11 campaigns with at least 190 hits are Rose (13) and Cobb (12). Players in the upper portion did it fewer times. Yount had four seasons with at least 190 hits, Carl Yastrzemski had one, and Eddie Murray never reached 190 hits in a season. This is not to say that players in the upper portion of Graph 4 weren't great players. They were. But from a pure hitting standpoint, relative to the players in the bottom portion, they were not as prolific.

As noted earlier, the extreme data points are often the most interesting. We started this section discussing Ty Cobb in the lower left portion of the graph; now it's time to turn to the upper right portion. The man who holds the distinction of taking the most games to reach 3,000 hits, and is tied with Ichiro Suzuki for the oldest to do it, is Rickey Henderson.

What's interesting about Henderson reaching the milestone is that unlike Pete Rose, Henderson was not motivated primarily by adding to his hit total during the latter portion of his lengthy career. Instead, he was motivated by the desire to break one of Ty Cobb's other career records, 2,245 career runs scored. Henderson said that was a goal of his after he broke Lou Brock's career stolen-base record in 1991.[2] It was a very ambitious goal. At the beginning of the 1991 season, Henderson had scored 1,290 runs and was already 32 years old. The math at the time indicated he would need to average about 130 runs per year over the next eight years to get there. That was a very tall order, even for Rickey Henderson.

But like Rose, who famously said he would run through Hell in a gasoline suit to play baseball, Henderson absolutely loved the game. Henderson's phrasing of that notion was not quite as vivid as Rose's,

Part I—Analysis of Players with 3,000 Hits

Rickey Henderson poised to steal a base in 1983. Henderson was almost 43 years old when he collected his 3,000th hit in 2001. His 1,406 career steals are a record that will never be broken (National Baseball Hall of Fame and Museum, Cooperstown, N.Y.).

but it conveyed the same message. "I have to play baseball to make me happy. I have to be an athlete," opined the Man of Steal.[3] His love of the game, and the desire to break Cobb's record, drove Henderson to play for not just eight, but 12 more years after he broke Brock's record. Henderson broke Cobb's record for career runs scored on October 4, 2001. His hit total also increasing over time, he was sitting on 2,998 hits after the game in which he broke the runs-scored record. Three games later,

12. Age and Game Number of 3,000th Hit

on the last day of the 2001 season, October 7, Henderson collected the hit that put him into the 3,000-Hit Club.

In the context of the earlier comparison of players in the lower half of Graph 4, to players in the upper half of the graph, Henderson provides the quintessential example of a player who reached the 3,000-hit milestone by dint of sheer longevity. Using the simple idea that it takes 20 years of 150 hits per year to get to 3,000 hits as a yardstick, Henderson reached 150 or more hits in just six seasons. His best season, in terms of hits, was 1980, when he collected 179 safeties. He needed to play more than 20 years to reach 3,000 hits. In the end, he reached the milestone on the last day of his 23rd season. Again, this is not to say Henderson was not a great player. But his skill as a hitter was inferior to the players in the lower portion of Graph 4. He made up for that by having a great eye for balls and strikes. His 2,190 career bases on balls is only exceeded by Barry Bonds (2,558). Bonds failed to reach the 3,000-hit milestone because of those walks. He finished with 2,935 hits, just 65 hits short of the plateau.

Dave Winfield and Craig Biggio are the next two players in the upper right corner of Graph 4. Although the details for each player's career are different from that of Henderson, the notion that the two players reached the milestone primarily because of their longevity is the same as for Henderson. Winfield collected his milestone hit at just short of 42 years old, towards the end of his 20th season. He was delayed because he missed the entire 1989 season due to back surgery.[4] Like others in this group of players, he had just one season with 190 or more hits. Biggio reached the milestone at about 41½ years old, during June of his 20th season. He managed two seasons with more than 190 hits. Biggio retired at the end of his 20th season, with a career total of 3,060 hits.

There is also a group of players in Graph 4 above 2,486 games, and below the data point for Robin Yount. We can think of these players as "average" for this group of outstanding hitters. The average number of games to reach 3,000 hits is 2,549, and the average age is 39.3 years old. This is very close to where George Brett's data point is located in Graph 4. The other players in this part of Graph 4 are all within about a year of the average, and within about 100 games of the average games to 3,000 hits. Besides Brett, this group of players includes Eddie Collins, Albert Pujols, Miguel Cabrera, Willie Mays, Álex Rodríguez, and Lou Brock.

You may chide this scribe for using the words "average" and "Willie Mays" together in any paragraph concerning baseball. To be clear, Mays' athletic ability on the diamond was unsurpassed. He is widely

Part I—Analysis of Players with 3,000 Hits

considered to be one of the best players to ever have graced the game. The word average in this context simply means that Mays was of average age, and took roughly an average number of games to reach 3,000 hits, compared to the other 31 players under discussion. For example, like Robin Yount, Mays finished with four seasons of 190 or more hits. But Mays had more 150-hit seasons than Yount, 13 versus 11, respectively.

Eddie Collins is the member of this subgroup with the fewest games to 3,000 hits. He got there in 2,503 games. This is just over the arbitrary cutoff of 2,486 games used earlier to define the best pure hitters in the 3,000-Hit Club. It's arguable that he should be included in that group. Bill James opined that Collins is one of the best second basemen to ever play the game.[5] Collins may be best remembered today for being a member of the 1919 White Sox team that threw the World Series. But, in addition to being one of the best players in the game at the time, he was a man of such integrity that the plotters didn't dare ask him to join the group for fear he would spill the beans about the fix.[6] In the context of the current discussion, Collins had as many seasons with 190 or more hits as Mays did, and he had 15 seasons (two more than the Say Hey Kid) of 150 or more hits. His 3,314 career hits put him in 11th place on the all-time list, one position above Mays, who is 12th with 3,293 hits.

Which of the players in this "average" group had the most seasons with 190 or more hits? Of course, Mays is the first player to come to mind. But the surprising answer is Lou Brock. Brock put together twice as many of these elite hitting seasons as Mays did. Brock had four seasons of 200 or more hits, and another four seasons with at least 190 hits. Just seven players in history had more 190-hit seasons than Brock. Six of those players fall below the 2,486-game line in Graph 4: Rose (13 seasons), Cobb (12 seasons), Jeter (11 seasons), Suzuki (10 seasons), Musial (10 seasons), and Waner (9 seasons). The seventh, Lou Gehrig (9 seasons), would be a member of the 3,000-Hit Club if his career had not been tragically cut short by disease. Miguel Cabrera has the second most 190-hit seasons in the average group in Graph 4. He did it seven times. Brock played in the major leagues for 19 years. In addition to his eight 190-hit seasons, he also collected 150 or more hits in 13 of those years. Brock does not get the recognition he deserves for being such an excellent hitter.

This analysis can be extended to include the player's age and game

Opposite: **Graph 5: Game Number of 3,000th Hit Graphed Against Age of Players with 3,000 Hits for Multiple Milestones**

12. Age and Game Number of 3,000th Hit

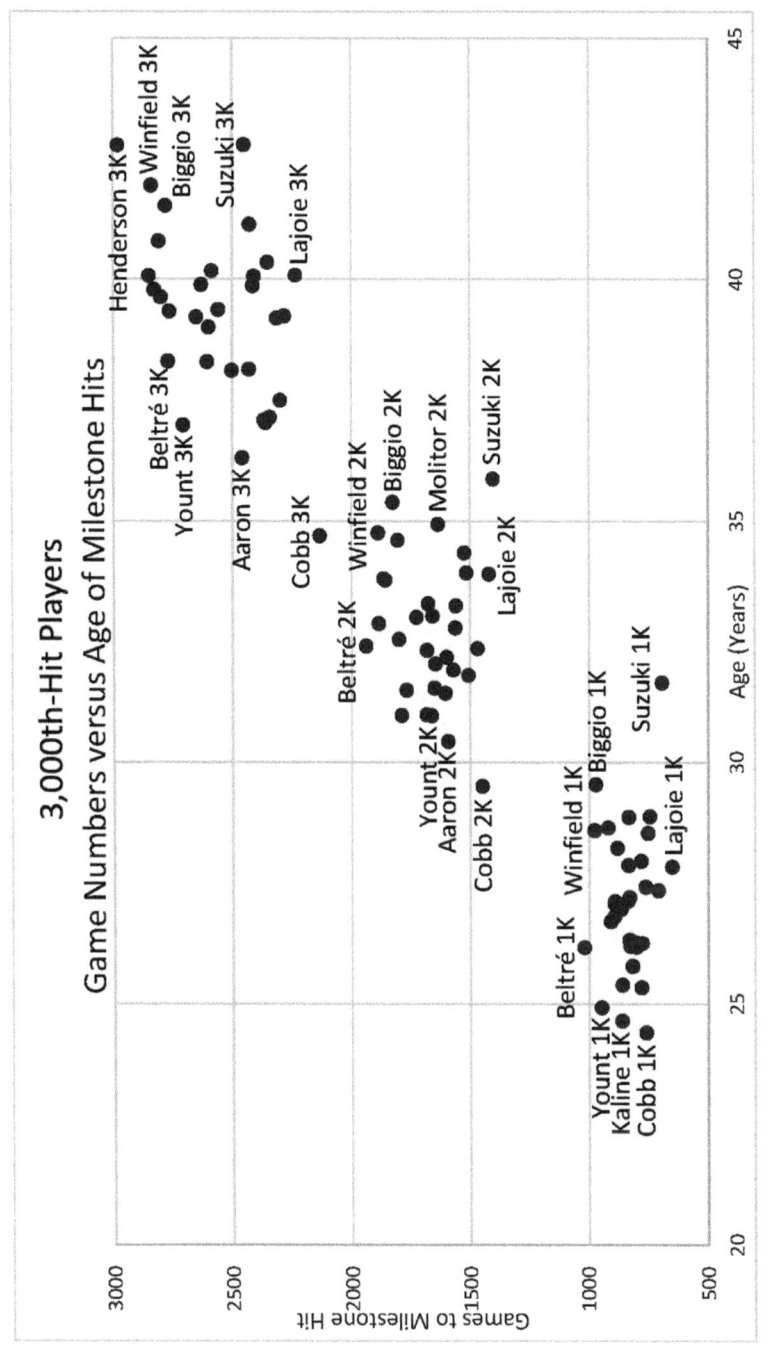

Part I—Analysis of Players with 3,000 Hits

number when he reached 1,000 and 2,000 hits. For the purpose of this discussion, these three hits (1,000, 2,000, 3,000) will all be referred to as milestone hits. However, rather than plotting each grouping of milestone hits individually, as was done in Graph 4 for the 3,000th hits, the three groups of hits will all be plotted on one graph in order to see the progression as the players aged. The results are shown in Graph 5. As in Graph 4, ages are shown to the fraction of a year. The Y-axis is scaled more conventionally because of the much wider range of games. In order to avoid cluttering up the graph too much, only the names of the players around the periphery of each grouping are shown.

As expected, there are three distinct groupings of data in Graph 5. The groupings correspond to the 1,000-hit, 2,000-hit, and 3,000-hit data. The spread of each grouping increases as the milestone hit number increases. This is especially noticeable along the games axis, although the spread of ages in the 3,000-hit group clearly exceeds the spread of ages in the 1,000-hit group, especially if the outlying data point for Ichiro Suzuki is ignored in the 1,000-hit group. Given that Ichiro didn't start playing in the U.S. until he was 27 years old, the fact that he lies well to the right of the rest of the 1,000-hit milestones (due to his greater age) is understandable.

Although there are three distinct groupings of data in Graph 5, Ty Cobb's 3,000th hit data point is notable. Without being labelled, the point could easily be assumed to be in the 2,000-hit milestone group. Cobb didn't get to 3,000 hits faster than any of the other players got to 2,000 hits, in terms of games. But he did reach 3,000 hits at a younger age (34.7 years old) than Dave Winfield (34.8), Paul Molitor (34.9), Craig Biggio (35.4), and Suzuki (35.9) reached 2,000 hits. Another general observation in Graph 5 is that a player's position within the three groups, relative to the other players, is fairly consistent over each milestone hit. Cobb is always at the lower left. Suzuki is always at the far right. Beltré is near the top of each group. Winfield and Biggio are in the upper right corner of each grouping. This is not surprising assuming that a player's hitting skills remain relatively constant over his career, but it is worth noting.

The Y-axis of the 1,000 hit grouping tells an interesting story that's worth examining in more detail. It is a direct measure of how many games each of these players needed in order to get to 1,000 hits. Although Graph 5 shows the relative positions of players compared to each other, it does not show the numerical details. These numbers are worth closer examination, so they're shown in Table 10. In addition,

12. Age and Game Number of 3,000th Hit

Table 10 shows how many games it took each player to go from 1,000 to 2,000 hits, and to go from 2,000 to 3,000 hits.

Table 10: Games Per 1,000 Hits

Player	Games to 1,000 Hits	Games 1,000 to 2,000 Hits	Games 2,000 to 3,000 Hits	Total Games to 3,000 Hits
Nap Lajoie	**653**	767	817	2237
Ichiro Suzuki	**696**	706	1050	2452
Paul Waner	711	757	847	2315
Wade Boggs	747	768	914	2429
Honus Wagner	755	769	830	2354
Ty Cobb	762	**687**	**686**	2135
Stan Musial	765	742	794	2301
Derek Jeter	780	791	791	2362
Hank Aaron	782	811	867	2460
Tony Gwynn	783	777	724	2284
Tris Speaker	803	801	740	2344
Albert Pujols	806	844	956	2606
Álex Rodríguez	819	865	947	2631
George Brett	828	831	900	2559
Pete Rose	831	769	770	2370
Eddie Collins	832	895	776	2503
Paul Molitor	835	800	776	2411
Rod Carew	837	725	854	2416
Willie Mays	838	844	970	2652
Miguel Cabrera	861	802	937	2600
Al Kaline	863	906	1058	2827
Roberto Clemente	866	781	785	2432
Lou Brock	882	796	908	2586
Eddie Murray	892	909	963	2764
Carl Yastrzemski	893	972	985	2850
Cal Ripken, Jr.	894	993	913	2800
Rickey Henderson	909	950	1120	2979

Part I—Analysis of Players with 3,000 Hits

Player	Games to 1,000 Hits	Games 1,000 to 2,000 Hits	Games 2,000 to 3,000 Hits	Total Games to 3,000 Hits
Rafael Palmeiro	921	885	1003	2809
Robin Yount	948	842	918	2708
Craig Biggio	972	855	954	2781
Dave Winfield	978	911	951	2840
Adrián Beltré	1020	919	832	2771
Average	836.3	827.2	885.5	2549

The first thing to note about the number of games it took each player to collect their first 1,000 hits, is that there are only two players, Nap Lajoie and Ichiro Suzuki, who did it in fewer than 700 games. There's a good reason for this. A player must average more than 1.43 hits per game for 700 games in order to reach 1,000 hits in this time frame. That is a very tall order, even for the best hitters.

For example, two 20th-century players to reach the 1,000-hit plateau in less than 700 games are Chuck Klein (683 games) and Suzuki (696 games). Lajoie is not included here because he started his career in 1896. It's not likely that Lajoie's 653 games is the all-time record for fastest to 1,000 hits, but poor record keeping during the 19th century makes it difficult to know who actually holds the record. For example, Baseball-Reference.com shows that Willie Keeler accumulated 931 hits in 556 games between 1892 and 1897. Keeler certainly reached 1,000 career hits in 1898 since he led the NL in hits with 216 that year. But it's not known exactly how many games into 1898 it took him to accumulate the 69 hits he needed to reach 1,000.

There are only two other numbers below 700 in Table 10. Both belong to Ty Cobb. It took Cobb under 700 games to go from 1,000 hits to 2,000 hits, and to go from 2,000 hits to 3,000 hits. This is another demonstration of Cobb's prowess as a hitter, and it also shows that he maintained that ability for an extended period of time. Cobb's three numbers in Table 10 (762, 686, and 687) beg the question of how many games it took him to reach 4,000 hits from 3,000. The answer is 749 games. No matter how you feel about Cobb, the man, there is no denying that Cobb, the hitter, was one of the best of all time.

Table 10 also shows that it isn't easy to accumulate 1,000 hits in under 800 games. Just eight players besides Lajoie and Suzuki achieved their first 1,000 hits in between 700 and 800 games. This means that 22

12. Age and Game Number of 3,000th Hit

Ichiro Suzuki displays his unique batting stance in 2003. Suzuki had a stellar nine-year career in Japan before moving to the Seattle Mariners in 2001. He played as a professional for 28 years and finished with 4,367 hits in Japan and the U.S. combined (Jerry Coli).

out of 32 (about 69 percent) of some of the greatest hitters of all time took at least 800 games to collect their first 1,000 hits. Six players took over 900 games to reach 1,000 hits, and one of those six players, Adrián

Part I—Analysis of Players with 3,000 Hits

Beltré, took over 1,000 games (1,020) to reach the first milestone. On average, it took 836 games for these players to collect 1,000 hits.

The data in Table 10 allows us to compare how many games it took each player to collect hits 1,001 to 2,000, and 2,001 to 3,000, versus their first 1,000 hits. Only Cobb took fewer than 700 games to collect his second 1,000 hits, but a dozen other players (versus eight in the first 1,000) needed between 700 and 800 games to collect those hits. In other words, 50 percent more players were able to collect their second 1,000 hits in 700 to 800 games, compared to their first 1,000 hits. In fact, 15 out of the 32 players (about 47 percent) took fewer games to collect their second 1,000 hits than it took to collect their first 1,000 hits. The average number of games for players to collect their second 1,000 hits was 827 games, compared to 836 games for the first 1,000 hits. These results for the second 1,000 hits are not surprising. Graph 5 shows that most of the players were 25–29 years old when they collected their 1,000th hit. This means that they were in, or moving into, their prime playing years, as they embarked on the second 1,000 hits.

The logic at the end of the previous paragraph is reversed when we consider the third 1,000 hits. Graph 5 shows that most players were 30–35 years old when they reached 2,000 hits. So they are usually past their prime as they pursue 3,000 hits. As would be expected, the numbers in Table 10 reflect this. Once again, Cobb is an outlier in this group. He went from 2,000 to 3,000 hits in under 700 games. However, the number of players who collect their third 1,000 hits in 700 to 800 games declines back down to eight, and 23 out of 32 players (about 72 percent) require at least 800 games to collect the third 1,000 hits. Seventeen of the players required 900 or more games to collect the third 1,000 hits (versus six in the first 1,000 group), including four who needed more than 1,000, and the overall average has increased from 827 games to 885 games. Just seven players (eight if you count Derek Jeter, who used the exact same number of games, 791) took fewer games to go from 2,000 to 3,000 hits as compared to going from 1,000 to 2,000 hits. Father Time is always victorious in the long run.

13

CLOSE, BUT NO CIGAR

This work examines, and celebrates, the men who reached the lofty plateau of 3,000 hits for their careers. It's fitting to do this, given the difficulty of the task, and the relatively few men who have accomplished the feat. However, we are guilty of round number bias when we focus exclusively on the players who reached 3,000 hits. Roberto Clemente finished his tragically truncated career with exactly 3,000 hits. Would he be less of a player, and less of a man, if he had finished with 2,999 hits? Would his contributions to the game both on and off the field be less worthy of celebration if he had come up a few hits short of 3,000? No, we would, and should, still celebrate him as a player and as a catalyst for change.

Therefore, this portion of the analysis will examine the players whose career hit-total came close to, but did not reach, 3,000 hits. Close to, in this case, means the players who finished with 2,900 or more career hits. This means they finished within 100 hits of 3,000 for their careers. That's fewer than five more hits per year over a 20-year career, or less than one more productive season of hits. Given that relatively small difference, it can be argued that (in terms of recognition) we should not penalize these players who came up just short of 3,000 career hits. The counter argument is that lines have to be drawn somewhere in order for an accomplishment to have meaning. There may not be a substantial difference between 2,900 career hits and 3,000 career hits. But what about fewer hits? Are 2,800 career hits or 2,600 career hits substantially different? At some point, the answer is clearly, yes. With those ideas in mind, we will now look at the eight players who finished their careers with more than 2,900 hits but fewer than 3,000 hits, and therefore came closest to being included formally in this study. The data are shown in Graph 6.

Sam Rice is the perfect example of a player whose name is not

Part I—Analysis of Players with 3,000 Hits

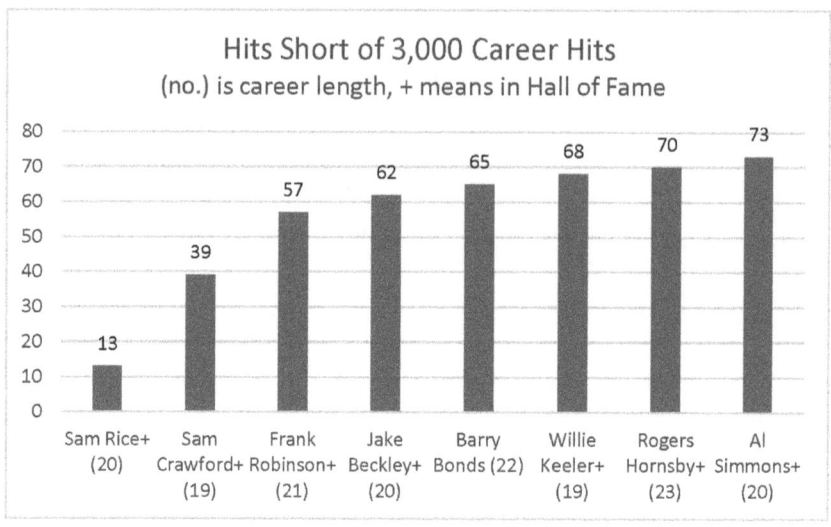

Graph 6: Players with More Than 2,900 Career Hits

widely recognized today because he came up 13 hits shy of 3,000 hits for his career. Even though he is in the Hall of Fame, he certainly would be more well known if his name was on the 3,000-hit list between Eddie Collins and Paul Waner (the most likely time period he would have reached 3,000 hits) because his moniker would be seen every time another player joined the 3,000-Hit Club. But like many players, including Willie Mays and Ted Williams, Rice's career numbers were reduced because of military service. In Rice's case, he was drafted when the U.S. entered World War I, and missed most of the 1918 season. Since he collected over 170 hits in the year before and the year after 1918, it's almost certain he would have reached 3,000 hits had he not been drafted.

Even missing that season, Rice was very close to 3,000 hits when he retired. Asked why he didn't stick around to collect those 13 hits, Rice replied, "The truth of the matter is I did not even know how many hits I had. A couple of years after I quit, [Senators owner] Clark Griffith told me about it, and asked me if I'd care to have a comeback with the Senators and pick up those 13 hits. But I was out of shape, and didn't want to go through all that would have been necessary to make the effort. Nowadays, with radio and television announcers spouting records every time a player comes to bat, I would have known about my hits and probably would have stayed to make 3,000 of them."[1]

There are two good reasons why a player of Rice's caliber is not

13. Close, but No Cigar

well known today. The first reason is that he played about a century ago, his 20-year career spanning 1915–34. And the second reason is that he played all but the last of those 20 years for the Washington Senators. Even though Rice played on three Senators teams that won the American League pennant (1924, 1925, and 1933) and won the World Series in 1924, the Senators spent so many years in the second division, and were out of the media glare of New York and Chicago, that players on the team other than Walter Johnson didn't get much national recognition.

Rice deserved better historical notice. Even considering the increased offense of that era, Rice put up excellent numbers. He batted .322 lifetime, and led the league in hits twice with 216 safeties in 1924 and 1926. His 63 steals led the major leagues in 1920. He scored more than 100 runs five times between 1923 and 1930. He compares favorably with the hitters who reached 3,000 hits using the 190- and 150-hit thresholds. Rice had seven seasons with more than 190 hits, and 13 seasons with more than 150 hits. That's the same number of 190-hit seasons as Aaron, Boggs, Cabrera, Gwynn, and Molitor. His accomplishments would be much better known if he had accumulated just 13 more hits during his career. Round number bias has done Sam Rice a great disservice.

Sam Crawford is the next player closest to 3,000 hits without getting there. Crawford came up 39 hits short of the milestone. Like Rice, he would be better known today if he had reached 3,000 hits. And also like Rice, part of the reason for his relative anonymity, even as a Hall of Famer, is that Crawford's career ended more than a century ago. Crawford made his major league debut with the Cincinnati Reds in 1899 as a 19-year-old. After four years with the Reds, he moved to Detroit in the fledgling American League. Crawford spent the next 15 years of his 19-year career with the Tigers. In another similarity with Rice, Crawford's Tigers teams won three pennants (1907–09), but none of those teams won the World Series. Crawford played with Ty Cobb from 1905 until he (Crawford) retired after the 1917 season.

How did Crawford wind up 39 hits short of 3,000 hits for his career? Although he had just two seasons with more than 190 hits, he had 14 seasons with more than 150 hits, in spite of spending his entire career in the dead-ball era. With a 19-year career, just two more hits per year would have gotten Crawford very close to 3,000 hits. But the real problem for Crawford was a very abrupt drop-off in his production in 1916. Crawford collected 183 hits in 156 games as the Tigers right fielder all season in 1915. But the 36-year-old Crawford made only 79

Part I—Analysis of Players with 3,000 Hits

Full length portrait of Sam Rice swinging a bat in 1924. Rice is not well known today in spite of an excellent 21-year career that got him into the Hall of Fame. He finished just 13 hits shy of 3,000 (Library of Congress).

13. Close, but No Cigar

starts in right field in 1916, because he began to share right field duties with a budding star, 21-year-old Harry Heilmann. As a result, Crawford notched just 92 hits in 1916. In 1917, he collected only 18 hits in 61 games, mostly as a pinch hitter, and retired after that season.

In addition to getting close to 3,000 hits, Crawford has another achievement that's worthy of note. Baseball-Reference.com has seasonal and career totals for every player in major league history. Career totals that are all-time records are highlighted in gold on the website. It's pretty special when you see one. For example, Pete Rose's all-time record of 4,256 career hits is highlighted in gold, and so are his records for games played, plate appearances, and at-bats. Tris Speaker's record of 792 career doubles is highlighted in gold. Sam Crawford joins them in having a career number with a gold highlight. Crawford holds the all-time record for career triples, with 309. He led the major leagues in triples five times, with a sixth season where he led the American League. His career best was 26 three-baggers in 1915, and he hit 25 triples in 1903. Those are impressive totals given that Amed Rosario led the majors with nine triples in 2022. So like Sam Rice, Sam Crawford's accomplishments should be better remembered than they are.

Frank Robinson is the next player listed in Graph 6. He finished his Hall of Fame career 57 hits below the 3,000-hit threshold. His stellar career exemplifies why it is so difficult to reach 3,000 hits. He checked all the boxes necessary to get there. He started young, took care of himself physically, and had a long career. In spite of those positives, he still came up short of 3,000 hits. However, unlike Rice and Crawford, Robinson's excellent reputation today would not be enhanced by much even if he had collected 57 more hits during his career.

Robinson broke in with the Cincinnati Reds as a 20-year-old in 1956. His excellent campaign that year resulted in the Rookie of the Year Award. He won the Most Valuable Player Award in 1961 as he sparked the Reds to the National League Pennant (although the team lost to the Yankees in the World Series). Robinson won another MVP Award and the triple crown in 1966, and led the Orioles to a World Series victory. But in late June 1967, he was knocked unconscious in a collision at second base. The collision left him with a concussion and double vision. Although he was out of action for only a month, he was never quite as good a hitter after the concussion as he was before. Robinson claimed the injury stunted his career: "I don't know how much I left at second base. … I haven't been the same hitter since."[2]

The numbers validate Robinson's assertion. His best season in

Part I—Analysis of Players with 3,000 Hits

terms of hits after the injury was 1969. He collected 166 hits that season as Baltimore won the pennant and advanced to the World Series, where they lost to the Mets. He had exceeded that hit total seven times before the concussion. His quest to become the first African American major league manager also probably reduced his hit total. Although he realized that goal in 1975 when he became the player / manager for the Cleveland Indians, he focused most of his attention on managing. He collected just 43 hits total in 1975 and 1976, before he ended his 21-year playing career in 1976. Robinson's career shows how difficult it is to reach 3,000 career hits. There are many ways to have the quest for 3,000 hits come up short.

Jake Beckley came up 62 hits short of 3,000. Like Rice and Crawford, he would be much better known today had he made it onto the 3,000-hit list. Beckley's 20-year career spanned 1888–1907. He came up short of 3,000 hits because, like Sam Crawford and Frank Robinson, his last two seasons were not very productive. He collected just 103 hits total in those two seasons.

Barry Bonds finished 65 hits short of 3,000, but Bonds is another player whose fame wouldn't be enhanced if he had reached 3,000 hits because he's already very well known for other reasons. Bonds' 22-year career was long enough to get there, but his problem, from a reaching 3,000 hit standpoint, was too many walks. Of course, Bonds' career total of 762 home runs is framed in gold on Baseball-Reference.com. But he has two more career numbers that are also gold-framed. His 2,558 career bases on balls is the all-time record, as are the 688 times that hurlers refused to pitch to him. In other words, he was intentionally walked almost 700 times! All those free passes greatly improved his on-base percentage, but also resulted in fewer opportunities to get a hit, and likely kept his hit total below 3,000. It needs to be pointed out that Bonds' 688 intentional walks is another record that will never be broken. The next man on the career list, Albert Pujols, has less than half of Bonds' total. Pujols did reach 3,000 hits, but he was issued "only" 316 free passes during his career. Bonds' total of 688 can't be touched.

Willie Keeler, Rogers Hornsby, and Al Simmons are three Hall of Famers who also came up less than 100 hits short of the 3,000-hit plateau. Keeler is another player, like Frank Robinson, whose career is a good example of how hard it is to reach 3,000 hits. Often referred to as Wee Willie because of his small stature (he stood 5-feet-4½-inches tall and weighed 140 pounds), Keeler employed the "hit 'em where they ain't" technique to achieve a .341 career batting average.[3] The technique

13. Close, but No Cigar

was effective enough that Keeler was able to collect at least 200 hits in eight consecutive seasons from 1894 to 1901. But age and injuries caught up to Keeler in 1907 when he was 35 years old. He batted under .300 for the first time in his career, and collected just 99 hits compared to his 1906 total of 180 safeties. Similar production the next two seasons meant his career hit total came up short of 3,000 hits. What Sam Rice said about not even realizing how close he was to 3,000 hits probably applies to Keeler too.

Al Simmons is another player who would be better known today if his name appeared on the 3,000-hit list. Simmons was a key member of the Philadelphia Athletics dynasty that won three American League pennants and two World Series from 1929 to 1931. He was second in MVP voting in 1925, and third in MVP voting in 1931. The 253 hits he collected in 1925 is the fifth-highest hit total ever for a single season. Simmons had eight seasons with more than 190 hits, and one dozen seasons with more than 150 safeties. But in contrast to Rice and Keeler, Simmons was fully aware that his hit total was below 3,000 toward the end of his career. He wanted to reach 3,000 hits, but like other hitters who came up a little short of the milestone, his production declined at the end of his career. Simmons finished 73 hits below the plateau.[4]

That leaves Rogers Hornsby as the final player from Graph 6 to not reach 3,000 hits during his career. Hornsby, like Bonds, would not have enhanced his reputation by collecting the 70 more hits he needed to increase his total to 3,000. This is because Hornsby is already widely considered the greatest right-handed batter in baseball history. Some very impressive batting statistics support this assertion. His .358 career batting average is the highest ever for a righty. He batted over .400 for five consecutive seasons from 1921 to 1925, with a high of .424 in 1924. His batting average for the whole five-year period was .402. Don't gloss over the last sentence. It's hard to believe he hit over .400 for half a decade! Hornsby won the triple crown twice (1922 and 1925) and was a two-time MVP (1925 and 1929). He had seven seasons with more than 200 hits (with none between 190 and 200 hits) and 13 seasons with more than 150 hits. He clearly deserves to be in the pantheon of the all-time great hitters.

That said, Hornsby is as famous for his unpleasant disposition as he is for his batting skill. Sportswriter John B. Sheridan said, "He is, as the French say, deficient in the social relation." Echoing that sentiment, Hall of Fame historian Lee Allen opined, "He was frank to the point of being cruel and as subtle as a belch." Joe Posnanski, who ranked

Part I—Analysis of Players with 3,000 Hits

Hornsby the 17th greatest of all-time in his 2020 series on the top 100 players, had this to say: "Looking back, it's fair to ask why Hornsby, rather than Ty Cobb, is not baseball's ultimate villain. He had all the attributes. To start with: Nobody liked him. The players didn't like him. The writers didn't like him. Baseball management hated him like no one else." Hornsby's defense against these allegations was that he was misunderstood. He argued that he was always focused on the two things that mattered, truth and baseball. Hornsby couldn't understand why that bothered so many people.[5]

So how did one of the greatest hitters in baseball history come up 70 hits short of 3,000 for his career when he played for 23 years? Foreshadowing Frank Robinson's career trajectory, Hornsby suffered injuries that derailed his career. In 1928, 14 years into his stellar career, Hornsby suffered a stone bruise on his right heel. The problem lingered into 1929, and even though his Chicago Cubs team held a comfortable lead in August and September, Hornsby played in every game that season, and won the MVP Award. By the end of the season, Hornsby's mobility was significantly affected by the now-calcified heel spur. This injury is probably why he played poorly (batting only .238) in the 1929 World Series where the Cubs lost to Philadelphia. He had surgery to remove bone spurs after the season.

Hornsby was not fully recovered when the 1930 season began. Although he did manage to work his way back into the lineup by mid–May, he broke his left ankle sliding into third at the end of that month, and was out of action until August.[6] He played in 42 games and collected just 32 hits during the 1930 season. In addition, it's clear that Hornsby focused more on his manager role than his player role during the last six years of his career, from 1932 to 1937. He collected just 75 hits during those six seasons. And so, like Frank Robinson, Hornsby didn't reach 3,000 hits due to injuries and managerial duties.

14

Who's Next to 3,000 Hits?

Humans always want to know what's going to happen next. Who will win the World Series? Who will be the MVP? In the context of this discussion, the question is: who will be the next player to reach 3,000 hits, and how long will it be before that happens? Unfortunately, these questions don't lend themselves to the type of analysis utilized thus far. Yogi Berra explained why when he said, "It's tough to make predictions, especially about the future." In spite of this reality, we can examine these questions, and try to make educated guesses about who will be the next player to join the 3,000-Hit Club and how soon it's likely to happen.

Before looking at specific players, some observations are in order that are likely to have bearing on the answers. First, since you must get 2,000 hits before you can reach 3,000 hits, the number of active players with 2,000 hits impacts the chances of another player joining the Club. The count of active players with 2,000 hits has varied dramatically through baseball history. Stan Musial was the only active player with 2,000 hits after the 1952 season. Following the 2004 season, there were 27 players who had accumulated 2,000 hits.[1] With a pool of candidates that large, it's not that surprising that six new players (about 18 percent of the total) reached the 3,000-hit milestone between 2011 and 2022.

But there were just five active players, Joey Votto, Freddie Freeman, Elvis Andrus, Andrew McCutchen, and Jose Altuve, who had more than 2,000 hits at the conclusion of the 2023 season. Given the difficulty of reaching the milestone, it's possible that no one in this quintet will reach 3,000 hits. However, in addition to these five players, there were two players with more than 1900 hits, and 17 players with over 1,500 hits after the 2023 campaign. Someone from these groups of players could be the next man to reach 3,000 hits. For the remainder of this

Part I—Analysis of Players with 3,000 Hits

section, the phrase "active players" will refer to hit totals for players at the end of the 2023 season.

One factor that will impact the likelihood of a player reaching 3,000 hits is how hard it is to get a hit during a particular season. In other words, players will get more hits when offense is strong compared to when pitching is dominant. We can measure this by looking at the major league batting average and team hits per game over time. Two data points will be used to make the point. The most recent peak of offensive production occurred in 1999, when the major league batting average was .271 and there were 9.33 hits per team in a game. By 2022, pitching was ascendant, driving the batting average down to .243 and hits to 8.16 per team game. That's a 10 percent reduction in batting average and about a 12 percent reduction in hits per game. Simply put, it's harder to get hits in a pitching-dominant era, so players will get fewer of them. Not a single player had 200 or more hits in 2021 or 2022. Obviously, having played during this time period will reduce a player's career total for hits and could prevent that player from amassing 3,000 hits.

However, major league baseball changed some rules for the 2023 season to encourage offense, and those changes had the intended effect. Batting average increased from .243 in 2022 to .248 in 2023. Per-team game hits went from 8.16 in 2022 to 8.40 in 2023. Per-team game runs increased to 4.62 from 4.28 over the same two years, and per-team game stolen bases increased from .51 to .72. And in contrast to 2021 and '22, three players had more than 200 hits during the 2023 season. Ronald Acuña (217), Freddie Freeman (211), and Luis Arráez (205) all breached the 200 mark in hits.

Unusual events can also impact a player's career totals. Many players have had their career totals reduced by service in a war. The strike by the players in 1994 shortened that season by an average of 48 games, and reduced the 1995 season by an average of 18 games. The loss of those games reduced the career totals for players active at the time. The most recent event that resulted in a loss of games was the COVID-19 pandemic of 2020. In addition to the tragic loss of life that the coronavirus caused, the major league baseball season was shortened to 60 games, played in mostly empty stadiums. The loss of roughly two-thirds of a season will reduce the hit total for all active players. Losing those games will make it less likely for active players to reach 3,000 hits, and will delay the achievement for those who do eventually get there.

Given all those factors, the question of who will be the next player to reach 3,000 hits will be explored using the age and games-to-milestone

14. Who's Next to 3,000 Hits?

graphs developed earlier. The idea is to compare the current crop of players with 2,000 and 1,500 hits, to the players in the 3,000-Hit Club in terms of the age and games to those milestones. The players in the Club in the upper right corner of those earlier graphs form an envelope that defines the oldest players who took the most games to reach the milestone. If a player in the current crop is below and to the left of the envelope, then the player is on a better pace than the slowest players in the Club to reach the milestone. Players who lie above and to the right of the envelope are slower and / or older than the slowest and / or oldest of the players in the Club. History suggests that those players are not likely to reach the milestone. The results are shown in Graph 7.

Graph 7 is a little confusing at first glance. The first thing to note is that the group of data points in the lower left of the graph (the 1,500-hit data) is separate from the data points in center to upper right of the graph (the 2,000-hit data). The large data points are for players who have already reached 3,000 hits. These large points are the same data that is shown in Graph 5 for the 2,000-hit data, but only the data points for the oldest, and slowest, players to 3,000 hits are shown. These are the data points for 3,000-Hit Club members Beltré, Winfield, Biggio, Molitor, and Ichiro. The larger data points form an envelope that creates an informal boundary of where a player must be when he reaches 2,000 hits in order to have a reasonable chance to eventually attain 3,000 hits. The smaller data points compare where the active players with 2,000 hits compare to the members of the Club when they reached 2,000 hits.

The 2,000-hit data points also include projections of the two active players with more than 1,900 hits. The projection was done by calculating hits per game for the player during the 2023 season, and using that number to estimate how many more games it will take the player to reach 2,000 hits. For example, Evan Longoria had 1,930 hits in 1,986 career games at the end of the 2023 season. During the 2023 season, he had 47 hits in 74 games for a hit rate of 0.64 hits per game. Assuming he maintains that hit rate during the 2024 season, it will take him 70 / 0.64 which equals 110 games to reach 2,000 hits. Adding those 110 games to his career total gives an estimate of 2,040 games for him to reach 2,000 hits. That, and his age during the 2024 season, combine to give the data point shown for Longoria in Graph 7. The same procedure was used to generate the data point for Paul Goldschmidt.

The following discussion is based on career totals at the end of the 2023 season. The active player closest to 3,000 hits is Joey Votto. Votto's career total of 2,135 hits leaves him 865 hits short of the milestone. But

Part I—Analysis of Players with 3,000 Hits

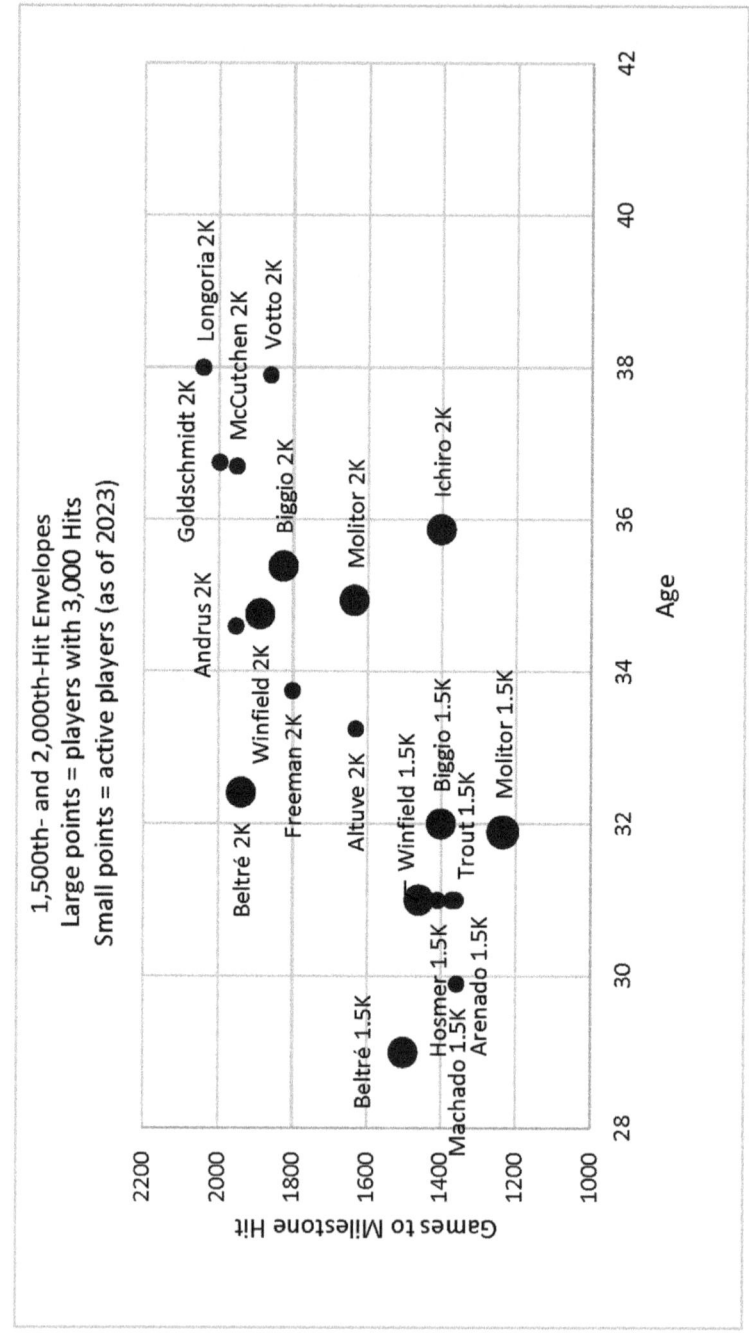

Graph 7: Age and Game Number Envelopes for 1,500 and 2,000 Hits

14. Who's Next to 3,000 Hits?

his data point in Graph 7 is well outside the envelope of the slowest players who did reach 3,000 hits, and he turned 40 during the 2023 season. He's not likely to get to the milestone. Andrew McCutchen has 2,048 hits, but like Votto, his data point is well outside the envelope of players to reach the milestone, so he probably won't get to 3,000 hits either. The projected 2,000 hit points for Goldschmidt and Longoria are also well outside the envelope. Neither player is likely to reach 3,000 hits.

Elvis Andrus was just three hits short of 2,000 hits at the end of the 2022 season. He reached the mark on April 5, 2023, and he finished the year with 2,091 hits. His data point in Graph 7 is between the data points for Club members Beltré and Winfield. This suggests that he has a chance to reach the 3,000-hit milestone. Andrus, who was 34 years old in 2023, had 133 hits in 2022 and 121 hits in 2021. He had 94 hits in 2023. Assuming 130 hits per season going forward, it will take Andrus about seven seasons to reach 3,000 hits. It seems unlikely that Andrus will be able to be productive enough, for long enough, to reach 3,000 hits, but it's within the realm of possibility.

Besides Andrus, the other active players with more than 2,000 hits are Jose Altuve (2,047 hits) and Freddie Freeman (2,114 hits). Graph 7 shows that the data points for Altuve and Freeman lie inside the Club member envelope. Even though both players have fewer career hits than Elvis Andrus, they were both a year younger (33 years old) than Andrus during the 2023 campaign. Setting aside the abbreviated 2020 campaign, Altuve collected 149, 167, and 158 hits from 2019 to 2022. He missed substantial time due to injury in 2023 and collected a modest 112 hits during that season. Assuming that he manages an average of 150 hits per year going forward, Altuve will need 953 / 150, or just over six seasons, to reach 3,000 hits. At that rate he would reach the milestone during his age-39 season in 2029 or age-40 season in 2030.

Freddie Freeman is arguably the most likely player to be next to reach 3,000 hits. Freeman has about 60 more hits than Altuve, and he has been much more productive from a hits perspective during his career. Since 2013, Freeman has had at least 170 hits in every season when he was healthy for the whole season. In 2021 and 2022, he got 180 and 199 hits, respectively. He did even better in 2023, collecting over 200 hits (211) for the first time in his career. Assuming 170 hits per year going forward, Freeman will need 886 / 170, or just over five years, to reach the 3,000-hit milestone. With roughly that rate of hit production, he could get to 3,000 hits in 2028 during his age-38 season.

You may take exception to these simple calculations for Altuve

Part I—Analysis of Players with 3,000 Hits

and Freeman on the basis that most players' hit production declines as they age, and that it's unlikely Freeman will be able to collect 170 hits per season when he is in his upper 30s. That's true, but the argument says he needs to average 170 hits per year, so he may have seasons with more, and seasons with fewer, hits going forward. It's also possible that he could play into his 40s and collect additional hits that way. Regardless of the arithmetic, the important point is that Graph 7 shows that both Altuve and Freeman are on a pace which suggests they could reach 3,000 hits for their careers. Of course, lots has to go right for either player in order to make that happen, but these two men are the most likely candidates to reach the 3,000-hit milestone next.

It's also possible that neither of them will reach the milestone. In that case, we need to move further down the active player list to find the next-best candidates to reach 3,000 hits. There are 17 active players with between 1,500 and 1,900 hits. In order to find the best candidates, we compared when these players reached 1,500 hits in terms of age and games with when Club members Beltré, Winfield, Biggio, and Molitor reached 1,500 hits. Most of the candidates were well outside the envelope defined by these four players. But four of the players were within the envelope. The data for all eight players is shown in the lower left corner of Graph 7.

The four players whose pace to 1,500 hits was faster than the Club members envelope are: Eric Hosmer (1,753 hits), Manny Machado (1,737 hits), Mike Trout (1,624 hits), and Nolan Arenado (1,669 hits). (It doesn't look like all four of these data points are shown in Graph 7 because the Trout and Arenado data points are almost on top of each other.) Although Hosmer has the most hits of this small group, he struggled offensively starting in 2021 and he managed only 22 hits during the 2023 season. Hosmer announced his retirement in February 2024.

Machado, Trout, and Arenado are all now well over 1,500 hits for their careers. It took them 12 years, 13 years, and 11 years, respectively (including pandemic-shortened 2020) to reach those career totals. This means that it should take slightly less than these time periods to collect another 1,400 hits in order for these players to join the 3,000-Hit Club. A decade (roughly) is a very long time, and many things can happen over that time span. For the sake of argument, we will discuss the chances of these players joining the Club, but it is by no means certain that their careers of will be long enough for them to reach the milestone.

The player in this trio of stars with the best chance of getting to 3,000 hits is Machado. He has the most hits in the group, and he is the

14. Who's Next to 3,000 Hits?

youngest of the three. Arenado and Trout are roughly 15 and 11 months, respectively, older than Machado. In fact, when Machado struck his 1,500th hit, on June 15, 2022 (about three weeks before his birthday on July 6), he became just the 17th player to have 1,500 hits and 250 home runs before turning 30 years old.[2]

The 17 players in this select group are: Machado, Miguel Cabrera, Albert Pujols, Andruw Jones, Álex Rodríguez, Ken Griffey, Jr., Eddie Murray, Ron Santo, Orlando Cepeda, Frank Robinson, Hank Aaron, Eddie Mathews, Mickey Mantle, Willie Mays, Mel Ott, Jimmie Foxx, and Lou Gehrig. The difficulty of getting to the 3,000-hit milestone is demonstrated by the fact that only six of these great players (Cabrera, Pujols, Rodríguez, Murray, Aaron, and Mays) achieved the milestone. Since six is roughly one-third of 17, this suggests that only one of the trio under discussion may eventually join the 3,000-Hit Club.

But we can't write off Mike Trout just because he's about a year older than Machado.

The superlatives associated with Trout's career could (and have) filled a book. Only 13 years into his career, he's already considered one of the greatest players in baseball history by having won three MVP awards before he was 28 years old. However, in terms of his chances of reaching 3,000 hits (or 700 home runs), there is something that might prevent him from piling up big career numbers. That something is that he seems to be somewhat injury prone. He missed over a season's worth of games between 2017 and 2023, having lost substantial time each season to injury. If that trend continues, it may prevent him from reaching the milestone. On the other hand, all of Trout's injuries have been to different parts of his body. This suggests he may simply have been unlucky, rather than prone to injury. And there is precedent that suggests injuries don't have to derail a player from reaching 3,000 hits. Club member Al Kaline lost substantial time to injury during his career, and yet he still reached the milestone.

Nolan Arenado is best known for his defensive prowess. He won the Gold Glove Award for his outstanding work at third base in each of his first 10 years in the big leagues. Although his offensive numbers are not as gaudy as Mike Trout's, Arenado led the league in home runs three times, and came in third in the MVP voting twice, so he contributes substantially on offense too. From a hits perspective, he has almost 1,700 hits in 11 years, which means he has averaged almost exactly 150 hits per year. One can argue that Arenado's offensive numbers are inflated because he spent the first eight years of his career in Colorado.

Part I—Analysis of Players with 3,000 Hits

His hit production did decline after he left the Rockies, but he still collected 151 and 163 hits in his first two years in St. Louis. Arenado's pursuit of 3,000 hits will be hindered by the fact that he didn't get to the major leagues until he was 22 years old (both Machado and Trout came up when they were 19), but he has a chance to get there if he can continue to average about 150 hits per year.

However, Arenado's chances of reaching 3,000 hits will be substantially reduced if he keeps to his plan to retire when he is 38 years old. Before the 2023 season he said, "I think 38 would be cool. I would like to play until 38, but I definitely don't want to do 40 like [Adam Wainwright] or Albert [Pujols]. I do want my daughter [Levi] to see me play, but my eyes are set on 38. That could change, but if I'm limping to the finish line I wouldn't mind going home then. But my sights are set on 38."[3] Arenado was 31 years old when he said this. Assuming he does retire at 38 years old, he's not likely to collect enough hits to reach 3,000 before he hangs up his cleats.

Part II

Analysis of Pitchers with 3,000 Strikeouts

Hitters are not the only baseball players that can strive for 3,000 as a round number. A pitcher who strikes out 150 batters for 20 years, or 200 batters for 15 years, will achieve 3,000 strikeouts during his career. But which is more rare, 3,000 hits or 3,000 strikeouts? In other words, are there more pitchers with 3,000 strikeouts, or are there more batters with 3,000 hits? Part I showed that there are 33 hitters with 3,000 hits. How many pitchers have 3,000 strikeouts?

It's not intuitively obvious which group has more members with 3,000 events. Recent data suggests the answer is pitchers. For example, in 2022 there were 36 batters who collected 150 or more hits (no one had 200 hits) while 52 pitchers had 150 or more strikeouts. Eleven of those pitchers had more than 200 strikeouts. But data from a century earlier suggests the opposite conclusion. Not a single pitcher collected 150 strikeouts in 1922 (Urban Shocker of the St. Louis Browns led with 149 strikeouts) while 64 hitters collected 150 or more hits, and a dozen of those batters had 200 or more hits. The 1922 data clearly suggests more batters have had an opportunity at 3,000 hits.

Of course, hitting dominated during the 1920s and pitching has had the advantage recently, so this rudimentary analysis is not sufficient to answer the question, but it does suggest that more hitters would reach 3,000 hits early in the 20th century, while more pitchers would reach 3,000 strikeouts in recent decades. As we will see shortly, the actual data verify this notion, but that doesn't answer the question of which group is smaller. The answer is pitchers. There are 33 hitters with 3,000 hits but just 19 pitchers with 3,000 strikeouts.

This data is accurate at the end of the 2023 season. However, by the time you read it, it's likely that the number of pitchers with 3,000 strikeouts will be 21. This is one of the perils of writing about an active

Part II—Analysis of Pitchers with 3,000 Strikeouts

data set. After the 2023 season, active pitchers Zach Greinke and Clayton Kershaw are both less than 60 strikeouts away from 3,000 for their careers. Assuming they both pitch in 2024, there is an excellent chance they both will reach 3,000 strikeouts during the 2024 season. Therefore, given the delay between writing and publishing, there will probably be 21 pitchers in the 3,000-strikeout club when you read this. These two pitchers are another example of how outside events can impact when (or if) baseball players reach milestones. Both of these men would probably have reached 3,000 strikeouts as this was being written immediately after the 2023 season if not for the pandemic shortened (teams played just 60 games) 2020 season.

That puts your humble scribe in a bit of a quandary. I can't assume both will get there and write as though that has already happened, but writing about the current 19 is likely to be inaccurate later. And waiting until they both get there to write the book is also an unattractive proposition since that would delay the project significantly, and because it is also possible one or both will not get there due to injury or retirement. With all of this in mind, the book has been written as the pitcher data exists in October 2023, and the previous paragraph is offered to explain the likely discrepancy for the reader.

Part II is organized along the same lines as Part I. Most of the topics about the hitters with 3,000 hits will also be discussed about the pitchers with 3,000 strikeouts. Comparisons between the two groups, when appropriate, will be made in the pitcher section where the topic is discussed. For example, teams that have had both, or neither, a 3,000th hit batter and a 3,000th strikeout pitcher will be compared in the Franchises and Teams for Pitchers section of Part II.

15

Who Are the Pitchers?

Baseball fans have always been fascinated by power hitters and power pitchers. Men who can consistently hit the ball over the fence, or throw a fastball near or above the century mark, get a lot of attention. Since power pitchers strike out numerous batters, this means that the names of many of the pitchers who have accumulated 3,000 career strikeouts will be familiar to most fans. It's no surprise that Nolan Ryan, Tom Seaver, Roger Clemens, and Randy Johnson are among the 19 men in the select group with 3,000 strikeouts. However, the names of some of the pitchers who join them on the list are surprising. It's likely that many fans would not expect that Bert Blyleven, Don Sutton, and Phil Niekro would join the previous quartet in the elite group. That's why we do this exercise, to give all of these men their due. The complete list is shown in Table 11.

As with the first hitter on the list in Table 1, Cap Anson, there is an issue with the date of Walter Johnson's 3,000th strikeout. Table 11 says he reached the milestone on June 18, 1923, but contemporary observers thought he collected his 3,000th strikeout on July 22. Paul W. Eaton reported, "Walter Johnson, who probably holds more records than any other pitcher ever in the game, made his 3,000th strikeout on July 22 and added four others to make it more binding. Johnson is sure to add a good many more, and there is little chance that his mark will ever be equaled."[1]

The dates are different because modern researchers have found discrepancies in the records from the time. For example, David W. Smith, the founder of Retrosheet, informed me that Retrosheet researchers credit Johnson with four strikeouts on May 2, 1923, but contemporary records had Johnson with zero strikeouts that day.[2] Other similar discrepancies mean that Johnson reached the milestone before his contemporaries thought he did. Retrosheet (and Baseball-Reference.com, which uses Retrosheet data) have Johnson collecting his 3,000th strikeout on June 18. Since this date is the best estimate from current research, that is what is reported in Table 11.

Table 11: Data About Pitchers with 3,000 Career Strikeouts

	Player	Throws	Date of 3,000th Strikeout	Age	Team	Game Number	3,000th K Hitter	Opposing Team	Home or Away	Career Strikeouts
1.	Walter Johnson	R	6/18/1923	35	Washington	658	Stan Coveleski	Cleveland	home	3,509
2.	Bob Gibson	R	7/17/1974	38	St. Louis	492	César Gerónimo	Cincinnati	home	3,117
3.	Gaylord Perry	R	10/1/1978	40	San Diego	626	Joe Simpson	Los Angeles	home	3,534
4.	Nolan Ryan	R	7/4/1980	33	Houston	413	César Gerónimo	Cincinnati	away	5,714
5.	Tom Seaver	R	4/18/1981	36	Cincinnati	484	Keith Hernandez	St. Louis	home	3,640
6.	Steve Carlton	L	4/29/1981	36	Philadelphia	530	Tim Wallach	Montréal	home	4,136
7.	Ferguson Jenkins	R	5/25/1982	39	Chicago	607	Garry Templeton	San Diego	away	3,192
8.	Don Sutton	R	6/24/1983	38	Milwaukee	605	Alan Bannister	Cleveland	home	3,574
9.	Phil Niekro	R	7/4/1984	45	NY Yankees	757	Larry Parrish	Texas	away	3,342
10.	Bert Blyleven	R	8/1/1986	35	Minnesota	529	Mike Davis	Oakland	home	3,701
11.	Roger Clemens	R	7/5/1998	36	Toronto	435	Randy Winn	Tampa Bay	home	4,672
12.	Randy Johnson	L	9/10/2000	37	Arizona	362	Mike Lowell	Florida	away	4,875
13.	Greg Maddux	R	7/26/2005	39	Chicago	630	Omar Vizquel	San Francisco	home	3,371
14.	Curt Schilling	R	8/30/2006	39	Boston	543	Nick Swisher	Oakland	away	3,116
15.	Pedro Martínez	R	9/3/2007	35	NY Mets	443	Aaron Harang	Cincinnati	away	3,154
16.	John Smoltz	R	4/22/2008	40	Atlanta	706	Felipe Lopez	Washington	home	3,084
17.	CC Sabathia	L	4/30/2019	38	NY Yankees	542	John Ryan Murphy	Arizona	away	3,093
18.	Justin Verlander	R	9/28/2019	36	Houston	453	Kole Calhoun	Anaheim	away	3,342+
19.	Max Scherzer	R	9/12/2021	37	LA Dodgers	404	Eric Hosmer	San Diego	home	3,367+

15. Who Are the Pitchers?

Eaton's remark about Johnson's career strikeout record never being broken deserves comment since your not-so-humble author has made similar assertions. First, since Johnson held the career strikeout record until 1982, Eaton was correct for 59 years. That's not never broken, but it's a long time. Eaton could not have foreseen the changes in the game that took place in the 1960s and 1970s that created the conditions for pitchers to strike out many more batters than during the 1920s. In addition, Eaton's assertion was based on about 40 seasons of data. There are over 100 seasons of data behind my proclamations. That larger time frame covers far more changes in the game and makes it less likely a particular record will be broken. I'm comfortable with the assertion that Rickey Henderson's career steals record of 1,406 will never be broken. Henderson was a tremendous outlier in terms of base stealing and longevity. Even with the new rules and larger bases in 2023 that encouraged more base stealing, it's highly unlikely anyone will be able to replicate Henderson's career steals.

As with the 3,000-hit players, we will start the discussion of these pitchers with the question: is 3,000 strikeouts an automatic ticket to the Hall of Fame? Sixteen of the 19 men on the list are eligible for Cooperstown. Sabathia retired after the 2019 season and will be eligible for induction in 2025. Verlander and Scherzer are still active. All but two of the other 16 players are in the Hall of Fame. The two who aren't are Roger Clemens and Curt Schilling.

There is no question that Clemens' numbers are Hall of Fame worthy. His 354 wins are ninth best all-time and his 4,672 strikeouts are third best. No other pitcher has matched the seven Cy Young Awards he won. But like Rafael Palmeiro and Álex Rodríguez, Clemens has been associated with performance enhancing drugs. That association is clearly keeping him out of Cooperstown. Schilling's case is more nuanced. His raw numbers, 216 wins and 3,116 strikeouts, are not as compelling as Clemens' are, but many people think that Schilling has been denied entry in Cooperstown because of his political views.[3] If that supposition is correct, it's fair to say that without off-the-field issues, 3,000 strikeouts will get a pitcher into the Hall of Fame. That should be the case for Sabathia, Verlander, and Scherzer when they become eligible.

16

How Frequently Does a Player Reach 3,000 Strikeouts?

The 19 hurlers in Table 11 are listed in chronological order according to when they reached their 3,000th strikeout. A visual representation of the dates is helpful.

Graph 8 shows that the majority of 3,000th strikeouts have come in two roughly decade-long periods. Almost half (nine) of the pitchers reached the milestone from Bob Gibson in 1974 to Bert Blyleven in 1986. Another six reached the mark from Roger Clemens in 1998 to John Smoltz in 2008. Sabathia, Verlander, and Scherzer got there from 2019 to 2021. That's 18 of the 19 great pitchers. The missing hurler stands on his own in the graph. Walter Johnson is the only pitcher before Gibson in 1974 to reach 3,000 strikeouts.

That fact by itself speaks volumes about how great a pitcher Walter Johnson was. Even though he spent the majority of his 21-year career (1907–27) in the dead-ball era (before 1920) and in spite of the fact that striking out was much more taboo than it is now, he still collected 3,509 strikeouts. Walter Johnson held the career strikeout record from 1921 through 1982. Steve Carlton surpassed Johnson in 1983, but in 1984 Carlton in turn was surpassed by Nolan Ryan, who has held the record since then.

It may seem surprising that Walter Johnson is the only pitcher before Gibson to get to 3,000 strikeouts, given that he wasn't the only excellent pitcher before Gibson. For example, Cy Young (1890–1911) came up about 200 strikeouts short (he finished with 2,803) in spite of a stellar 22-year career. Christy Mathewson (1900–16) missed by about 500 strikeouts after a 17-year career. Lefty Grove (1925–41), who is

16. How Frequently Does a Player Reach 3,000 Strikeouts?

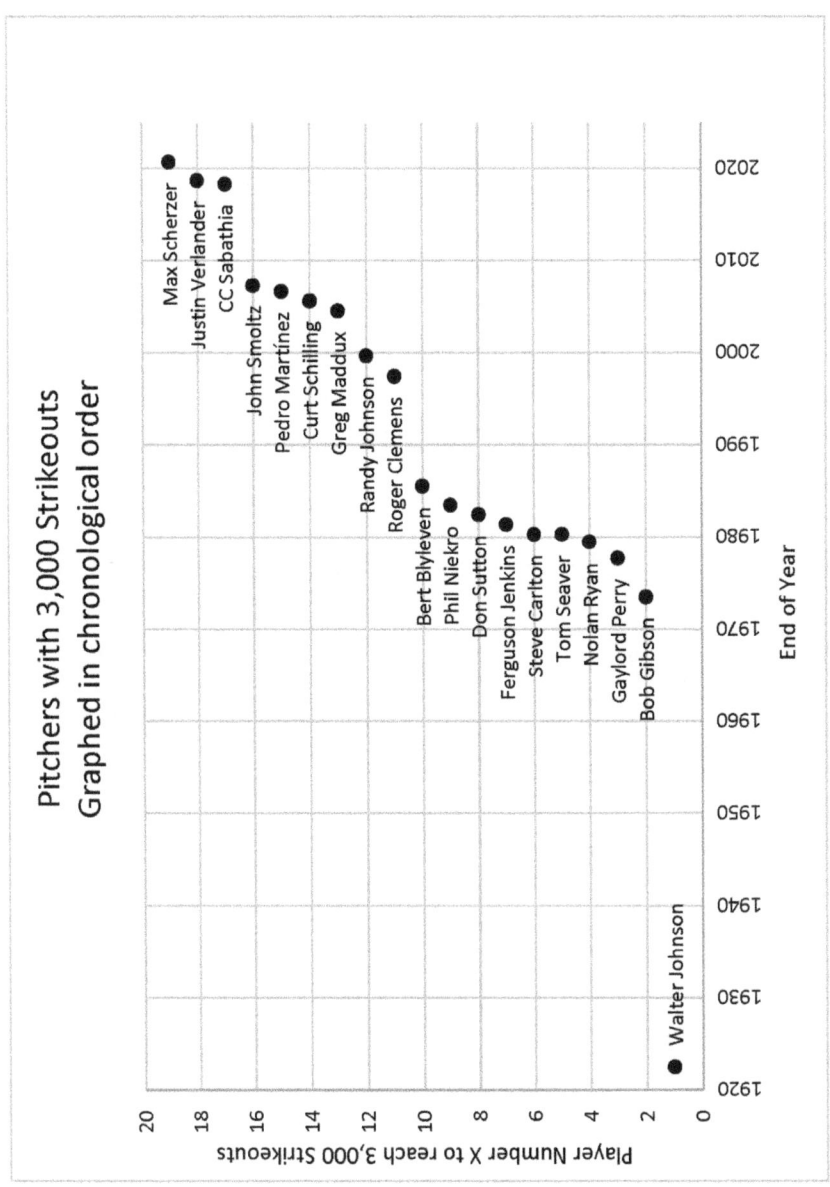

Graph 8: Pitchers with 3,000 Strikeouts Graphed in Chronological Order

often referred to as one of the best pitchers in baseball history, finished over 700 short after a 17-year career.

That said, just like the gap between Eddie Collins and Paul Waner

Part II—Analysis of Pitchers with 3,000 Strikeouts

for the hitters, there is a good reason for the long gap in time between W. Johnson and Gibson. That reason is World War II. It's likely that two pitchers would have reached the milestone before Gibson if they hadn't had to miss playing time while serving in the war. Those two pitchers are Bob Feller and Warren Spahn.

Feller's fastball was legendary. There is a famous short film of him throwing his fastball past a speeding motorcycle.[1] He grew up on a farm where his father built a baseball field to showcase the boy's talent. Feller got national attention from a young age and made his major league debut in 1936 as a 17-year-old high school student.[2] He led all of baseball in strikeouts from 1938 to 1941 with 240 or more per year in that span. But his promising career was interrupted by the attack on Pearl Harbor. Feller immediately enlisted in the Navy and he missed the next three full seasons. He returned to baseball in late August 1945 and collected 59 strikeouts for the season.

Bucky Jacobs (left) speaking with Bob Feller in 1937. Feller had one of the best fastballs in baseball history. He finished his career with 266 wins and 2,581 strikeouts. His four years in the service during World War II likely prevented him from reaching both 300 wins and 3,000 strikeouts (Library of Congress).

16. How Frequently Does a Player Reach 3,000 Strikeouts?

Feller had a career year in 1946. He went 26–15 with a 2.18 ERA for a sixth place Cleveland Indians team that won only 68 games. The 27-year-old led all of baseball in wins (26), games started (42), complete games (36), shutouts (10), innings pitched (371), and strikeouts (348). By today's standards, every one of those numbers is very impressive. Pitchers simply don't do that anymore. His 348 strikeouts were the most since Rube Waddell struck out 349 in 1904.

This has bearing on the current topic because Feller struck out 260 batters in his last full season before the war and 348 batters in his first full season after the war. It's very likely that he would have struck out over 200 batters per year during the four years he served in the Navy. Since he finished his career with 2,581 strikeouts (419 short of 3,000), that makes it very likely that he would have reached the milestone if he had not missed time because of the war. His data point in Graph 8 would have been around 1950 if not for World War II. Feller finished his career with 266 wins. His time in the service also prevented him from reaching 300 wins.

Warren Spahn's case in terms of 3,000 strikeouts is similar to Feller's. He also missed three full years because of his time in the service and in an interesting coincidence, he finished with just two more career strikeouts (2,583) than Feller did. This left Spahn 417 strikeouts short of the milestone. But the left-handed Spahn wasn't the strikeout machine that Feller was, so it's less certain he would have gotten the extra strikeouts if he hadn't missed time. Spahn was three years younger than Feller, so his missed time came right at the outset of his career. He pitched in four games in 1941 and then missed the next three years due to his service time. In his first full season after the war, 1947, he struck out 123 batters. Spahn would have needed about 140 strikeouts per year during the three years he missed to reach 3,000. He exceeded 140 strikeouts eight seasons of his career, but it's harder to argue he would have certainly gotten an additional 417 strikeouts during the first three full years of his career without the war. But it's possible he could have, especially if he got close enough by the end of his career to target 3,000 strikeouts. Had he done so, his data point in Graph 8 would be at roughly 1964.

Walter Johnson

Now to return to the pitchers who are on the list. The very brief career descriptions that follow in this section are not intended to be

Part II—Analysis of Pitchers with 3,000 Strikeouts

President Calvin Coolidge (left) shaking hands with Walter Johnson at Griffith Stadium in Washington, D.C., between 1923 and 1927. Johnson collected his 3,000th strikeout in 1923. He was the only pitcher to hold that distinction until Bob Gibson joined him in 1974 (Library of Congress).

comprehensive. They simply contain some career related statistics and stories about the pitchers that I think are interesting. Like Bob Feller, Walter Johnson is said to have had one of the best fastballs of all time. No less an authority than Ty Cobb, whose 24-year career completely overlapped Johnson's 21-year career, said this of Johnson's fastball: "The first time I faced him, I watched him take that easy windup. And then something went past me that made me flinch. The thing just hissed with danger." Cobb added, "We couldn't touch him ... every one of us knew we'd met the most powerful arm ever turned loose in a ball park."[3]

Johnson used that powerful arm to great effect. Even though he played for the usually hapless Washington Senators his whole career, he still finished with 417 wins, second only to Cy Young's 511 wins. The 1919 season provides a good example of what Johnson was capable of. The Senators won just 56 games that year and finished seventh (of eight)

16. How Frequently Does a Player Reach 3,000 Strikeouts?

in the American League. But Johnson went 20–14 with a 1.49 ERA that led all of baseball. He won 20 or more games 12 years, and had two years with 33 and 36 wins. And, of course, he struck out many batters, leading the American League in strikeouts 12 times, with a career high 313 in 1910.

Those are all very impressive numbers. But the statistic that most testifies to the greatness of Walter Johnson is the only number on his Baseball-Reference.com page that is highlighted in gold. He threw more shutouts than any other pitcher in baseball history. How many? An almost unbelievable 110 shutouts. Grover Alexander is second on the list with 90. The most recent player on the list (assuming retiring in the 1990s is recent) is Nolan Ryan with 61 shutouts. Like many pitching records, it's pretty safe to say Johnson's shutout record will never be broken.

A summary of Johnson's stellar career would not be complete with mentioning the 1924 season. The 36-year-old hurler went 23–7 to lead the Senators past the defending champion Yankees by two games. This gave Washington the opportunity to play the veteran N.Y. Giants who were appearing in their fourth consecutive World Series. Johnson pitched poorly by his standards in Games One and Five and he lost both games. The Senators forced a Game Seven with a 2–1 win in Game Six. The drama of the final game is one of the highlights of baseball history.

Before describing what happened, it needs to be made clear that in addition to being one of the best pitchers of all time, Johnson was a gentleman who was beloved across baseball. With the exception of Giants fans, the baseball world was pulling for the veteran Johnson to win his first World Series after toiling since 1907 in the pit of Senators mediocrity. The Giants led 3–1 in the middle of the seventh inning of Game Seven but the Senators tied the score with two runs in the bottom of the eighth. With the game and the Series in the balance, Senators manager Bucky Harris called on Johnson to pitch the ninth on two days' rest. Johnson's slow walk to the mound is part of baseball lore. Johnson escaped trouble in the ninth and kept the Giants off the board over the next three innings.

Most baseball fans have seen a catcher fling his mask well out of the way when attempting to field a pop-up. Catchers do that because of what happened in the bottom of the 12th inning of the 1924 World Series. With one out, Senators catcher Muddy Ruel popped up behind home plate. The Giants catcher, Hank Gowdy, threw his mask aside but he still stumbled over it and dropped the pop-up. Given another chance,

Part II—Analysis of Pitchers with 3,000 Strikeouts

Ruel doubled to get into scoring position. Two batters later, a ground ball down the third base line hit a pebble and got into left field. Ruel scored, and Washington had its first World Championship. The city wouldn't see another for almost a century, when the Nationals won a thrilling seven-game World Series in 2019 with neither team winning a game at home.

In my research, I stumbled across recently discovered footage of the Game Seven described above. The surprisingly high-quality four minutes of footage shows Griffith Stadium, key moments from the game, Walter Johnson pitching, and Senators fans storming the field after what we now call the walk-off single. It's definitely worth watching. The link is given in an endnote.[4]

The long gap in Graph 8 between Walter Johnson and Bob Gibson is partially accounted for by World War II. However, that doesn't explain why after a 50-year hiatus there were nine pitchers to reach the milestone in a dozen years between 1974 and 1986. The answer to that question is revealed by historic strikeout rates. Strikeout rates for the National League are shown in Graph 9. The trends in the American League (not shown) are very similar.

A complete explanation of the year-to-year variation in strikeout rates could be a book on its own. The rules of the game were evolving before 1900, resulting in a large variance in strikeout rates between 1876 and 1900. The strikeout rate stayed relatively stable from 1900 to 1945, but after 1945 there is a clear, almost unbroken, uptrend in strikeout rates. The uptrend through the 1950s was initiated by a change to the strike zone in 1950. The new strike zone was technically smaller than the old one but, batters were swinging for the fences (doesn't that sound familiar to modern fans) and strikeouts increased.

Although National League runs per team per game had decreased to 4.24 in 1960 from 4.66 in 1950, there was a misperception in the baseball establishment that there was too much offense in the game after the 1961 expansion. This prompted baseball to change back to the larger, pre–1950, strike zone in 1963.[5] Naturally, this helped the pitchers who already had the upper hand, to put a stranglehold on offense. The pitcher domination culminated in 1968 with Bob Gibson's 1.12 ERA. In response, baseball famously lowered the mound and restored the 1950–62 strike zone in 1969 in order to better balance pitching and offense. And even though the strikeout rate declined between 1970 and 1981, the rate in 1981 (4.92 strikeouts per team game) was still far above the rates that prevailed before World War II.

16. How Frequently Does a Player Reach 3,000 Strikeouts?

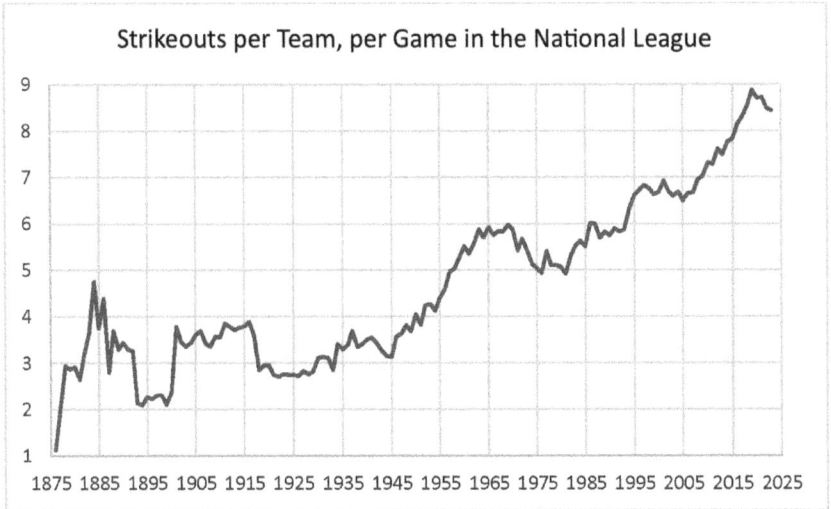

Graph 9: National League Strikeout Rates Since 1876

That set the stage for the next nine pitchers to reach the milestone. All but two of them, Bob Gibson who started his 17-year career in 1959 and Bert Blyleven whose 22-year career commenced in 1970, began their careers during the 1960s. These pitchers dominated the game. That, combined with a pitching philosophy of the time that said a pitcher should finish what he started, meant the group usually pitched deep into games and put up commensurately lofty strikeout totals. Although all the above applied to other pitchers also, only these nine from that era had the career longevity to reach the 3,000-strikeout plateau.

Bob Gibson

The main claims to fame of Omaha, Nebraska, are Warren Buffett and the College World Series. Teams in the College World Series began playing in Omaha in 1950, and Buffett began playing there (ok, I'll come clean, he was born there) in 1930. Baseball fans can add two great stars to the list. Both Bob Gibson and Wade Boggs were born in Omaha. It may not be a coincidence that Gibson, born in 1935 and therefore of the same generation as Buffett and from the same home town, dominated his chosen field in the same way that Buffett has dominated investing.

Gibson's 1968 season was one of the best ever. He went 22–9 with

Part II—Analysis of Pitchers with 3,000 Strikeouts

a league-leading 268 strikeouts that season. His 1.12 ERA and 13 shutouts made him the face of "The Year of the Pitcher." It was the lowest ERA since Dutch Leonard had a 0.96 ERA in 1914 (during the deadball era) and hasn't been equaled by any pitcher since then. Gibson's performance that year is so well-known that the number 1.12 has become one of the iconic numbers from baseball history. Gibson, and Denny McLain (who won 31 games in 1968), won both the Cy Young and MVP Awards that year. How can a pitcher with an ERA that low lose nine games? A closer look at Gibson's 1968 season can answer the question.

The short answer is lack of run support. Gibson lost 1–0 twice, 2–0 once, and the Cardinals scored just one or two runs in five of his other losses. He didn't allow more than three earned runs in any of the nine losses. The other aspect of the season that exemplifies how great Gibson was that season is that he allowed just three earned runs (in the form of single runs in three separate games) in 11 complete games between June 6 and July 30. Read the last sentence again and give it some thought. That is a two-month run of sustained excellence.

Gibson's ERA was 0.96 after his July 30 start. He didn't pitch quite as well in August but after his 12th shutout of the season on September 2, his ERA stood at 0.99. So Gibson had a sub-1.0 ERA into September of 1968. He faltered slightly on September 11 when he allowed four earned runs for just the second time that season. That relatively poor outing increased his ERA to 1.13, and he finished at 1.12 after another shutout in his final start of the season.

Intimidation was said to be one of the weapons that made Gibson effective. Cardinals catcher Tim McCarver reflected the thinking of many when he said, "For my money, the most intimidating, arrogant pitcher ever to kick up dirt on a mound is Bob Gibson. If you ever saw Gibson work, you'd never forget his style: his cap pulled down low over his eyes, the ball gripped—almost mashed—behind his right hip, the eyes smoldering at each batter almost accusingly."[6]

But later comments by the pitcher make this a good example of how looks can be deceiving, and that we have to be very careful when we think we know what someone else is thinking. Gibson wasn't scowling at hitters, he just couldn't see very well without the glasses he wore off the field so he was squinting to better see the signs from the catcher. He explained, "I got a lot of mileage out of looking angry. Sometimes it wasn't intentional—like when I was squinting in for the signs and the batters thought I was glowering at them—but the fact is, I was

16. How Frequently Does a Player Reach 3,000 Strikeouts?

deliberately unfriendly to the opposition. I wouldn't even say hello to hitters on the other teams."[7]

In spite of the rightful recognition that his 1968 season gets, Gibson is arguably more famous for his postseason performance in three World Series (1964, '67, '68). He threw three complete games in each Series and took home the World Series MVP Trophy in the first two. Gibson earned those two trophies by going 5–1 with a 2.0 ERA and winning Game Seven in both Series.

He could have won Game Seven of the 1968 Series too. That game was scoreless after six innings and Gibson retired the first two Detroit Tiger hitters in the top of the seventh. The next two batters singled to bring Jim Northrup to the plate. Northrup hit a long fly ball to left-center field. The Cardinals Gold Glove center fielder, Curt Flood, appeared to have a play on the ball, but he stumbled as he ran after the ball and could not catch up to it. The two runs that scored proved to be the difference in the game and Gibson took the loss. If Flood makes that catch (and this observer thinks he would have if he hadn't stumbled), Gibson could have had three Game Seven wins. Bill James argues that Gibson is the second best big-game pitcher in baseball history.[8] James' best big-game pitcher is Roy Oswalt, but that's a story for another day.

Gaylord Perry

The first two pitchers to reach 3,000 strikeouts, Johnson and Gibson, had reputations as flame-throwing power pitchers. The third man to reach the milestone had a very different reputation. The first thing many fans think of when they hear the name Gaylord Perry is the spitball. Perry was notorious for using the illegal pitch, but he always denied wrongdoing with a twinkle in his eye and a grin on his face. Regardless of the legality of some of his pitches, Perry used his pitching arsenal to craft an impressive 22-year career.

Perry pitched a lot. With the exception of 1965 (when he pitched 195 innings), Perry threw more than 200 innings every year from 1964 to 1980. During six of those seasons he pitched more than 300 innings. He epitomized the start-what-you-finish philosophy of the time, compiling the most complete games, 303, of any pitcher since 1960. From 1967 to 1975 he started at least 37 games per year with a career best 41 starts in 1970 and 1973. It's not an exaggeration to say that Perry was very durable. Only five men threw more innings during their careers than he did.[9]

Perry wasn't just a mediocre volume pitcher. Between 1966 and 1978 he won 19 or more games seven times. He led the league in wins three times, and had a career-best 24 wins in 1972. That was the year he won his first Cy Young Award with the Cleveland Indians after a decade in San Francisco. He threw a league-leading 29 complete games, including five shutouts, out of his 40 starts, and finished 24–16 with a 1.92 ERA. Six years later he became the first man to win a Cy Young Award in both leagues when he went 21–6 with the San Diego Padres. Perry had just five complete games that year. But that's what happens when you have Rollie Fingers to finish the game. Fingers finished 41 games for the Padres in 1979.

Unfortunately for Perry, the only time he saw postseason action was 1971 when the Giants lost to Pittsburgh in the NLCS. He started two games in that series, winning one and losing one. However, he did pitch a noteworthy regular season game. Perry threw a no-hitter on September 17, 1968. That contest was briefly noted earlier in the Bob Gibson section. Gibson lost two games in 1968 by a 1–0 score. This game against Perry was one of them. Both men went the distance, but Perry threw a no-hitter and Gibson allowed just four hits in the game. However, one of those four hits left the ballpark, so Gibson took one of his nine losses in 1968 because of Perry's no-hitter.

Nolan Ryan

Sometimes you just get lucky enough to be in the right place at the right time to witness history in person. That happened to me twice with respect to the Ryan Express. The Oakland A's were coming to Arlington, Texas, in August 1989 and I wanted to see McGwire, Canseco, Lansford, and the two Hendersons (Rickey and Dave) in person. It was a three-game series and I randomly picked one of the games about a month in advance. I was fortunate because that contest turned out to be the game where Nolan Ryan had a chance to reach 5,000 career strikeouts. Someone offered me hundreds of dollars for my tickets on the way into the game. It was tempting, but I am glad I declined because I'm still writing about the game over 30 years later. Of course, Ryan did get his milestone strikeout, Rickey Henderson was the victim, and I was fortunate enough to be there.

16. How Frequently Does a Player Reach 3,000 Strikeouts?

A similar thing happened four years later. By then I was living in Seattle and the Rangers were coming through at the end of the season. This time I deliberately went to see the game where Ryan was pitching and as he was nearing the end of his illustrious career, I knew there wouldn't be many more chances for me to see him pitch in person. What I didn't know was that there actually wouldn't be *any* more chances to see him pitch. Ryan walked three batters in the bottom of the first inning and allowed a grand slam to Dann Howitt. He later said he felt a burning sensation in his arm while pitching to the next batter and had to come out of the game.[10] Those turned out to be the last pitches Ryan ever threw and I'd been there to see them. That's a pretty low probability event given the end came unexpectedly and Ryan pitched for an astounding 27 years.

Portrait of Nolan Ryan in 1991. Ryan became the fourth pitcher to reach 3,000 strikeouts when he struck out César Gerónimo in 1980. Over the course of his 27-year career, he collected 324 wins and 5,714 strikeouts. Ryan's strikeout total is another record that will never be broken (National Baseball Hall of Fame and Museum, Cooperstown, N.Y.).

The previous statement is not an exaggeration. Pitching for 27 years *is* astounding. The only other player to have a 27-year major league career in the United States was Cap Anson. But Ryan's career actually spanned 28 years. After pitching in just two games as a rookie at the end of the 1966 season, he missed the entire 1967 season due to a combination of an arm injury and service time with the Army Reserve. If he had appeared in just one game in 1967, he would have had a 28-year career. It needs to be noted that Ichiro Suzuki did have a 28-year professional baseball career. He played for nine seasons in Japan before his 19-year major league career.

Part II—Analysis of Pitchers with 3,000 Strikeouts

The number that Ryan is most famous for is 5,714. That is, of course, the number of career strikeouts he had. We are celebrating the men who achieved 3,000 career strikeouts and Ryan's total is almost twice that. No other pitcher has even 5,000 strikeouts. Randy Johnson is second with 4,875. Once again, I'm comfortable with the assertion that this is another record that will never be broken.

Ryan also owns two other records that are highlighted in gold in Baseball-Reference.com. Not surprisingly, the second one is bases on balls. It's fair to say that Ryan was not a control pitcher. Part of what allowed him to compile so many strikeouts is that he was also effectively wild. That increased his strikeout total and his walk total. He finished with the all-time record 2,795 free passes. Ryan's third all-time record is for the fewest hits allowed per nine innings pitched. He allowed just 6.6 hits per nine innings over his entire career. Sandy Koufax is second on this list at 6.8 hits per nine innings. Koufax had fewer than 6.6 hits per nine innings from 1962 to 1965 but he was not as effective earlier in his career. Clayton Kershaw, another southpaw like Koufax, is right behind Koufax with just over 6.8 hits per nine innings.

Ryan compiled so many career strikeouts because his individual season strikeout totals were very high. He had over 300 strikeouts six times, and between 200 and 300 another nine times. His career best 383 strikeouts in 1973 is the modern single-season record. The story behind how he set that record is interesting. Sandy Koufax, one of those dominant pitchers from the 1960s who didn't reach 3,000 career strikeouts, struck out 382 batters in 1965. That number became the target as Ryan was having a career year in terms of strikeouts in 1973.

On September 23, 1973, Ryan struck out 12 batters to get to 367 strikeouts for the season. He would need 15 strikeouts in his final start of the season to tie Koufax. That's a tall order, even for a strikeout specialist like Ryan. He had done 17 once, 14 once, and 12 or 13 a dozen times that season, so it was possible but not likely. The Twins were visiting Anaheim on September 27 for what would be Ryan's last game of the campaign.

Ryan struggled in the top of the first. The first four batters reached base and three runs scored before Ryan settled in and struck out the side. The Angels answered with three runs in the bottom half of the inning. The next six innings Ryan struck out 2, 1, 3, 2, 0, and 3 batters to get to 14 strikeouts on the day. Each team had tallied one more run so the game was tied at 4–4 after the seventh inning. Ryan tied Koufax with a strikeout that ended the eighth inning, but he failed to register a strikeout in the top of the ninth.

16. How Frequently Does a Player Reach 3,000 Strikeouts?

Neither team could push across another run, so the game went into extra innings. Naturally, (would you have had the courage to try and remove him from the game?) Ryan pitched the 10th inning—no strikeouts. And the 11th inning—no strikeouts. And the 12th inning, wherein he finally recorded his 383rd strikeout of the season on the final out of the inning. The Angels emerged with a walk-off victory in the bottom of the 12th. So without extra innings during his final start of the 1973 season, Ryan would have tied Koufax rather than holding the single-season strikeout record himself.

Tom Seaver and Steve Carlton

The data points for Tom Seaver and Steve Carlton in Graph 8 are almost perfectly aligned vertically. That's because Carlton collected his 3,000th strikeout just nine days after Seaver in April 1981. That seems appropriate since Carlton was also born a little over a month after Seaver in late 1944. Although Seaver was from California and Carlton was born in Florida, the two great hurlers had similar career arcs like George Brett and Robin Yount. Carlton made his debut with the Cardinals in 1965 but didn't become a full-time starting pitcher until 1967. Seaver debuted in 1967 because he spent a few years in college, but he was immediately thrust into the Mets rotation so both men became starters the same year.

Seaver made an immediate impact by going 16–13 for a Mets team that won only

Portrait of Tom Seaver in Cincinnati Reds livery (between 1977 and 1982). Future teammate Keith Hernandez was Seaver's 3,000th strikeout victim in 1981. Seaver won the Rookie of the Year Award and two Cy Young Awards with the Mets (Library of Congress).

Part II—Analysis of Pitchers with 3,000 Strikeouts

61 games and taking home the Rookie of the Year Award in 1967. Two years later he was the ace of the Mets staff and he carried the team down the stretch to its first divisional title. The Mets trailed the Cubs by five games after play on August 25, 1969. From August 26 until the end of the season Seaver pitched eight consecutive complete game victories allowing just eight earned runs during that span. The Mets finished with 100 wins, eight games ahead of the Cubs. Seaver finished the year with a 25–7 record, a 2.21 ERA, and his first Cy Young Award. The Mets went on to beat the heavily favored Baltimore Orioles in the World Series. It was the only World Series victory that Seaver enjoyed during his 20-year career.

Three years later Carlton put together his own stretch of excellent pitching. From June 7 to August 17, 1972, Carlton went 15–0 with a 1.51 ERA. Over this 18-game stretch, he threw 14 complete games which included five shutouts. It would have been 15 complete games except that Carlton pitched 10 innings of a game that went 11 innings, so he didn't get credit for a complete game in that start. Carlton's final record was 27–10 with a league-best 1.97 ERA. Like Seaver, he was rewarded with his first Cy Young Award after the campaign. But unlike Seaver, there was no postseason glory for Carlton that year. The Phillies struggled all season and finished 59–97. Carlton won an all-time high 46 percent of the Phillies' victories.[11]

Stellar pitching from these two men continued through the 1970s. From 1969 to 1977 the pair won five of nine Cy Young Awards. Seaver won two more Cy Youngs in 1973 and '75. Carlton added his second in 1977, then two more in 1980 and '82. His performance in 1980 was particularly notable. He went 24–9 with a 2.34 ERA to lead the Phillies to their fourth divisional title in five years. But this time the team got past the NLCS as Carlton's Phillies team upended Nolan Ryan's Astros to advance to the World Series for the first time since 1950. Carlton went 2–0 in the World Series against the Kansas City Royals to lead the Phillies to the first championship in franchise history. That was no small feat since the franchise was established in 1883. It was Carlton's second championship. He'd won his first during his first full year as a starter with the Cardinals in 1967. In another parallel, it also means that both pitchers won a championship during their third year in major league baseball.

Both pitchers also moved around quite a bit toward the ends of their careers. Over the last five years of his career Seaver played for the Reds, Mets, and White Sox, before ending his career in 1986 with the Red Sox. In a tremendous irony, only a knee injury prevented him from

16. How Frequently Does a Player Reach 3,000 Strikeouts?

pitching *against* the Mets in the 1986 World Series. During the last three years of his career Carlton pitched for the Phillies, Giants, White Sox, and Indians before closing out with the Twins in 1988. Carlton's 24-year career began two years before Seaver's and ended two years after.

Part of the attraction of baseball is that the numbers can ostensibly allow answers to highly subjective questions such as: who was a better pitcher, Carlton or Seaver? Carlton won more games (329 versus 311) and had more strikeouts (4,136 versus 3,640), but Seaver had a better career ERA (2.86 versus 3.22), and dominated their head-to-head pitching matchups. The pair faced each other 17 times. Seaver went 11–3 in those matchups while Carlton was 3–12.[12] This superficial analysis suggests Seaver was the better pitcher. Yet, in spite of its simplicity, it agrees with what Daniel Marks concluded in 2021 when he ranked the top 10 starting pitchers of the last 50 years in Bill James Online. Marks has Carlton seventh and Seaver third.[13]

Bill James went further with his praise of Seaver in his 2001 *The New Bill James Historical Baseball Abstract*. "There's actually a good argument that Tom Seaver should be regarded as the greatest pitcher of all time," wrote James. "Where Seaver rates … depends to a large extent on how steep one believes the incline of history to be. Since no one can say with any confidence how much tougher the game has become, it is certainly reasonable to argue that the accomplishments of early pitchers should have been marked off by more than I have discounted them, and thus that Seaver's record, in context, is more impressive than [Walter Johnson's]."

Fergie Jenkins

During the summer of 2022 my son and I visited Victoria, British Columbia on vacation. As we walked around the lovely town, at one point we heard shouting and banging from up ahead. We couldn't figure out what the noise was. As we crested a small hill, we saw that there was a hockey rink with a game in progress. Canadians don't let a lack of ice stop them from playing hockey. But our friends to the north don't play just hockey. They've also left their mark on baseball. Joey Votto, Justin Morneau, Eric Gagné, and Larry Walker all hail from Canada. When Walker was inducted into the Hall of Fame in 2020, he became the second Canadian so honored. The first was Ferguson Jenkins.

Part II—Analysis of Pitchers with 3,000 Strikeouts

Jenkins came up with the Phillies in 1965, the same year Carlton made his debut. If the Phillies had had the wisdom to keep Jenkins instead of sending him to the Cubs in 1966, the team could have had both Carlton and Jenkins for most of the 1970s. That didn't happen, but it's intriguing to think about. Jenkins was best known for his control. He allowed fewer than two bases on balls per nine innings for nine consecutive years (1970–78) and led the league in the category five times over that span. He also led all of baseball in strikeout-to-walk ratio five times, with a career best ratio of 7.11 in 1971 when he walked just 1.0 batter per nine innings. His control allowed him to become the first pitcher with 3,000 strikeouts to have fewer than 1,000 walks. It took almost 25 years before Greg Maddux joined him with both those distinctions. Curt Schilling, Pedro Martínez, Justin Verlander, and Max Scherzer joined the pair after Maddux.

Jenkins won 20 or more games for six consecutive years (1967–72). During this span he came in third in the Cy Young Award voting twice, second in the voting once, and he won the Cy Young Award once in 1971. (Seaver was second in the voting that year.) However, Jenkins had a relatively down year in 1973, going 14–16, so the Cubs traded him to the Texas Rangers before the 1974 season. Jenkins responded with one of the best seasons in Rangers history. He led all of baseball with 25 wins against 12 losses and a 2.82 ERA as the team finished five games behind the defending champion Oakland A's. The A's would go on to win their third consecutive title in 1974. Although his overall numbers were very good that year, Jenkins' performance was especially noteworthy over the last three months of the season.

He started the season with a 5–1 record, but by the end of June he was 9–9 with a 4.01 ERA. Jenkins turned things around in July, August, and September. Over 21 starts from July 3 to October 2, he went 16–3 with a 1.79 ERA. As was customary for pitchers during this time period, 16 of his starts were complete games, and four of those 16 were shutouts. In another seven of those complete game starts he allowed just one run. The voting for the American League Cy Young Award was close. Jenkins got 10 first place votes and a total of 75 vote points. But Catfish Hunter, who also won 25 games against 12 losses, had a slightly better ERA of 2.49. Hunter got 12 first place votes and 90 vote points to win the award. It was the second time Jenkins had come in second in the Cy Young voting. That was the closest the Rangers have ever come to having a pitcher win the Cy Young Award. They are the only AL team without one.

16. How Frequently Does a Player Reach 3,000 Strikeouts?

Don Sutton

In addition to being a great pitcher, Tom Seaver was wise. He said, "In baseball, my theory is to strive for consistency, not to worry about the numbers. If you dwell on statistics you get shortsighted, if you aim for consistency, the numbers will be there at the end."[14] That philosophy helped Seaver to be on the short list of men in the conversation about the greatest pitchers of all time. But the eighth pitcher to reach the 3,000-strikeout milestone is the embodiment of Seaver's argument. Don Sutton's career was a model of consistency. And that's how Sutton wanted it. He said, "I never wanted to be a superstar, or the highest paid player. [A]ll I wanted was to be appreciated for the fact that I was consistent, dependable, and you could count on me."[15]

Sutton broke in with the Dodgers in 1966 and pitched for the next 22 years. He was astoundingly consistent. He had double-digit wins every year of his career except for 1983 and the last year. But he won over 20 games just once when he got to 21 wins in 1976. He started over 30 games every year but 1968, strike-shortened 1981, and his final season. He pitched between 200 and 300 innings every year except for 1981 and his last two seasons. He collected 100 or more strikeouts in 21 seasons. Greg Maddux also did this, but only Roger Clemens (22) and Nolan Ryan (24) have more 100 strikeout seasons.[16] Sutton would have had 22 seasons with 100 strikeouts but he came up one strikeout short in his penultimate season, 1987. Round number bias strikes again. Sutton's consistency and longevity put him seventh on both the career innings pitched list and the career strikeout list. This is exactly what Seaver was talking about.

The downside of Sutton's consistency is that he never had a season with eye-popping numbers. He was selected to the All-Star Team just four times, and he never won the Cy Young Award, although he did place third in the voting in 1976. His postseason record is exactly what you would expect given his consistency. Sutton started 14 games over nine postseason series and finished with a 6–4 record and 3.68 ERA. He appeared in four World Series (1974, '77, '78, '82) but never won a championship.

Phil Niekro

Gaylord Perry's name and the spitball are forever linked. There's a similar linkage for Phil Niekro. He's the most famous practitioner of an

Part II—Analysis of Pitchers with 3,000 Strikeouts

arcane pitch that's almost extinct, the knuckleball. Niekro learned the pitch from his father who was forced to throw it himself after an arm injury. Niekro said, "I never knew how to throw a fastball, never learned how to throw a curveball, a slider, split-finger, whatever they're throwing nowadays. I was a one-pitch pitcher."[17]

He rode that pitch for a very long time. In spite of not making his big-league debut until he was 25 years old, Niekro's knuckleball allowed him to craft a 24-year career from 1964 to 1987, pitching until he was 48 years old. And like Perry and Sutton who reached 3,000 strikeouts before him, Niekro pitched a lot. Except for the strike-shortened 1981, he made at least 32 starts per year from 1968 until 1986. Once he became a starter in 1967, Niekro pitched at least 200 innings per year through 1986 (again excepting 1981). This included four years where he exceeded 300 innings, pitching a career high 342 innings in 1979. Just three pitchers: Cy Young, Pud Galvin, and Walter Johnson, threw more innings than Niekro.

Niekro's best year was 1969 when he went 23–13 with a 2.56 ERA. He came in second to Seaver in the Cy Young Award voting. That was the closest he ever got to winning the award. In 1979 the 40-year-old Niekro put together an interesting season. He led the league in starts (44), complete games (23), innings pitched (342), and victories (21). But he also led the league in losses with 20. It was the second time in his career he lost 20 games. Niekro was unfortunate to pitch for the Atlanta Braves during a time period when the team was not very good. He pitched in the NLCS twice (1969 and '82) but the Braves lost both series.

Niekro and Perry share another interesting connection. Both players had a brother who also pitched in the major leagues. Niekro's brother, Joe, won 221 games in 22 years from 1967 to 1988. Perry's brother, Jim, won 215 games over his 17-year career. These pairs of brothers are first and second in combined victories by siblings. The Niekro brothers have 539 combined wins, while the Perry brothers have 529. Joe Niekro's career illustrates why we are celebrating the 19 men who reached 3,000 strikeouts. You have to be a very good pitcher to pitch for 22 years and to win over 200 games. But in spite of his longevity and skill, Joe Niekro finished with 1,747 career strikeouts. It is very difficult to reach the 3,000-strikeout plateau.

Bert Blyleven

The 10th pitcher to record a 3,000th strikeout was the only man in the group who came into this world as a European. Bert Blyleven was

16. How Frequently Does a Player Reach 3,000 Strikeouts?

born in Zeist, Netherlands in 1951. Baseball fans would likely not know his name except that his family moved to Canada and then to Southern California when he was young, so he grew up playing baseball.[18] His career path is similar to Don Sutton's. Blyleven never had a truly remarkable season, but he had many good ones. And like Perry, Sutton, and Niekro, he pitched a lot. He threw 200 or more innings in 16 of his 22 seasons and sits 14th on the career innings pitched list. Blyleven threw 242 complete games, and he struck out 100 or more batters in 19 seasons. Like Sutton, he was consistent over a lengthy career.

But Blyleven managed a few career accomplishments that eluded Sutton. He threw a no-hitter while pitching for the Texas Rangers in 1977. Sutton never had one. Two years later Blyleven went 12–5 for the "We Are Family" Pirates as they came back from being down three games to one to win the World Series. Blyleven pitched four shutout innings in relief to get the win in the crucial fifth game. In 1987 he was instrumental in the Minnesota Twins' run to the World Series title. He got two wins in two starts in the ALCS against Detroit, including beating Jack Morris in Game Two. Blyleven won Game Two of the World Series, although he took the loss in Game Five. But the Twins prevailed in a World Series where the home team won every game to give Blyleven his second championship. It's interesting to note that four years later, pitching for, not against, the Twins, Morris would be the World Series MVP on the back of a famous 10-inning shutout in Game Seven against the Braves.

The longest gap in time between 3,000th strikeouts occurred from Walter Johnson to Bob Gibson. Graph 8 shows that there was another substantial gap after Blyleven collected his milestone strikeout in 1986. It was a dozen years before the next pitcher, Roger Clemens, tallied 3,000 strikeouts. There isn't any particular reason for this gap other than the fact that it's very difficult to strike out that many men. However, the group of six pitchers from Clemens to Smoltz did benefit from a baseball environment that was characterized by increased numbers of strikeouts. All six of these hurlers spent the bulk of their careers pitching in the 1990s and early 2000s. Graph 9 shows that strikeouts per team game were near an all-time high (at the time) of just under seven. It was a good time to be a strikeout pitcher.

Roger Clemens

Bill James developed what is known as the black ink test as one way to analyze how well qualified a player is to be in the Hall of Fame. The

Part II—Analysis of Pitchers with 3,000 Strikeouts

test gives points to players for leading the league in various important statistical categories. It's called a black ink test because the numbers are shown in bold black ink on the player's career summary page. However, even without assigning points, the black ink test is a quick and dirty way of looking at a player's career. Great players have a lot of black numbers on their career summary page. Average players don't usually have many black numbers. The quintessential example of this phenomenon is Babe Ruth. His career summary is full of black numbers.

Even among the elite group of great pitchers in this study there are substantial differences in black ink. Gaylord Perry, Don Sutton, and Bert Blyleven have a few scattered numbers in black ink on their career pages. That is not the case for Roger Clemens. There is a lot of black ink on his page. That by itself is a pretty good indication of how good he was. This is not an appropriate venue to address the allegations of steroid use by Clemens so his career accomplishments will be taken at face value in the following discussion.

As great as many of the numbers associated with Clemens' career are, there is really one number that stands out. That number is seven. The man won seven Cy Young Awards. That's about all you need to know to get a feel for how great a pitcher Clemens was. Nobody else has won more than five of those awards (Randy Johnson won five, he's discussed next). That puts Clemens in a class by himself. And he is almost in a class by himself when it comes to career strikeouts. He is one of just four men with more than 4,000 career strikeouts. The other three are Nolan Ryan, Steve Carlton, and Randy Johnson.

Although Clemens was excellent throughout his 24-year career, his third season, in 1986 was arguably his best. His record was unblemished for the first three months of the season as he won 14 of his first 15 starts and was 14–0 entering July. He lost four of his next seven starts, but didn't lose another game after August 4, finishing the year 24–4 with a league-leading 2.48 ERA. He was rewarded with his first Cy Young Award and the MVP Award for the American League. His dominance that year is also demonstrated by his performance on April 29 when he struck out a record 20 Seattle Mariners batters. Clemens excellence over time is evidenced by the fact that he repeated the 20-strikeout performance a decade later on September 18, 1996, against the Detroit Tigers.

There are enough highlights from Clemens' career to fill another book, but one more regular season game anecdote will suffice for now. Clemens was pitching for the Yankees in 2003, and by early June he had recorded his 299th win to go along with 3,996 career strikeouts. On

16. How Frequently Does a Player Reach 3,000 Strikeouts?

June 13 he had the opportunity to reach two significant career milestones in the same game. Naturally, he didn't waste that opportunity; Clemens collected his 300th win and his 4,000th strikeout during the same contest. But there is a little more to the story than that. Two players who would later reach 3,000 hits also played in the game. Derek Jeter had just over 1,400 hits at the time and Albert Pujols, in just the third season of his career, had less than 500 hits to his credit. Pujols came very close to being Clemens' 4,000th strikeout victim. He was strikeout number 3,999 when Clemens struck him out for the third out of the first inning. Edgar Rentería, the 2010 World Series MVP, was the 4,000th strikeout the next inning.

Randy Johnson

It's an interesting coincidence that the two men who are third and second, respectively, on the career strikeout list, Clemens (4,672 strikeouts) and Randy Johnson (4,875 strikeouts), collected their 3,000th strikeouts just over two years apart. Like Seaver and Carlton, the careers of Clemens and Johnson overlap significantly. Clemens pitched for four years before Johnson made his debut in 1988, but the two men were both active over the next 19 years until Clemens retired in 2007. Johnson's career page, like Clemens,' has a lot of black ink on it. They were both great pitchers. How can we measure that? How about by Cy Young Awards?

Clemens won seven of the awards between his first in 1986 and his last in 2004 when he became the oldest player to win the award at 42 years old. Which pitcher has the second most Cy Young Awards? It's Johnson with five. He won those five awards over eight seasons between 1995 and 2002, with four of the awards coming in consecutive seasons from 1999 to 2002. His last Cy Young Award-winning season was especially noteworthy. Johnson won the pitching triple crown in 2002. He led the league in wins (24), ERA (2.32), and strikeouts (334). However, the pitching triple crown is more common than the batting triple crown (leading the league in home runs, runs batted in, and batting average). Four other pitchers in this study have also won pitching triple crowns. Clemens has two (1997, '98), Walter Johnson did it three times (1913, '18, and '24), and Carlton (1972) and Verlander (2011) each did it once as Randy Johnson did.

Although Clemens was unarguably very good at collecting strike-

Part II—Analysis of Pitchers with 3,000 Strikeouts

outs, there is also no doubt that Johnson was better. Clemens had two games with 20 strikeouts to Johnson's one, but Johnson also had two other games with 19 strikeouts, while Clemens' next best game was an 18-strikeout effort. Clemens led the league in strikeouts five times while Johnson led the league nine times in a 22-year career. He most likely would have had 10 league-leading campaigns except that he was traded from Seattle in the AL to Houston in the NL at the trading deadline in 1998. Had he been in one league the whole season, his 329 strikeouts almost certainly would have led either league. To put that in perspective, Walter Johnson led the league in strikeouts 12 times. Nolan Ryan did it 11 times.

There's more. Johnson had six seasons with more than 300 strikeouts. Clemens never struck out 300 batters in a season. Nolan Ryan set the single-season strikeout record of 383 in 1973. That's an incredible number that seems unapproachable, but Johnson collected his career-best 372 strikeouts in 2001. With one more start, he might have broken Ryan's record. All that said, Johnson's

Randy Johnson preparing to deliver a pitch in 1994. Johnson struck out Mike Lowell on his (Johnson's) 37th birthday for his 3,000th strikeout. He is second to Nolan Ryan on the all-time career strikeout list with 4,875. Johnson and Ryan both had six seasons with more than 300 strikeouts (National Baseball Hall of Fame and Museum, Cooperstown, N.Y.).

strikeouts per nine innings numbers are his most impressive statistics. During that 2001 season, he averaged 13.4 strikeouts per nine innings. That was the all-time record until Gerrit Cole broke it in 2019 with 13.8

16. How Frequently Does a Player Reach 3,000 Strikeouts?

strikeouts per nine innings. Johnson averaged 10.6 strikeouts per nine innings over his entire career. As of 2023, that's the highest among all retired pitchers.

The other connection between Clemens and Johnson concerns one of the most memorable games in baseball history. The 2001 World Series featured the Yankees and the Diamondbacks. Johnson started Games Two and Six, getting the win for the Diamondbacks in both. Clemens started, and won, Game Three for the Yankees. Johnson's Game Six victory sent the Series to a winner-take-all Game Seven with Clemens facing off against another 3,000-strikeout pitcher, Curt Schilling. Both men pitched well and the game was tied at one run each after seven innings. The Yankees took a one-run lead in the top of the eighth inning on an Alphonso Soriano home run. Johnson, after pitching seven innings in Game Six the previous day, came in to get the final out of the eighth, and then held the Yankees scoreless in the top of the ninth. He was awarded the win when Luis Gonzalez famously singled off Mariano Rivera to give the Diamondbacks the World Series victory. This famous Game Seven was the only postseason contest that Clemens and Johnson appeared in together.

Greg Maddux

Most of the hurlers in this study were power pitchers who overpowered batters on their way to 3,000 strikeouts. But the next man to reach the milestone, five years after Johnson did, was the exact opposite. Greg Maddux looked more like a college instructor—hence one of his nicknames, The Professor—than a professional pitcher. His hallmark was control, not power, and his pitching was often very efficient. For Maddux, pitching was an art form. But that didn't stop him from collecting many strikeouts over his 23-year career in order to join this elite group. The following quote from Wade Boggs is as good an explanation of how Maddux reached 3,000 strikeouts as any: "It seems like he's inside your mind with you. When he knows you're not going to swing, he throws a straight one. He sees into the future. It's like he has a crystal ball hidden inside his glove."[19]

Clemens, Johnson, and Maddux were the 11th, 12th, and 13th pitchers to reach 3,000 strikeouts. It's interesting that those three men are also first, second, and third in Cy Young Awards with seven, five, and four, respectively. It's also interesting that Johnson and Maddux reached

Part II—Analysis of Pitchers with 3,000 Strikeouts

the milestone consecutively, and that they are the only men to win four consecutive Cy Youngs. Steve Carlton also won four Cy Young Awards, but not consecutively. Maddux might have won a fifth award in 1997 when he went 19–4 with a 2.20 ERA, but he came in second in the voting to Pedro Martínez, who'd put together an excellent 1.90 ERA for the campaign to bring home the award.

The focus of these brief pitcher discussions has been innings pitched for many of the first group of pitchers and appropriately, strikeouts for Clemens and Johnson so far in this group. But for Maddux, it's most appropriate to discuss walks—or more specifically, lack of walks. But before we look at his numbers, let's first get a feel for what was typical for this time period. In the year 2000 the average number of bases on balls per nine innings across major league baseball was 3.8. In other words, the average pitcher walked almost four batters per nine innings.

Portrait of Greg Maddux in 1993. Maddux struck out 11-time Gold Glove winner Omar Vizquel for his 3,000th strikeout in 2005. He is the only pitcher in history with 3,000 strikeouts, 300 wins, and less than 1,000 walks (National Baseball Hall of Fame and Museum, Cooperstown, N.Y.).

Maddux won the first of his four Cy Young Awards in 1992. His walk rate that year was 2.4 bases on balls per nine innings. The next two years those rates declined to 1.8 and 1.4. Those numbers are all substantially better than average. But Maddux got even better by this measure over the next three years. During his final Cy Young season (1995) his walk rate was 1.0 per nine innings. He repeated that tremendous performance the next year and then exceeded it with a career best 0.8 walks per nine innings in 1997. Maddux issued just 20 bases on balls in the 33 games he started that year. That is simply amazing. Over the course of

16. How Frequently Does a Player Reach 3,000 Strikeouts?

his 23 seasons Maddux led the league in fewest bases on balls per nine innings a total of nine times. His career rate was 1.8 bases on balls per nine innings. That's the best of any pitcher in the elite 19 under discussion. Curt Schilling and Ferguson Jenkins are next best at 2.0 walks per nine innings over their careers. Nolan Ryan is the highest in the group at 4.7 walks per nine innings in his career.

My favorite Maddux story is walks related. The Professor finished his career in 2008 with the Dodgers. At the end of August that year he had issued 997 bases on balls over the course of his career. He pitched into the sixth inning of a start on September 1 without walking any batters, but he allowed two walks during a six-inning outing on the 8th. He now had 999 career bases on balls. Maddux *really* wanted to finish his career with less than 1,000 walks but he had to make three more starts for the playoff-bound Dodgers. Could he pitch those games without issuing even one more base on balls? That's difficult, even if your name is Greg Maddux.

On the 14th he pitched seven shutout innings without issuing a walk in the thin air of Coors Field. On the 19th he allowed seven earned runs in five innings, but it was another game with no walks. The final start of his career came on the 27th. Maddux allowed just one run in six innings while collecting the 355th win of his illustrious career. And of course, he didn't walk a single batter. He pitched the final 18 innings of his career without allowing a base on balls to keep his career walks total under 1,000. By doing so, he became the only pitcher in history with 3,000 strikeouts, 300 wins, and less than 1,000 walks.

Sometimes, in spite of a lengthy, accomplished career, players are best known for one thing. An unfortunate player may be best remembered for a mistake. Fred Merkle and Bill Buckner are two players in this category. After Merkle passed away in 1956, the first line of his obituary in the *New York Times* said, "Fred Merkle, former major league baseball player who was best remembered for a 'boner' that cost the New York Giants the pennant in 1908, died today. He was 67 years old." Buckner got the same treatment. When he passed in 2019 the *Los Angeles Times* obituary led with, "Bill Buckner, a veteran of 22 Major League Baseball seasons who debuted with the Dodgers in 1969 and persevered after a calamitous fielding error in the 1986 World Series for the Boston Red Sox, died Monday. He was 69." It's not fair to these players, and others like them, that their long careers are defined by a single mistake.

Other players are remembered for a positive contribution that came in the national spotlight. Kirk Gibson's home run in Game One of

Part II—Analysis of Pitchers with 3,000 Strikeouts

the 1988 World Series is the quintessential example of this. The performance of David Freese in the late innings of Game Six of the 2011 World Series is another. Pitchers in this category include Madison Bumgarner for his 2014 World Series performance and Jack Morris for his complete game shutout in Game Seven of the 1991 World Series. The next pitcher to reach 3,000 career strikeouts is in this category. In spite of a successful 20-year career, Curt Schilling is best remembered for his postseason performances.

Curt Schilling

Schilling's regular season career is not as impressive as some of the other pitchers in this group, but he still has some significant accomplishments to his credit. Although he never won a Cy Young Award, he was second in the voting three times between 2001 and 2004. In spite of winning 22 and 23 games, respectively, during the first two of those years, he was second to teammate Randy Johnson in the voting. This means that the Diamondbacks had the two best pitchers in the National League for back-to-back years. No wonder the team advanced to the World Series in 2001. Schilling did not quite have the control that Maddux exhibited, but he still led the league in fewest bases on balls per nine innings with 1.1 and 1.2 in 2002 and 2006, respectively. That good control, combined with his ability to strike batters out, yielded five years wherein he led the league in strikeout-to-walk ratio.

But it was in the postseason that Schilling really shined. He started 19 postseason games over the course of his career and went 11–2 with a 2.23 ERA. Schilling started seven World Series games and finished with a 4–1 record and a 2.06 ERA. He gave up a total of 11 earned runs in his World Series starts, but six of those runs (and his only loss) came in his first World Series start for the Phillies in 1993. He made up for that by pitching a complete game shutout in Game Five which sent the Series back to Toronto. That was the first of five must-win-or-go-home games that Schilling started in the postseason. His team won every one of those games. He was co–MVP with Randy Johnson during the 2001 World Series, and he took home three championship rings.

One of his famous postseason starts came against Clemens in the 2001 World Series Game Seven discussed earlier. But arguably, his two "Bloody Sock" starts in the 2004 postseason are what he's most famous for. Schilling had injured his ankle in the 2004 Division Series and was

16. How Frequently Does a Player Reach 3,000 Strikeouts?

ineffective in the Red Sox Game One loss in the ALCS against the Yankees. After falling behind three games to none, the Red Sox had won two games to force a Game Six. Schilling and his doctor agreed on a radical surgery on the tendons in Schilling's ankle that might allow him to start the sixth game.[20] Television cameras caught blood seeping through Shilling's sock as he warmed up to pitch and shots of the bloody sock were shown throughout the game. Schilling was able to pitch effectively in spite of the bleeding, and the Red Sox won the game, and the series, to become the only team to recover after being down three games to none in a seven-game series. A similar series of events happened before and during Schilling's Game Two start in the World Series. But once again, he pitched well in spite of the blood on his sock and the Red Sox won the game. The team famously went on to win its first World Series since 1918. It's an interesting coincidence that the bloody (red) sock episodes happened to a Red Sox pitcher.

Pedro Martínez

Sandy Koufax is not in this group of 19 elite pitchers because his 12-year career was too short for him to accumulate 3,000 strikeouts. Koufax was so dominant from 1963 to 1966 that he earned the nickname "The Left Arm of God." It can be argued that those four years were the best any pitcher ever had. Koufax had a 1.74 ERA in 1964 and a 1.73 ERA in 1966. There's no denying those were two great seasons. But as Graph 9 shows, pitching dominated hitting in the mid–1960s and Koufax wasn't the only pitcher who was having success. The league average ERA in 1966 was 3.52.

However, the delicate balance between pitching and hitting had swung toward the hitters by the late 1990s. The league average ERA was 4.76 in 2000. That's the year that Pedro Martínez had his best campaign. His 1.74 ERA was equal to Koufax's ERA in 1964. Whose pitching performance is more impressive? Sabermetric analysis (named after the Society for American Baseball Research where it originated) can help us to answer that question.

Earned run average by itself is a flawed measure of pitcher effectiveness because the overall ERA in baseball varies over time. It's not an apples-to-apples comparison to compare the ERA for a pitcher in the pitching-dominant dead-ball era or the 1960s to an ERA from the hitting dominant 1930s or 1990s. The sabermetric statistic ERA+ was

Part II—Analysis of Pitchers with 3,000 Strikeouts

developed to account for this. ERA+ compares a pitcher's ERA to the league average ERA during that year and then also adjusts for ballpark effects. For example, setting aside ballpark effects, a pitcher whose ERA is exactly the league average ERA will have an ERA+ of 100 that year. A pitcher with an ERA that is half the league average will have an ERA+ of 200 for the season. We need to understand this statistic because by this measure Pedro Martínez is the greatest retired starting pitcher in AL or NL history.

Like Clemens and Randy Johnson, there are a lot of black numbers on Pedro Martínez's career page. Martínez led all of baseball in ERA five times between 1997 and 2003, with an ERA of 1.90 and 1.74 in 1997 and 2000, respectively, and 2.26 or lower three times. Those same five years he also led the league in ERA+. That's very good, but what's more impressive is that his ERA+ was over 200 all five years. In 1999 he had an ERA+ of 243, and he did even better in 2000, with an ERA+ of 291. How good are those numbers? The ERA+ of 291 is the highest single-season ERA+ since 1900 of any AL or NL pitcher with at least 200 innings pitched. His 243 ERA+ in 1999 is eighth best under the same restrictions.[21] Greg Maddux has the third and fourth best ERA+ seasons with 271 and 260 in 1994 and '95, respectively. Bob Gibson's famous 1968 season with a 1.12 ERA had a 253 ERA+, which is sixth best.

That peak performance is part of what drives the assertion that Martínez is the best ever starting pitcher as measured by ERA+. But those five great seasons are not the full story. Martínez didn't have a few good seasons and then lapse into mediocrity. He was much better than an average pitcher for his entire career as indicated by his career ERA+ of 154. Compared to his best seasons that number isn't very impressive, but it's the best career ERA+ mark of any retired AL or NL starting hurler.[22] The caveats in that statement are necessary because closer Mariano Rivera has the highest career ERA+ at 205, and two currently active pitchers, Clayton Kershaw and Jacob deGrom, also have a career ERA+ slightly better than Martínez. But neither caveat diminishes how great Martínez was over the course of his whole career.

The downside to looking at the career pages for all of these great pitchers is that one can start to take great pitching feats for granted. For example, Martínez led the league in strikeouts three times, and he had over 300 strikeouts in both 1997 and 1999. But citing the 300 strikeouts statistic without context doesn't do justice to the feat. How many pitchers since 1900 have multiple 300-strikeout years?[23] Take a guess before going on. The answer: just nine. Nolan Ryan and Randy Johnson

16. How Frequently Does a Player Reach 3,000 Strikeouts?

did it six times each. Schilling and Koufax each did it three times, and four other pitchers besides Martínez (one of which was Walter Johnson) did it twice. In an interesting coincidence, just as there are 19 pitchers with 3,000 career strikeouts, there are also a total of 19 pitchers who have ever had at least one season with 300 or more strikeouts. It's not an accomplishment to be taken lightly.

John Smoltz

Like Don Sutton and Bert Blyleven, the 16th man to reach 3,000 strikeouts doesn't have too many black numbers on his career summary page. But he does possess one black number that none of the other pitchers in this study have. John Smoltz was a starting pitcher for the first dozen years of his career. However, he missed the entire 2000 season because a nagging elbow injury required Tommy John surgery. Smoltz wasn't sure if his surgically repaired arm would hold up to the rigors of starting, so he came back at 34 years old as a relief pitcher. A very good one. In 2002 he led all of baseball with 55 saves (the black number no other elite pitcher has). That's tied for fourth on the all-time single-season saves list. He continued his excellent performance as a closer when he saved 45 and 44 games the next two years. Smoltz earned a total of 154 saves during the four years he spent as a reliever.

This initial focus on Smoltz's prowess as a closer is simply because he's the only one of these 19 elite pitchers who spent a significant portion of his career in a relief role. But he wouldn't be part of the group if he wasn't also an excellent starting pitcher. Smoltz, Greg Maddux, and Tom Glavine were the core of an Atlanta Braves rotation that helped the team win the NL East Division a record 14 consecutive times between 1991 and 2005. The trio won five of the six NL Cy Young Awards between 1993 and '98. Smoltz contributed to that by winning the award in 1996 when he went 24–8 with a 2.94 ERA. Had Smoltz remained in a relief role, he wouldn't have reached 3,000 strikeouts. But he returned to starting in 2005 and spent the last five years of his career in that role. The 686 strikeouts he recorded during those five years allowed him to reach the 3,000-strikeout milestone. He finished just 84 strikeouts above the mark.

Although Smoltz is well known for being one of the few pitchers who excelled as both a starter and a reliever, he is arguably better known for his performance in the postseason. Over 14 years, Smoltz

Part II—Analysis of Pitchers with 3,000 Strikeouts

started 27 postseason games and pitched 209 innings. The innings total is the third highest of all time. His postseason record is an impressive 15–4, with 15 wins also being the third highest of all time. Smoltz was the starting pitcher in three win-or-go-home Game Sevens during his career. He started Game Seven of both the 1991 and 1992 NLCS against the Pirates, and the Braves won both games to advance to the World Series each time.

The most famous start of his career happened in Game Seven of the 1991 World Series. Smoltz faced off against Jack Morris of the Twins. Morris is remembered for his 10-inning complete game shutout to get the victory. But what may be forgotten is that Smoltz matched him zero for zero until he was pulled from the game after getting one out in the eighth inning. Smoltz did not want to be removed but it wasn't his call. The Twins went on to a walk-off victory in the bottom of the 10th. Bill James rates Smoltz as the fifth best big-game pitcher ever.[24]

CC Sabathia

There's an 11-year gap in Graph 8 after Smoltz reached the 3,000-strikeout milestone in 2008, before CC Sabathia became the 17th pitcher with 3,000 strikeouts in 2019. Sabathia is another pitcher in the elite group with just a smattering of black numbers on his career page. He led baseball in wins twice (19 in 2009 and 21 in 2010) and he also led the league twice in starts. His 241 innings pitched in 2007 were the most in the majors. That workload, combined with a 19–7 record and 3.21 ERA netted Sabathia the only Cy Young Award of his career. Like Don Sutton, Sabathia reached 3,000 strikeouts by being consistent over an extended time period. Although he never struck out 300 batters in a season, he struck out over 200 three times, and he had over 100 strikeouts every year of his 19-year career except for 2014 when he underwent knee surgery. Just six pitchers (Ryan, Clemens, Maddux, Sutton, Blyleven and Carlton) had more 100 strikeout seasons than Sabathia. (See Endnote 19 for details.)

CC (Carsten Charles) was no stranger to the postseason. His 23 starts over 10 postseasons are tied for the eighth-most all time. Although his overall postseason record is not that impressive at 10–7, he was particularly effective in Division Series play, compiling a 6–1 mark. Sabathia's best postseason year was 2009. After earning a win in the Yankees sweep of the Twins in the Division Series, Sabathia got two

16. How Frequently Does a Player Reach 3,000 Strikeouts?

more wins in the ALCS against the Angels, and took home the MVP trophy for that league championship series. He faced reigning Cy Young Award winner Cliff Lee in Game One of the World Series and took a loss. But his Game Four victory helped the Yankees win the championship. Those were the only two World Series appearances in Sabathia's career.

Sabathia's reputation was also enhanced by his performance for the Milwaukee Brewers during the second half of the 2008 season. He'd spent the first seven years of his career with the Indians, but he and the club could not come to terms after his Cy Young Award-winning season in 2007. Suspecting they would not be able to sign the free-agent-to-be after the 2008 season, Cleveland traded Sabathia to Milwaukee in early July. Sabathia entranced fans in Milwaukee, and kept the Brewers in the hunt for both the division crown and wild-card position, by going 9–0 in his first 11 starts during July and August. Knowing the team needed his services, Sabathia made his last three starts of the season on three days' rest. His victory on the last day of the season made Milwaukee the NL wild-card entry for the playoffs. It was the first postseason appearance for the Brewers since 1982. The fact that Milwaukee lost to the eventual champion Phillies in the Division Series does not diminish Sabathia's accomplishments over the second half of the season.

Justin Verlander and Max Scherzer

The final two pitchers who have reached 3,000 career strikeouts were both still active at this writing (after the 2023 regular season), so the final chapters of their stories are unknown. Nonetheless, Justin Verlander and Max Scherzer have accomplished enough in their careers that they both can be celebrated for more than the accumulation of 3,000 strikeouts. In fact, it's difficult to decide what to include in a short summary for both of them.

Let's start with their Cy Young Awards. There are seven pitchers who have won the Cy Young Award three times. Four of those seven are in this elite group of 19 men. We've already mentioned Tom Seaver and Pedro Martínez as being three-time winners. The other two are Verlander and Scherzer. Scherzer won his three in the five years between 2013 and '17. But Verlander's Cy Youngs are more spread out. His campaign in 2011 was so outstanding (24–5 record, 2.40 ERA, 250 strikeouts) that he won the pitching triple crown, the Cy Young Award, and

Part II—Analysis of Pitchers with 3,000 Strikeouts

the American League MVP Award. His next Cy Young didn't come until 2019 and he won his third in 2022. The 2022 award is special because Verlander became the fourth-oldest man to win a Cy Young just a few months short of his 40th birthday.

How these two pitchers got to 3,000 strikeouts is also interesting. Graph 9 shows that they both spent their careers in a strikeout-friendly era. Verlander led the league in strikeouts five times. Surprisingly, his career best in 2019, when he registered exactly 300 strikeouts, did not lead the AL in strikeouts that year. He was second to Gerrit Cole who rang up 326 batters. Verlander struck out more than 200 batters nine times and over 100 batters 17 times. The strikeout statistics for Scherzer are eerily similar to those of Verlander. His career high is also 300 strikeouts exactly (although that figure did lead the majors for Scherzer) in 2018. And like Verlander, he also exceeded 200 strikeouts nine times. Including the 2023 season, Scherzer has 16 seasons above 100 strikeouts, compared to Verlander's 17 campaigns.

There are other interesting parallels in the careers of these two outstanding pitchers. They were teammates on the Detroit Tigers from 2010 to 2014, and then again for most of the 2023 season with the N.Y. Mets before the team let both of them go because of a highly disappointing season. Both men have thrown multiple no-hitters, with Verlander having three to his credit and Scherzer having two. In 2016 Scherzer joined Clemens, Randy Johnson, and Kerry Woods as the only pitchers with 20 strikeouts in a nine-inning game. Verlander's best single-game strikeout total was 15 in 2019.

Both men have reached the postseason 10 times during their careers. Over those 10 seasons, Verlander's 37 postseason starts exceed Scherzer's 25 starts, but both are in the top 10 all time in postseason starts. The pair have similar postseason ERAs, with Verlander at 3.58 and Scherzer at 3.78. After leaving the Mets during the 2023 season, Verlander went back to Houston and Scherzer went to Texas. The pair then helped their respective teams into the postseason. The Astros met the Rangers in the 2023 ALCS with Scherzer and Texas advancing to the World Series in seven games. Although they didn't start against each other, both Scherzer and Verlander went 0–1 during the series. Finally, both men have two championship rings. Verlander won twice with Houston (2017 and 2022). Scherzer earned his second ring when Texas won the 2023 World Series. He added that one to the ring he won in 2019 when the Nationals defeated Verlander's Astros. The visiting team won every game of the seven-game World Series in 2019.

17

Age

Now that we've seen how frequently a pitcher reaches 3,000 strikeouts and learned a little about the men who got there, it's time to learn about some characteristics of these pitchers as a group. We'll start with how old each of the pitchers was when they recorded their 3,000th strikeout. The results are shown in Graph 10.

Graph 10 shows that Nolan Ryan was the youngest pitcher to reach the milestone at 33 years old, while Phil Niekro was the oldest at 45 years old. The next three youngest were Walter Johnson, Bert Blyleven, and Pedro Martínez, who were all 35 years old. There is a gap of four years between Niekro and the next oldest pitchers, Gaylord Perry and John Smoltz. Besides Ryan and Niekro, the other 17 pitchers accumulated their 3,000th strikeout between 35 and 40 years old. Four men were 36 years old when they reached the milestone, with nine other pitchers spread equally between the ages of 35, 38, and 39 years old. Using integer ages, the average age of the 19 men with 3,000 strikeouts is about 37½ years old.

As is often the case, the outlying data points are the most interesting. The most obvious outlier in Graph 10 is Phil Niekro. He was five years older than any other pitcher when he recorded his 3,000th strikeout. Why was that? The answer is that he started later. Niekro had a difficult time getting up to the major leagues. He didn't start his professional career as a minor leaguer until he was 20 years old, and then spent four years in the minors (and one in the Army) before he made his major league debut at 25. At the end of his age-40 season (the age of the next oldest players) in 1979, Niekro had accumulated just over 2,400 strikeouts. But because he specialized in the knuckleball, he still had plenty of bullets left in his arm. Five years later in 1984, he reached his milestone 3,000th strikeout on the Fourth of July, and Niekro pitched for three more seasons after that to finish with 3,342 strikeouts in his career. He

Part II—Analysis of Pitchers with 3,000 Strikeouts

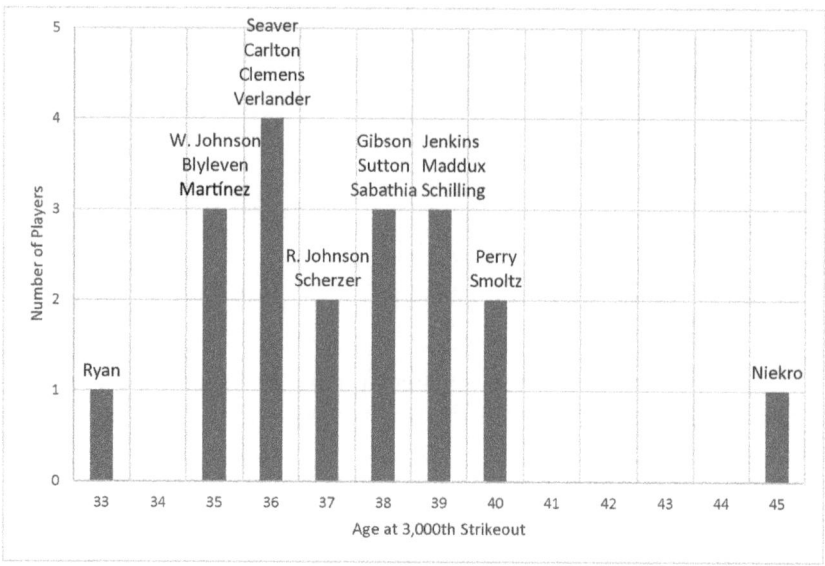

Graph 10: Pitchers with 3,000 Strikeouts by Age at 3,000th Strikeout

threw his last pitch at the ripe old age of 48 years old. It almost makes you wish you could throw a knuckleball.

The outlier at the other end of the spectrum is Nolan Ryan. Ryan was two years younger than any other pitcher, 33 years old, when he reached 3,000 strikeouts. How did he do that? It's pretty simple. He struck out *a lot* of hitters. He got to 1,000 strikeouts in 1973 when he was 26 years old. But it took Ryan just 122 games over three years to collect his next 1,000 strikeouts. That's what happens when you strike out 367 hitters (1974) and 327 batters (1976) in two seasons. He collected his 2,000th strikeout at age 29 in 1976. It's hard to believe, but Ryan kept up that strikeout rate over the next few seasons, too. It was four years on the calendar, but only 126 games later, when Ryan collected his 3,000th strikeout on the Fourth of July in 1980 as a 33 year old. It's an interesting coincidence that the two outlying pitchers in Graph 10 both collected their milestone 3,000th strikeout on the nation's birthday. They are also the only two pitchers of these 19 who collected the milestone hit on the same calendar day.

Ryan, of course, didn't stop pitching in 1980. He had 13 more years to ply his craft. Almost exactly five years later, 153 games after his 3,000th strikeout, he reached the next milestone. In 1985, at age 38,

17. Age

Ryan became the first man to strike out 4,000 batters during his career. He wasn't the only man to do that for long. Steve Carlton reached 4,000 strikeouts in 1986. Incredibly, it took Ryan fewer games (137) to get to the 5,000-strikeout milestone than it had for him to get to 4,000. He reached that mark in August 1989 when he was 42 years old. When his arm gave out in 1993 he had 5,714 strikeouts. That's another record that will never be broken.

How do the ages of the 3,000-strikeout pitchers compare to the ages of the 3,000-hit batters? Given that there are more hitters than pitchers, it seems easier to reach the mark as a hitter, and therefore that the pitchers would be older, in general. But that simplistic reasoning overlooks one important statistical fact. That is, while it's possible to strike out 300 or more hitters in a season, it's not possible (at least to date) to get 300 hits in a season. That gives great pitchers an advantage over great hitters in terms of how long it takes to reach the 3,000 threshold. The data bears this out. The average age for 3,000-strikeout pitchers is 37½ years old, while the average age for hitters is two months shy of 39 years old. On average, the hitters were a little more than a year older than the pitchers when they reached the milestone.

Averages, of course, obscure a lot of detail. We can learn more by comparing Graph 2 for the hitters to Graph 10 for the pitchers. The youngest hitter or pitcher to reach the 3,000 plateau was Nolan Ryan at 33 years old. But given Ryan's advantage in being able to strike out so many batters (over 300) each year, it says a lot about how great a hitter Ty Cobb was that he reached 3,000 hits at 34 years old. To do that, Cobb needed seven seasons with more than 200 hits (including a career-best 248 in 1911), and another nine campaigns with more than 100 hits. He also had to make his major league debut as an 18-year-old. All of that was required for Cobb to reach 3,000 hits two years before anybody else.

Setting the 45-year-old Phil Niekro aside as a true outlier in Graph 10, every other pitcher reached 3,000 strikeouts no later than age 40. But for the hitters, three players reached the milestone at age 41, and two more at age 42. Outside of Ryan and Niekro, all of the pitchers reached the milestone between 35 and 40 years old. Outside of Cobb, the spread of ages for the hitters is shifted right one year, and is wider, from age 36 to age 42. These statistics testify to the difficulty of hitters achieving the simple arithmetic of 150 hits times 20 years. That's not to say it's easy for pitchers to reach 3,000 strikeouts. But this data suggests that great pitchers can reach 3,000 strikeouts faster than great hitters can reach 3,000 hits.

18

Franchises and Teams

As was done for the 3,000-hit players, we can examine which franchises and teams have had the opportunity to celebrate a 3,000th strikeout. The results are shown in Table 12.

Table 12:
Pitchers with 3,000 Strikeouts by Franchise and Team

	1903 Franchise	Expansion Franchise	City	Team Name	No. 3,000 Strikeout Pitchers	Players
1.		x	Arizona	Diamondbacks	1	R. Johnson
2.	x		Atlanta	Braves	1	Smoltz
3.	x		Boston	Red Sox	1	Schilling
4.	x		Chicago	Cubs	2	Jenkins, Maddux
5.	x		Cincinnati	Reds	1	Seaver
6.		x	Houston	Astros	2	Ryan, Verlander
7.	x		Los Angeles	Dodgers	1	Scherzer
8.		x	Milwaukee	Brewers	1	Sutton
9.	x		Minnesota	Twins	1	Blyleven
10.		x	New York (N)	Mets	1	Martínez
11.	x		New York (A)	Yankees	2	Niekro, Sabathia
12.	x		Philadelphia	Phillies	1	Carlton
13.		x	San Diego	Padres	1	Perry
14.	x		St. Louis	Cardinals	1	Gibson
15.		x	Toronto	Blue Jays	1	Clemens

18. Franchises and Teams

1903 Franchise	Expansion Franchise	City	Team Name	No. 3,000 Strikeout Pitchers	Players
16.	x		Washington	Senators	1	W. Johnson
Total	10	6			19	

There are 16 teams that have had the good fortune to celebrate a pitcher reaching his 3,000th strikeout. That means that about half of the teams in MLB have had one of these celebrations. Ten of those teams have been around at least since 1903. The other six are expansion teams that came into existence in 1961 or later. The Cubs, Astros, and Yankees have had two celebrations of a 3,000th strikeout milestone, while 13 teams have had one. But even though there have been 16 teams with a 3,000-strikeout pitcher, there have been only 15 franchises. That's because Bert Blyleven and Walter Johnson both got their 3,000th strikeout while playing for the same franchise even though the team had changed locations, and names, when it moved from Washington to Minneapolis.

Most of this tome is factual, but there's a "what might have been" aspect to this discussion that deserves to be mentioned. John Smoltz spent almost all of his career with Atlanta and collected his milestone strikeout while with the club. But there easily could have been two more Atlanta Braves pitchers to get their 3,000th strikeout with the team. This would have given the franchise three pitchers with the milestone strikeout. Most fans know that both Phil Niekro and Greg Maddux spent the bulk of their careers with the Braves. What's also true, and much less well known, is that they both left the club shortly before they reached the milestone.

That's especially true in Niekro's case. Niekro had a relatively poor year in 1983. He was 44 years old and went 11–10 during the 1983 campaign. The Braves coaching staff thought he should retire, but Niekro, who wanted to remain with the Braves, felt like he had a few more good years left.[1] In the end, Niekro went to the Yankees for the 1984 season. That's why he collected his milestone strikeout playing for New York. Niekro won 16 games for the Yanks in 1984 and '85. With a little better foresight, the Braves could have had his services for those years, and with it, the ninth pitcher to reach 3,000 strikeouts. The argument in Maddux's case is not quite as clear-cut. After 11 years with the team, Maddux left the Braves as a free agent following the 2003 season. He reached the milestone two seasons later with the Cubs. Had he re-signed

Part II—Analysis of Pitchers with 3,000 Strikeouts

with Atlanta, the Braves would be the only team with three pitchers to collect their 3,000th strikeout with one team. It could have been four if Warren Spahn had not lost time to World War II.

The proliferation of strikeouts since the 1960s, shown in Graph 9, means that in general, expansion franchises have had shorter waits to see a 3,000th milestone strikeout than the 16 original franchises. The best example of this is the Arizona Diamondbacks. The franchise came into existence in 1998, along with Tampa Bay. The team signed Randy Johnson as a free agent in 1999, and Johnson collected his 3,000th strikeout on September 10, 2000. So the franchise had a pitching milestone to celebrate during its third season in existence. It's an interesting coincidence that September 10 also happens to be Johnson's birthday. That's a pretty good present to give yourself on your 37th birthday. He's the only pitcher in the group to collect the milestone strikeout on his birthday. The Tampa Bay franchise, born in the same year as the Diamondbacks, has yet to see a 3,000th strikeout celebration.

The biggest one-year expansion in major league history occurred in 1969. San Diego, Seattle, Kansas City, and Montréal all began playing that year. The Padres and the Brewers franchises would both see a 3,000th strikeout milestone relatively quickly. Gaylord Perry was traded from Texas to the Padres before the 1978 season. Perry had one of the best campaigns in his long career for the Padres in 1978, winning the Cy Young Award and collecting his 3,000th strikeout on the final game of the season with a complete game, 10-inning effort. It took just 10 campaigns for the franchise to celebrate the milestone. The Brewers weren't far behind. When Don Sutton collected his milestone strikeout while pitching for Milwaukee in 1983, the franchise had been in existence for 15 years.

The first expansion in major league baseball, as opposed to a franchise relocation, occurred in 1961. There were two unique aspects to it. First, it involved expansion and relocation at the same time. In the American League, the existing Washington Senators franchise moved to Minneapolis and was replaced by an expansion franchise of the same name. The American League also expanded at the same time by adding the Los Angeles Angels. Then, in order to make the schedule work, the American League played a 162-game season in 1961, while the eight-team (not yet expanded) National League played a 154-game schedule. So the two leagues played schedules of different lengths in 1961.

This is relevant to the current discussion because both of the teams

18. Franchises and Teams

that were added to the National League in 1962, the Houston Colt .45s and the New York Mets, have had 3,000th strikeouts to celebrate. Nolan Ryan was born in Refugio, Texas, which is about 160 miles from Houston. Because of that (and a then-record over $1 million-per-year contract), when he became a free agent after the 1979 season, Ryan signed with the Astros.[2] He proved his worth immediately. Not only did he help the Astros get to the postseason for the first time in their history in 1980, but he also collected his milestone 3,000th strikeout on July 4. The franchise had been in existence for 19 years. It would have been even better if Ryan had been able to reach the coveted plateau at a home game in Houston, but that was not to be. He was pitching in Cincinnati when he reached the milestone. The Mets had to wait considerably longer. It was 46 years before Pedro Martínez got there while pitching for the Metropolitans in 2007.

Three of the five teams involved in the 1961–62 expansion / relocation have seen a 3,000th strikeout celebration. The Twins got to Minneapolis in 1961. They became the third team in this quintet with a milestone celebration when Bert Blyleven struck out his 3,000th batter in 1986. In this case we must make a distinction between franchise and city when looking at how long it took. From a franchise perspective, it's an interesting coincidence that the Washington Senators had been in existence for 23 years when Walter Johnson reached the 3,000th strikeout plateau in 1923. Fans in the Twin Cities had to wait 26 years to celebrate Blyleven's achievement of the same feat.

The last two teams in the group, the Los Angeles Angels and the expansion Senators / Texas Rangers, have not seen a 3,000th strikeout celebration. But that simple statement comes with a big qualification for the Rangers. Although no pitcher has struck out his 3,000th hitter while wearing a Ranger uniform, the franchise did get to celebrate the only 5,000th strikeout in baseball history. It's very likely the second clause in the previous sentence will always be true. If Randy Johnson could not get to 5,000 career strikeouts, it probable that no one else besides Nolan Ryan can either. There's a small qualification for the Angels too. Ryan pitched for the Angels for eight years and had over 2,400 strikeouts with the team. Had he stayed in California for just one more year, he would have reached the 3,000-strikeout milestone wearing an Angels uniform.

The long gap between Walter Johnson and Bob Gibson in Graph 8 means all of the other franchises that had been established in 1901 or earlier had to wait much longer before they could celebrate a 3,000th strikeout. It's not necessary to do precise calculations of times here,

Part II—Analysis of Pitchers with 3,000 Strikeouts

other than to note that in all cases it is at least a 75 to 85-years wait. This is the case for St. Louis, Cincinnati, Philadelphia, Chicago (NL), and the Yankees. The Braves franchise and the Dodgers franchise both had to wait over a century. The Braves drought likely would have ended much sooner had Warren Spahn been able to reach the milestone. It's surprising that the pitching-centric Dodgers franchise had to wait until 2021 before celebrating a 3,000th strikeout by Max Scherzer. The Dodgers drought could have ended sooner, but Don Sutton, who collected almost 2,700 strikeouts in a Dodgers uniform, finished his career elsewhere and wasn't with the team when he reached the milestone.

The franchises with 3,000-hit players section in Part I concluded with a discussion of the nine franchises that never celebrated that milestone hit. That data, combined with the pitching franchise data in this section, allows us to determine which franchises have never had a batter collect a 3,000th hit or a pitcher reach 3,000 strikeouts. Six expansion franchises never had a hitter with 3,000 hits. However, three of those franchises did get to have a 3,000th strikeout celebration. Roger Clemens collected his for the Blue Jays in 1998. Randy Johnson did the same for the Diamondbacks in 2000, and Pedro Martínez reached the milestone with the Mets in 2007. That leaves the Nationals (established in 1969), Mariners (established in 1977), and the Rockies (established in 1993) as the three expansion franchises without a 3,000th hit or strikeout celebration. For the Nationals, that's over 50 years without one of these milestones. That's a pretty long time, but other franchises have had much longer droughts.

The hitters discussion in Part I noted that there were three franchises which have been around since 1903 that haven't had a 3,000th hit player. Two of those franchises did get to have a 3,000th strikeout celebration. The Philadelphia Phillies got to celebrate the milestone when Steve Carlton reached 3,000 strikeouts in 1981. Max Scherzer broke the drought for the Dodgers in 1921. The Phillies franchise was established in 1883. So it took just under a century before the franchise had a 3,000th-something celebration. The Dodgers franchise came into existence in 1884. That makes it almost 140 years for that franchise to see a 3,000th-something celebration. Those are pretty long time periods. But there is one original franchise that has not seen either celebration. Do you remember what the third original franchise without a 3,000th-hit celebration was? That team has also not had a 3,000th strikeout celebration. The unfortunate franchise is the Philadelphia / Kansas City / Oakland Athletics.

18. Franchises and Teams

Why haven't the Athletics had either celebration? The team has certainly had its share of great players, but reaching either milestone is so difficult that none of those excellent players could get there in an Athletics uniform. Rickey Henderson is one of two special cases for the A's. Henderson played for the A's for 14 years and collected over 1,700 of his 3,055 hits while playing in Oakland. But he was on five teams over the last four years of his career and was wearing a Padres uniform when he struck his 3,000th hit. Who is the other player with 3,000 hits that played for the Athletics? Since his career ended almost a century ago, it's easy to forget that Eddie Collins was a key cog in two Philadelphia Athletics dynasties. He won five of his six championships with the A's: three from 1910 to 1913 and then two more later in 1929 and '30. He was on the team for 13 years (the first nine years of his career and the last four) while collecting over 1,300 hits for the franchise. But Collins also spent a dozen years with the White Sox and was playing for Chicago when he collected his 3,000th hit.

A similar situation happened on the pitching side. Don Sutton spent the first 16 years of his career with the Dodgers. He accumulated almost 2,700 strikeouts during that time period. Sutton moved on to Houston, Milwaukee, and then Oakland but he was pitching for the Brewers when he reached the 3,000-strikeout milestone. Therefore, like Collins during his second stint with the team, but not Henderson, Sutton had already attained the

Portrait of Eddie Collins in 1913. Bill James argues that Collins was one of the best second basemen to ever play the game. Collins was a member of the 1919 White Sox team that threw the World Series but he was not in on the fix (Library of Congress).

Part II—Analysis of Pitchers with 3,000 Strikeouts

milestone while playing for the A's. The A's franchise leader for strikeouts is Eddie Plank. He collected almost 2,000 strikeouts over 14 years with the team, from 1901 to 1914. But Plank finished his career with 2,246 strikeouts, well short of the next milestone.

19

THE 3,000TH STRIKEOUT HITTERS

A portion of the discussion in Part I was an examination of the 33 pitchers who gave up a 3,000th hit. Those pitchers are listed in Table 2. The analogous situation in this part of the book is to look at the 18 hitters who became a 3,000th strikeout. We'll find out shortly why there aren't 19 hitters. The names of the hitters are given in Table 11. There is only one name that appears in both Table 2 and Table 11. In other words, there is only one pitcher who gave up a 3,000th hit and also reached 3,000 strikeouts. Who is this unique hurler? When Álex Rodríguez collected his 3,000th hit with a home run in Yankee Stadium in 2015, it was Justin Verlander who delivered the pitch. Four years later, Verlander struck out Kole Calhoun to reach the 3,000-strikeout plateau. Even though Calhoun reached first base on a wild pitch, the strikeout made Verlander the only pitcher to allow a 3,000th hit and record a 3,000th strikeout. That's a pretty good trivia question to inject into your next baseball discussion with friends.

Since there are 19 pitchers with 3,000 strikeouts, why are there only 18 hitters who have been a 3,000th strikeout? A close look at Table 11 provides the answer: César Gerónimo was unlucky enough to be at the plate at the wrong time as the 3,000th strikeout for both Bob Gibson in 1974 and Nolan Ryan in 1980. In between the two historic strikeouts Gerónimo was a cog in the Big Red Machine that won back-to-back championships in 1975–76. He batted .307 and won a Gold Glove Award for his play in center field in 1976.

The only other first name that appears twice in Table 11 is Mike. Bert Blyleven retired Mike Davis for his milestone strikeout, while Randy Johnson's 3,000th strikeout victim was Mike Lowell. There aren't any other names that appear both in Table 2 and Table 11, but there is

Part II—Analysis of Pitchers with 3,000 Strikeouts

one other player who was mentioned in Part I who also shows up in Table 11: Eric Hosmer. He was mentioned in the context of who might be the next player to reach 3,000 hits. Although the conclusion was that he will not reach 3,000 hits because he retired, had he managed to do so, he would be the only player to be a 3,000th strikeout victim and collect 3,000 hits. Max Scherzer struck Hosmer out in 2021 for his milestone 3,000th strikeout.

All but five of the pitchers shown in Table 11 (Clemens, Schilling, Sabathia, Verlander, and Scherzer) are in the Hall of Fame. Are any of the hitters who became a 3,000th strikeout victim in the Hall of Fame? To a modern fan, the names of the hitters in Table 11 that standout in this regard are Keith Hernandez and Omar Vizquel. Although a case can be made that both of them should be in Cooperstown, neither man is, as of 2023. Setting the Hall of Fame discussion aside, Vizquel almost made it into this book. He came close to being a hitter with 3,000 hits as well as a 3,000th strikeout victim. Vizquel is best remembered for his stellar defense. He won 11 Gold Gloves for his play at shortstop. But he had a long career, 24 years, and collected a surprising (to me) 2,877 hits. That left him just 23 hits short of being in the Close, But No Cigar section of this book and only 123 hits short of the 3,000-hit milestone. Round number bias is probably partly to blame for keeping Vizquel out of the Hall of Fame. If he had reached 3,000 hits, he might have made it to Cooperstown.

One of the hitters listed in Table 11 is in the Hall of Fame. But it's likely that most fans have never heard of him because he *pitched* about a century ago. Walter Johnson struck out Stan Coveleski for his 3,000th strikeout in 1923. The fact that Coveleski was a pitcher isn't that surprising since all pitchers had to hit before the American League instituted the designated hitter in 1973. However, it is somewhat surprising that Coveleski is in the Hall of Fame given that his name isn't exactly a household word today. Nonetheless, Coveleski had a distinguished career from 1912 to 1928.

Coveleski was a renowned spitball pitcher (the spitball was not illegal when he started pitching) who also had great control.[1] His career walk rate was 2.3 bases on balls per nine innings. That walk rate compares favorably with Walter Johnson's 2.1 career rate. Coveleski had a career high 24 wins in 1920 as he helped the Cleveland Indians win 98 games and their first American League pennant. He dominated the Brooklyn Robins (later the Dodgers) in the 1920 World Series, going 3–0 and allowing just two earned runs in three complete games to help the

19. The 3,000th Strikeout Hitters

Indians win their first (of two, the other being in 1948) championship. There was another sad but noteworthy event for the Indians in 1920. N.Y. Yankees pitcher Carl Mays hit Indians shortstop, Ray Chapman, in the head with a pitch on August 16 and Chapman died the next day. That terrible tragedy is well known to baseball fans, but what is less well known is that Coveleski was on the mound for the Indians versus Mays and was awarded the win for the contest.

Although Keith Hernandez is not a Hall of Famer, there is an interesting story associated with his connection to Tom Seaver. Seaver was pitching for the Cincinnati Reds against St. Louis when he retired Hernandez for his 3,000th strikeout in 1981. But Seaver had the worst year of his career in 1982, and the Reds traded him back to the Mets before the 1983 season. Similarly, Hernandez spent the season after the historic strikeout with the Cardinals, but his ongoing problems with drug abuse caused St. Louis to trade him to the Mets in June 1983. Therefore, not only are the two men connected because of the historic strikeout, but they were teammates two years later. There's another connection between the pair also. Seaver was born and raised in Fresno, California, while Hernandez is a native San Franciscan. Fresno is roughly 150 miles from San Francisco so the two men share northern California roots.

Graph 10 shows how old the pitchers in this study were when they collected their 3,000th strikeout. We found that the average age for the pitchers was 37 years old. We can do the same analysis for their 3,000th strikeout victims. The results are shown in Graph 11.

The average age (once again using the integer ages) of the hitters shown in Graph 11 is just over 28 years old. Given how long it takes to accumulate 3,000 strikeouts, it's not surprising that the average age of the hitters who were their victims for the milestone strikeout is almost a decade younger than the pitchers who delivered the pitches. The youngest strikeout victim was 23-year-old Tim Wallach. Wallach had a productive 17-year career where he made five All-Star appearances and won three Gold Glove Awards. He was called up by the Montréal Expos late in the 1980 season and hit a home run in his first official at-bat (he walked in his first plate appearance), but played in just five games that September and October.

Wallach had appeared in five more games for the Expos early in the 1981 season before the Expos travelled to Philadelphia for a series against the Phillies. He started the third game of the series. So did Steve Carlton. The veteran Carlton, coming off a Cy Young Award-winning season in 1980, was sitting on 2,997 career strikeouts going into the

Part II—Analysis of Pitchers with 3,000 Strikeouts

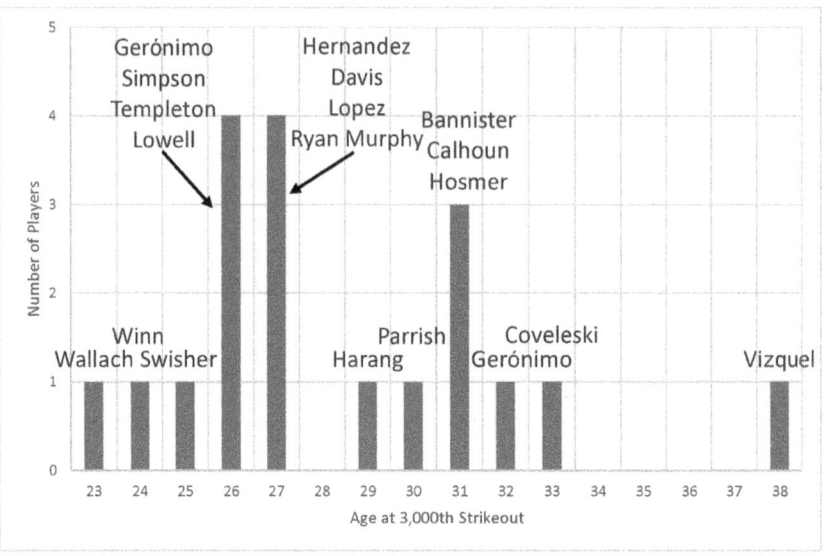

Graph 11: Age of Hitters When They Became a 3,000th Strikeout Victim

game against the Expos. Wallach was third in the Expo batting order. Carlton fanned the first two Expo batters in the top of the first to bring Wallach to the plate as the potential 3,000th strikeout of Carlton's career. Wallach must have been very nervous coming to the plate against one of the greatest pitchers in the game. So naturally, he struck out, becoming a footnote to history.

The next youngest player in Graph 11 is Randy Winn. Although the 24-year-old Winn was a year older than Tim Wallach when he became a 3,000th strikeout, there are interesting parallels with Wallach's experience. First, both players were rookies. Winn did have more games under his belt going into the milestone contest (41 to Wallach's 10), but he was still a relatively inexperienced player. The pitcher that Winn was facing on July 5, 1998, Roger Clemens, was (like Carlton) coming off a Cy Young Award-winning campaign the previous year. In fact, Clemens went 11–0 after the July 5 contest and won his second consecutive Cy Young (and fifth overall) in 1998. Finally, both Wallach and Winn stepped to the plate as the potential milestone strikeout after the first two batters of the inning had struck out. Winn must have been as nervous as Wallach was stepping into the box, so it's not surprising he became Clemens' milestone-strikeout victim.

On the far-right side of Graph 11 is Omar Vizquel. The 38-year-old

19. The 3,000th Strikeout Hitters

Vizquel was five years older than any other player when he became the 3,000th strikeout victim of Greg Maddux in 2005. There are a few interesting similarities in the careers of these two players. First, Maddux (born April 14, 1966) is almost exactly one year older than Vizquel who was born on April 24, 1967. Maddux had a 23-year major league career while Vizquel was in the big leagues for 24 years. Vizquel was in the 17th year of his career when the fateful strikeout occurred, and Maddux was in his 20th year. The difference is primarily because Maddux started his career at 20 years old while Vizquel didn't make it to the majors until he was 22. However, unlike Carlton and Clemens, Maddux's last Cy Young Award was a decade behind him when he caught Vizquel looking to reach the 3,000-strikeout plateau.

20

The Stadiums

As we did for the players with 3,000 hits, we can also look at the stadiums that hosted a 3,000th strikeout. There are 19 pitchers with 3,000 strikeouts and 18 hitters who were victims of a 3,000th strikeout because César Gerónimo was victimized twice. But there are only 17 stadiums where one of the historic strikeouts took place. That's because Riverfront Stadium and Jack Murphy stadium were each the site of two of these historic strikeouts. The stadiums that have hosted a 3,000th strikeout are shown in Table 13.

Table 13: Stadiums Where 3,000th Strikeouts Took Place

	Stadium	3,000th Strikeouts	Pitcher(s)	When Stadium Closed*
1.	Angel Stadium of Anaheim	1	Justin Verlander	
2.	Arlington Stadium, Arlington, Texas	1	Phil Niekro	1993
3.	Busch Stadium II, St. Louis	1	Bob Gibson	2005
4.	Chase Field, Phoenix	1	CC Sabathia	
5.	County Stadium, Milwaukee	1	Don Sutton	2000
6.	Dodger Stadium, Los Angeles	1	Max Scherzer	
7.	Great American Ballpark, Cincinnati	1	Pedro Martínez	
8.	Griffith Stadium, Washington, D.C.	1	Walter Johnson	1961
9.	Hubert H. Humphrey Metrodome, Minneapolis	1	Bert Blyleven	2009
10.	McAfee Coliseum, Oakland	1	Curt Schilling	

20. The Stadiums

	Stadium	3,000th Strikeouts	Pitcher(s)	When Stadium Closed*
11.	Pro Player Stadium, Miami	1	Randy Johnson	2011
12.	Riverfront Stadium, Cincinnati	2	Nolan Ryan, Tom Seaver	2002
13.	San Diego Stadium / Jack Murphy Stadium, San Diego	2	Gaylord Perry, Ferguson Jenkins	2003
14.	SkyDome, Toronto	1	Roger Clemens	
15.	Turner Field, Atlanta	1	John Smoltz	2016
16.	Veterans Stadium, Philadelphia	1	Steve Carlton	2003
17.	Wrigley Field, Chicago	1	Greg Maddux	

*When the stadium closed for baseball. Some venues continued to be used for other events.

Although it went unnoticed at the time (see Who Are the Pitchers?), the first 3,000th strikeout occurred on June 18, 1923, at Griffith Stadium in Washington, D.C., when Walter Johnson struck out Stan Coveleski. The Senators had moved into National Park (renamed Griffith Stadium during 1920) in 1911 after a fire destroyed the wooden ballpark they had been playing in. The new park had one unique feature: a Presidential box near the first base dugout for use when the President threw out the ceremonial first pitch at the beginning of the season. Howard Taft initiated the tradition in 1910, and every President from Taft to John F. Kennedy threw a ceremonial first pitch at Griffith Stadium.[1] Although the Senators struggled for most of their history, the ballpark hosted major league baseball until 1961. Fifty years is a pretty good run for any ballpark, even if Fenway and Wrigley are twice as old.

The mid-1920s were a special time in Washington from a baseball perspective. Johnson's historic strikeout occurred in 1923 and Griffith Stadium hosted the World Series in 1924 and '25. The first of these Series has already been discussed, but there is an interesting coincidence associated with the 1925 World Series. Coveleski, who was pitching for Cleveland in 1923 when he was Johnson's 3,000th strikeout victim, was traded to the Senators in 1925. He went 20–5 and Johnson went 20–7, together leading the Senators to the American League pennant. They faced the Pittsburgh Pirates in the World Series. Johnson won the first two games he pitched, but Coveleski lost his first two games and, as in 1924, the Series went to a seventh game. Johnson started Game Seven

Part II—Analysis of Pitchers with 3,000 Strikeouts

for the Senators, but this time there was no fairy tale ending for The Big Train, as the Pirates won the game 9–7 to win the championship.

One of the things that immediately stands out in Table 13 is that Riverfront Stadium hosted two 3,000th strikeouts while all but one of the other venues had one. It's another interesting coincidence that the two pitchers who reached the milestone at Riverfront were Nolan Ryan and Tom Seaver. Both men started their careers with the Mets in the late 1960s and they were teammates in New York for four years from 1968 to 1971. Seaver, Jerry Koosman, and Gary Gentry were the mainstays of the pitching staff in 1969, but Ryan made 10 starts as the "Miracle Mets" won the first championship since the franchise had been established in 1962. That would be the only World Series Ryan and Seaver would win in their long, distinguished careers.

Unfortunately for Mets fans, the question of what might have been lingers over the franchise. Ryan struggled early in his career during his time with the Mets and he wasn't yet the pitcher he would later become. The team lost patience and traded him to the California Angels after the 1971 season. In an acrimonious split, Seaver was traded to the Reds during the 1977 season. What if these two great pitchers had both stayed in New York? Would the franchise have had to wait until 1986 for its next championship? It's impossible to know. Ignoring these hypothetical questions, in 1980 Ryan was pitching for Houston when he collected his 3,000th strikeout at Riverfront Stadium to become the fourth man to reach the milestone. Less than a year later, early in the 1981 season, Seaver became the fifth man to reach 3,000 strikeouts while pitching for the Reds at Riverfront. They are the only pair of pitchers in the group who recorded their 3,000th strikeout in the same venue consecutively.

As with the stadium section in the 3,000-hit players portion of the book, we're not going to look at every one of the stadiums in Table 13. But a few words about Dodger Stadium are appropriate given its iconic status. When the Dodgers moved to Los Angeles in 1958 they played in the Los Angeles Memorial Coliseum. The Coliseum had been built for the 1932 Olympics and was not really an appropriate venue for baseball, but the Dodgers had to play somewhere so they squeezed a baseball field into what was essentially a football stadium. It's worth the time to go to the website ballparksofbaseball.com to see a picture of the odd configuration. The one advantage was that the Coliseum was very large. When the Dodgers played the White Sox in the 1959 World Series, attendance at Games Three, Four, and Five was over 90,000 each game. These

20. The Stadiums

figures still stand as the all-time highest attendance records for a major league non-exhibition game.[2]

The Dodgers spent four seasons at the Coliseum while Dodger Stadium was being built, moving into Dodger Stadium for the 1962 season. What's interesting is that they had to share the venue with the Los Angeles Angels for four years until Anaheim Stadium was completed in 1966. But the owner of the Dodgers, Walter O'Malley, didn't mind sharing too much. He leased the stadium to the Angels in exchange for 7½ percent of the annual gate receipts, or $200,000, whichever was higher.[3] The move to Los Angeles was very profitable for O'Malley, but not so much for Brooklyn.

Dodger Stadium deserves its iconic status. It's an idyllic setting for a ballgame, and many historic events have taken place there. Great baseball-related moments include Kirk Gibson's home run in Game One of the 1988 World Series (if you are not an Oakland A's fan), Sandy Koufax's perfect game in 1965, Clayton Kershaw's no-hitter in 2014, the hoopla surrounding Fernando Valenzuela in 1981, and clinching the 1963 World Series victory with a win at the ballpark. That was one of 10 World Series that have been played at Dodger Stadium, with the Dodgers bringing home five titles in those 10 series. Outstanding non-baseball related moments include concerts by the Beatles and Elvis Presley in 1966, Elton John (1975 and 2023), The Jacksons (1984), The Three Tenors (1994), and Madonna (2008). Pope John Paul II made a historic visit to the stadium in 1987.[4]

Getting back to the subject at hand, 3,000th hits and strikeouts, Table 9 (the stadiums where the 3,000th hits took place) does not include Dodger Stadium. Table 13 shows that Max Scherzer was the pitcher who collected his 3,000th strikeout at Dodger Stadium. But Scherzer was the last pitcher (as of this writing) to reach the milestone and he didn't get there until 2021. That means that Dodger Stadium, which has been in use since 1962, did not see a 3,000th hit or a 3,000th strikeout for almost 60 years. This is a little surprising since the stadium is now the third oldest in baseball behind Fenway Park and Wrigley Field. That said, although Fenway did host Carl Yastrzemski's 3,000th hit in 1979, there hasn't been a 3,000th strikeout there in over a century. And although Wrigley has hosted both a 3,000th hit (Musial in 1958) and a 3,000th strikeout (Maddux in 2005), the ballpark was open over 90 years before Maddux's historic strikeout took place. This just shows both milestones are very rare.

However, the fact that Wrigley Field hosted both events raises the

Part II—Analysis of Pitchers with 3,000 Strikeouts

following question. Are there any other venues besides Wrigley that have had both a 3,000th hit and a 3,000th strikeout? This question is easily answered by combining the data in Tables 9 and 13. The results are shown in Table 14.

Table 14:
Stadiums with a 3,000th Hit and a 3,000th Strikeout

	Stadium	3,000th hits or Strikeouts	Position Player(s)	Pitcher(s)	When Stadium Closed*
1	Angel Stadium of Anaheim	3	Carew (1985), Brett (1992)	Verlander (2019)	
2	Busch Stadium II, St. Louis	2	Brock (1979)	Gibson (1974)	2005
3	County Stadium, Milwaukee	2	Yount (1992)	Sutton (1983)	2000
4	Hubert H. Humphrey Metrodome, Minneapolis	4	Winfield (1993), Murray (1995), Ripken Jr. (2000)	Blyleven (1986)	2009
5	Jack Murphy Stadium, San Diego	3	Henderson (2001)	Perry (1978), Jenkins (1982)	2003
6	Riverfront Stadium, Cincinnati	3	Rose (1978)	Ryan (1980), Seaver (1981)	2002
7	Wrigley Field, Chicago	2	Musial (1958)	Maddux (2005)	

*When the stadium closed for baseball. Some venues continued to be used for other events.

There are seven stadiums that have hosted both a 3,000th hit and a 3,000th strikeout. The venue with the most 3,000th events is the Metrodome. In the 15 seasons from Bert Blyleven collecting his 3,000th strikeout in 1986 to Cal Ripken, Jr., striking his 3,000th hit in 2000, the Metrodome saw four of these events. In half of those (Winfield and Blyleven) the star of the day was wearing a Twins uniform, so the hometown fans got to cheer on their hero. Three other stadiums, Angel Stadium in Anaheim, Jack Murphy Stadium in San Diego, and Riverfront Stadium in Cincinnati, have hosted three of these special moments each. Rod Carew, George Brett, and Justin Verlander all reached the milestone in Anaheim, but none of the three players was playing for the Angels when they did so.

Another venue with three of these milestone events is Riverfront Stadium. We already discussed Ryan and Seaver reaching the milestone

20. The Stadiums

there just months apart. In addition, Pete Rose collected his 3,000th hit at Riverfront only two years before Ryan's milestone 1980 strikeout. So, three of these events occurred within three years at Riverfront Stadium. To make it even more memorable, both Rose and Seaver wore hometown livery on the big day. If we expand the focus beyond 3,000th events, we find that it was a very exciting time to be a baseball fan in Cincinnati during the decade or so after Riverfront opened in July 1970. The stadium played host to the World Series in 1970, '72, '75, and '76, with the Reds winning the title the last two of those years. In addition, Henry Aaron hit his 714th home run (tying him with Babe Ruth) at Riverfront on Opening Day in 1974. Four days later Aaron would famously break Ruth's record at home in Atlanta. History was made almost annually for the first decade of Riverfront Stadium's existence.

The third venue that hosted three milestone events was Jack Murphy Stadium. Although the stadium had hosted football starting in 1967, the first major league baseball game wasn't played there until the expansion Padres entered the National League in 1969. The primary events at San Diego Stadium (it was renamed Jack Murphy Stadium in 1981) over its first half-decade were not player related. The team was purchased by the founder of McDonald's, Ray Kroc, in 1974. That same year the San Diego Chicken (played by Ted Giannoulas) made its debut at the stadium.[5] The Chicken's antics became famous nationwide and prompted other teams to also adopt mascots.

Kroc's willingness to spend money on the team bore fruit on the field. Randy Jones won the team's first Cy Young Award in 1976. Just two years later, Gaylord Perry took home the franchise's second Cy Young and collected his 3,000th strikeout at the San Diego stadium on the final day of the 1978 season. Four years after Perry (at the now Jack Murphy Stadium), Ferguson Jenkins reached the 3,000-strikeout plateau while playing for the Cubs.

After 15 years of futility, the Padres finally won the National League West Division in 1984. San Diego lost the first two games of the last five-game NLCS against the Cubs before returning to the "The Murph" to finish the series. Steve Garvey's walk-off home run in the bottom of the ninth in Game Four is one of the famous moments in baseball history (at least in San Diego). The Padres completed the comeback with a come-from-behind victory in Game Five. That allowed the stadium to host the first two games of the World Series against Detroit. But the Tigers prevailed in five games behind two victories by *Jack* Morris (the first in Game One in *Jack* Murphy Stadium).

Part II—Analysis of Pitchers with 3,000 Strikeouts

The stadium was renamed Qualcomm Stadium in 1997 and San Diego made a second appearance in the World Series in 1998. Unfortunately for fans in Southern California, the Padres ran into one of the greatest teams of all time in that series. The 1998 Yankees won 114 games (only exceeded by the 1906 Cubs and the 2001 Mariners who both won 116 games) and swept San Diego. The Padres are still looking (as of 2023) for their first championship. Three years later Qualcomm was the site of another 3,000th milestone event. Rickey Henderson, at 42 years old, punched his 3,000th hit on the final day of the 2001 season. It was also the final game of Tony Gwynn's career.

Besides Wrigley, two other stadiums have hosted both a 3,000th strikeout and a 3,000th hit. It's interesting to note that in both cases, the four featured players were all on the hometown team when they reached their respective milestones. Busch Stadium II in St. Louis opened in 1966. The first decade of its existence was almost as exciting as the first 10 years at Riverfront. The MLB All-Star game was played there during the inaugural season, and the Cardinals took the National League pennant in 1967 and '68 so there were World Series games at Busch Stadium the next two years. Fans in St. Louis watched Bob Gibson win the National League Cy Young Award in 1968 and '70 before Gibson collected his milestone strikeout at the stadium in July 1974. Less than two months later, St. Louis fans witnessed Lou Brock set the single-season stolen-base record on September 10 when he stole his 105th base of the season. Brock set the career record for stolen bases (later broken by Rickey Henderson) in 1977 and he collected his 3,000th hit at Busch Stadium in 1979, crowning an exciting decade or so in St. Louis.

The other stadium to see both a 3,000th hit and a 3,000th strikeout was County Stadium in Milwaukee. County Stadium has an unusual history. Like Dodger Stadium and Riverfront Stadium, it hosted World Series games early on. The stadium opened in 1953 when the Braves moved to Milwaukee from Boston. The Braves won the National League pennant in 1957 and '58, so the World Series was played at the stadium in the fifth year of its existence. But the Braves moved to Atlanta in 1966 so Milwaukee (and County Stadium) lost its major league team after just 13 seasons. For those of us, like your scribe, not from the upper Midwest it may come as a surprise that County Stadium was not tenantless after the Braves left. The Green Bay Packers played about half their home games there from the 1950s until the 1990s.[6]

But County Stadium was without big-league baseball for just four years. The expansion Seattle Pilots lasted only one year in the Northwest

20. The Stadiums

Bob Gibson delivering a pitch in 1970. Gibson became the second man with 3,000 strikeouts when he struck out César Gerónimo (who was also Nolan Ryan's 3,000th strikeout) in 1974. Gibson's ERA was below 1.0 entering September 1968. He finished the season with a 1.12 ERA (National Baseball Hall of Fame and Museum, Cooperstown, N.Y.).

before moving to Milwaukee as the Brewers in 1970. Five years later, Henry Aaron returned to Milwaukee to end his career where he had spent a dozen years before moving to Atlanta. County Stadium was the site of his 755th and final home run in 1976.

After Don Sutton defeated Jim Palmer on the final day of the 1982 season to give the Brewers the American League East Division title by one game over the Orioles, the Brewers made it to the World Series against the Cardinals, and County Stadium hosted its first World Series game since 1957. Sutton collected his 3,000th strikeout in front of home fans the following year at County Stadium. Another pitcher on the 3,000th strikeout list made history at the stadium in 1990. Nolan Ryan won his 300th game there two years before Robin Yount struck his milestone hit in the same ballpark.

21

Birthdays and Birthplaces

As we did for the players with 3,000 hits, we can examine the group of pitchers with 3,000 strikeouts to see when and where these men were born. As before, the goal is to better understand the distribution of their birthdays and the distribution of their birth locations, within or outside, the country. The results are shown in Figure 2.

Beginning with the distribution of birth locations, Figure 2 shows that 15 of these elite pitchers were born in the continental United States. The state with the most births was California. Three of the pitchers, Tom Seaver, Randy Johnson, and CC Sabathia hail from the Golden State. Two other states, Texas and Ohio, also had multiple births. Texas produced Nolan Ryan and Greg Maddux while Phil Niekro and Roger Clemens are from Ohio. Eight other continental states were home to just one of the pitchers. Three of the hurlers came from the center of the country. Walter Johnson, Bob Gibson, and Max Scherzer were born in Kansas, Nebraska, and Missouri, respectively. Steve Carlton and Don Sutton were born in the deep South (Florida and Alabama, respectively) and the Mid–Atlantic region was home to Gaylord Perry (North Carolina) and Justin Verlander (Virginia). John Smoltz was born in Michigan.

California is a large state. It's about 1,000 miles north to south. But the three elite pitchers native to the state were born within about 150 miles of each other. In fact, Randy Johnson and CC Sabathia were born about 20 miles apart in the San Francisco Bay Area, Johnson entering the world in Walnut Creek and Sabathia in Vallejo. Both cities are a bit east of San Francisco, with Vallejo being north of Walnut Creek. To complete the trifecta, Tom Seaver was born in Fresno, which is roughly 150 miles south of the Bay Area. This isn't actually too surprising since the climate in the area is conducive to baseball most of the year. That's

21. Birthdays and Birthplaces

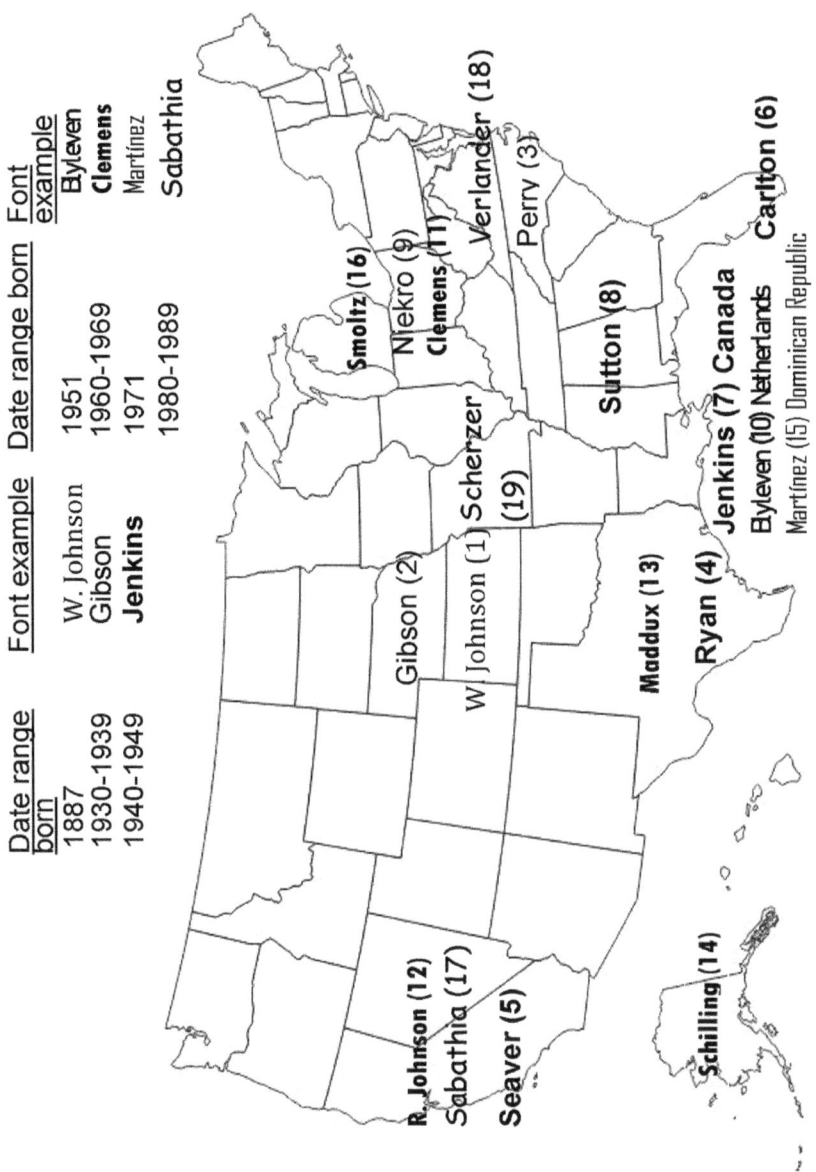

Figure 2: Where and When Pitchers with 3,000 Strikeouts Were Born

why these are not the only three players from that region to make it to the big leagues. Jimmy Rollins, Brandon Crawford, Troy Tulowitski, and Joc Pederson also hail from the area.

Part II—Analysis of Pitchers with 3,000 Strikeouts

Two other pitchers were born roughly 150 miles apart. But in this second case at that distance, there is a state line between the two locations. Gaylord Perry was born in Williamston, North Carolina. Williamston is in the eastern portion of the state, about 50 miles south of the Virginia border. Continuing north past the border for another 100 miles or so you come to Richmond, Virginia. Justin Verlander entered the world in the Richmond suburb of Manakin Sabot. In an interesting numerical coincidence, Perry was born in 1938 and Verlander arrived 45 years later in 1983 ('38 versus '83). It also mildly interesting that these two men from the East Coast both collected their 3,000th strikeout on the West Coast. Perry got his in San Diego and Verlander in Anaheim.

Two of the pitchers were born over Texas soil. With that phrase, a short digression is in order. My wife is from Texas. We were living in California when our twin sons were born. Being a born and bred Texan, my better half asked her father to send some dirt from Texas to her before the boys were born. She insisted the dirt be put under the table where the births took place so her sons would be born over Texas soil. It's a true story, no kidding. The mothers of Nolan Ryan and Greg Maddux didn't have to go to such lengths for their sons to be considered Texans. But since Texas is another large state, Ryan, from Refugio in the far south, and Maddux, from San Angelo in central Texas, were born roughly 300 miles apart.

There seem to be some almost magical distances associated with the births of these hurlers. It's about 300 miles from Omaha, Nebraska, to Humbolt, Kansas. It's also about 300 miles from Humbolt, Kansas, to St. Louis, Missouri. Why do we care? Because the three pitchers in this study from the center of the country came from these three cities. Bob Gibson was born in Omaha, Walter Johnson in Humbolt, and Max Scherzer in St. Louis. And although it doesn't quite fit the pattern, it's about 350 miles from Omaha to St. Louis. That means that Bob Gibson, who collected his 3,000th strikeout in St. Louis, wasn't that far (on a national scale) from where he was born and raised when he reached the milestone.

Ohio is much smaller than California or Texas (about 220 miles east to west) but two of these great pitchers are from that state. Phil Niekro was born in Blaine, while Roger Clemens entered the world in Dayton. These two cities are almost on the eastern and western edges of Ohio, respectively, so the hurlers were actually born further apart than the three Californians. But what is interesting is that Blaine is only about 40 miles from Chartiers, Pennsylvania. So we can add one

21. Birthdays and Birthplaces

more great player, Phil Niekro, to the list of luminaries that include Stan Musial, Honus Wagner, Griffey Sr. and Jr., and Joe Namath who were all born near Pittsburgh.

One of the other 19 pitchers was also born in the United States. But it wasn't the continental United States. Curt Schilling was born in Anchorage, Alaska. How does an Alaskan make it to the big leagues given the cold and short summer season? The answer, Schilling's father was in the Army. Curt was born in Anchorage and the family moved around quite a bit before settling in Phoenix, Arizona, where he grew up.[1] There's plenty of sunshine and baseball conducive weather there. The remaining three pitchers were not born in the United States. In fact, two of the three came from locations that are not usually associated with producing baseball players. Ferguson Jenkins was born in Canada. As a child, he developed a strong arm by throwing rocks at ice chutes and boxcars. His raw talent was recognized by a scout for the Phillies and he signed with the team in 1962.[2] And then, there is the only man born in Europe to reach 3,000 events on a major league baseball field. Bert Blyleven was born in the Netherlands not too long after World War II, but he honed his baseball skills growing up in Southern California. The last of these elite pitchers was born in the Dominican Republic. Pedro Martínez was the first Dominican to celebrate a 3,000th event. He was later joined by his countrymen, Adrián Beltré and Albert Pujols. The Dominican Republic is the only country besides the United States to have multiple members of these two groups of players.

Now let's examine the distribution of the pitchers according to birthday. Walter Johnson is the only pitcher on the list born before 1900. Given the long gap in Graph 8 after Johnson reached the milestone, it's not surprising that there is also a gap before the birthday of the next pitcher on the list, who wasn't born until the 1930s. Three of these elite pitchers were born during that decade: Bob Gibson (born 1935), Gaylord Perry (born 1938), and Phil Niekro in 1939. It's interesting that although Niekro was the fourth of the 19 pitchers to be born, he was the ninth hurler to reach 3,000 strikeouts. That's primarily because Niekro didn't make it to the big leagues until he was 25 years old and pitched until he was 48. We can also observe that since Johnson was born in 1887, it was almost 50 years (48 to be exact) before another pitcher was born who would reach 3,000 strikeouts. That's another measure of how great Johnson was.

The 1940s and the 1960s are tied for the decade with the most hurlers who reached 3,000 strikeouts. Both periods saw the births of five

Part II—Analysis of Pitchers with 3,000 Strikeouts

pitchers who eventually reached the milestone. The five for the '40s were Jenkins (born 1942), Seaver (born 1944), Carlton (born 1944), Sutton (born 1945), and Ryan (born 1947). Ryan is a special case. Reversing positions with Niekro, he was the ninth of the group to be born, but the fourth to reach the milestone. Ryan reached 3,000 strikeouts sooner than five of the other pitchers who were born before he was. For example, Ryan was born about eight years after Niekro, and yet reached the milestone four years earlier. But that's what happens when you have five seasons with more than 300 strikeouts by the time you are 30 years old. Incredibly, Ryan added one more 300-strikeout season to his resume when he struck out 301 batters at 42 years old in 1989. To put that in perspective, as great as Roger Clemens was, he never struck out 300 batters in a season.

Five of the pitchers were born in the 1960s: Clemens (born 1962), R. Johnson (born 1963), Maddux (born 1966), Schilling (born 1966), and Smoltz (born 1967). The first four of these men reached the 3,000-strikeout milestone in birth order, starting with Clemens in 1998. Schilling was born exactly seven months after Maddux in 1966 (November 14 and April 14, respectively). The two collected strikeouts at roughly the same pace because Schilling reached the 3,000 milestone about 13 months after Maddux in 2005. However, the only one of these pitchers born in the 1970s, Pedro Martínez (1971), reached the milestone before John Smoltz did. Martínez collected his 3,000th strikeout at the end of the 2007 campaign, while Smoltz reached the plateau early in the 2008 season.

The last three pitchers were born in the 1980s. CC Sabathia debuted in 1980 while Justin Verlander arrived in 1983. The last of the group, Max Scherzer, was born in 1984. This sub-group reached their 3,000th strikeouts in birth order, with Scherzer being last in 2021.

Hitters and Pitchers Combined Birth Locations

In Part I, Figure 1, we examined where the 33 hitters with 3,000 hits were born. The previous section of Part II looked at where the pitchers with 3,000 strikeouts came from. What happens, in terms of most common birth locations, when we combine the two data sets? However, before we get to that analysis, in comparing Figure 1 to Figure 2, it's interesting to observe that none of the pitchers with 3,000 strikeouts came from the Northeast, while six (or eight if you count western

21. Birthdays and Birthplaces

Pennsylvania as part of the Northeast) of the players with 3,000 hits were born in the Northeast. This is likely to just be a coincidence, but it may also reflect the broader western migration in the United States following World War II, since almost half of the pitchers in the elite group were born after 1960. The other observation from both figures is that there are no states west of Texas, with the exception of California, where any player in these two groups were born. There is a large blank space in the western portion of both maps. This is most likely a reflection of the lower population destiny in that part of the country, but it is clearly visible on both figures.

For the following portion of the discussion, the combined group of hitters (H) with 3,000 hits, and pitchers (P) with 3,000 strikeouts, will be referred to as H/P3000. California is home to the most players in the H/P3000 group. Five of the players were born there. In addition to the fact that it's where most of the H/P3000 group entered the world, what's interesting is that the three pitchers from the Golden State, Tom Seaver, Randy Johnson, and CC Sabathia, are all from the Bay Area in Northern California, while the two hitters, Eddie Murray and Tony Gwynn, are both from Los Angeles in Southern California.

One of the other states in the previous pitcher-oriented discussion, Texas, was home to three of the H/P3000 group. Like Greg Maddux, Tris Speaker was also born in central Texas, giving the state three of the group when Nolan Ryan is added in. Speaker's home town, Hubbard, is about 200 miles east of San Angelo where Maddux was born.

Two other states are home to three of the H/P3000 group. Don Sutton entered the world in Clio, Alabama. That's just 90 miles south of Westfield, Alabama, where Willie Mays was born. The third player from the state is Henry Aaron. So we can add Sutton to the list of great players from Alabama, that includes these three along with Satchel Paige and Willie McCovey. The third state that was home to three of the H/P3000 group is Ohio. Pete Rose joins the two hurlers, Phil Niekro and Roger Clemens, as Ohio natives. It's just a 50-mile jaunt north on I-75 from Cincinnati where Rose was born, to Clemen's arrival location in Dayton. We already discussed the fact that the Dominican Republic was also home to three members: Pedro Martínez, Adrián Beltré, and Albert Pujols.

We learned during the discussion of the players with 3,000 hits in Part I that Dave Winfield and Paul Molitor are both from St. Paul, Minnesota. Eddie Murray and Tony Gwynn are both from Los Angeles. Looking a little more broadly at the term "hometown," Al Kaline

Part II—Analysis of Pitchers with 3,000 Strikeouts

and Cal Ripken, Jr., also share Baltimore as a hometown, if you count the Baltimore suburb of Havre de Grace where Ripken Jr. was born as Baltimore. These are the only cases of two players in the hitters group being from the same hometown. None of the pitchers in the elite group were born in the same city. But when we expand the examination to the H/P3000 group as a whole, we gain one more common hometown. That location is Omaha, Nebraska. Bob Gibson entered the world in Omaha in 1935 and Wade Boggs followed him in the same city in 1958. However, the Boggs family moved to Tampa Bay when Wade was young, while Gibson was raised and went to high school in Omaha.

22

Age and Game Number at 3,000th Strikeout

As we did for the players with 3,000 hits, we can investigate how long it took each of these 19 pitchers to reach 3,000 strikeouts. But rather than simply look at how old the pitchers were when they collected their milestone strikeout, we can also compare them in terms of how many games it took to get there. The results are shown in Graph 12. As with Graph 4 for the hitters, in order to prevent all of the age data points from being on the integer values of the ages, the exact ages of the players are used rather than the more typical integer ages. For example, we would normally say Walter Johnson was 35 years old when he threw his 3,000th strikeout. But Johnson was born in November and threw the historic pitch in June, so he was about 35 years and seven months old at the time. Converting the months to years shows that Johnson was actually 35.6 years old when he reached 3,000 strikeouts. That's where Johnson's data point is in terms of his age in Graph 12. The same procedure is used for age of all of the pitchers.

A common way to get a better understanding of a data set is to look at the average value. But which average should we use for age in Graph 12, the integer age average or the exact age average? Using the more common integer values of the ages for pitchers, the average age when pitchers reached 3,000 strikeouts was 37.5 years old. Of course, the average is going to be higher when using the exact ages. Using the true ages, the average is 37.9 years old. The average age is about five months older using the exact ages. This result makes sense. Some pitchers reached the milestone just after their birthday while others reached it just before their next birthday. In a large data set, the difference would be very close to six months. But these pitchers form a relatively small data set, so the true average is not exactly six months higher than the integer average.

Part II—Analysis of Pitchers with 3,000 Strikeouts

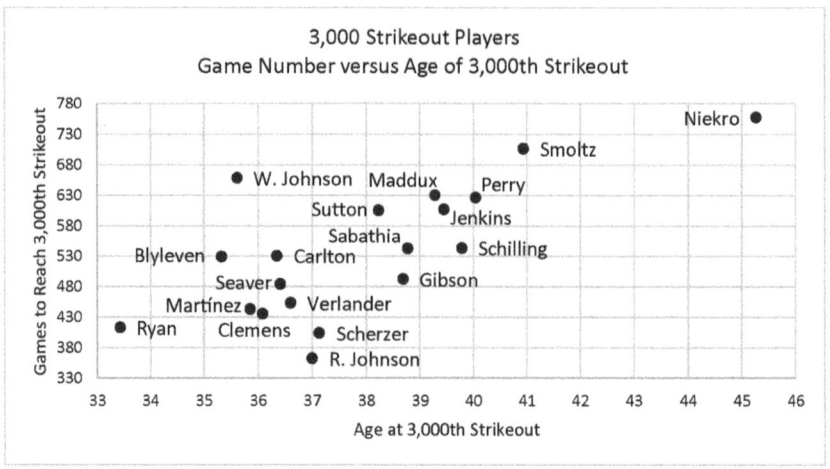

Graph 12: Pitchers with 3,000th Strikeouts, Age and Game Number at 3,000th Strikeout

The average number of games for these 19 men to collect 3,000 strikeouts is 538 games. When the two averages are plotted on Graph 12, the data point falls near the second letter "a" in Sabathia. Data points above this point mean the pitcher took longer than average (in terms of the number of games) to collect their 3,000 strikeouts. Pitchers who were older than about 38 years old took longer than average. But it's important to remember that average in this context is not what is usually meant by average. None of the hurlers in this study are average pitchers.

If we consider within 1½ years of 38 years old to be roughly average, the pitchers in this category are R. Johnson, Scherzer, Verlander, Seaver, Carlton, Sutton, Gibson, Sabathia, Maddux, and Jenkins. The significantly younger than average group then includes Clemens, Martínez, W. Johnson, Blyleven, and Ryan. Schilling, Perry, Smoltz, and Niekro were significantly older than average when they reached the 3,000-strikeout milestone.

In general, the pitchers in the latter two groups are there because of how old they were when they made their big-league debut. In the younger than average group, Ryan, Blyleven, and W. Johnson all debuted at 19 years old. Martínez was 20 when he got to the majors. Clemens was 21 years old when he started, but his tremendous proficiency at striking out batters allowed him to reach the 3,000-strikeout milestone just after he turned 36 years old. Moving up to the older than average group,

22. Age and Game Number at 3,000th Strikeout

Schilling, like Clemens, made his debut at 21 years old. But Schilling was almost 40 years old when he collected his milestone strikeout. That four-year lag is an indication of the difference between a great strikeout pitcher (Clemens) and a very good strikeout pitcher (Schilling). John Smoltz also got to the big leagues when he was 21 years old, but he is a special case among these elite pitchers. He's the only one who spent a considerable amount of time (four years) as a relief pitcher, which limited his strikeout totals during those seasons. He also missed the entire 2000 season due to arm surgery. That's why he is the second-oldest pitcher to reach 3,000 strikeouts at just under 41 years old.

Gaylord Perry is the third of the four pitchers in the older than average group. Perry started his career when he was 23 years old. This is at least two years older than the other pitchers discussed in this section. He collected his milestone strikeout when he was just past his 40th birthday. That makes him the third oldest pitcher to reach 3,000 strikeouts. Only two special cases, Smoltz and Phil Niekro, were older. And Phil Niekro is a very special case. He didn't reach the majors until he was 25 years old, and he specialized in the knuckleball. Both of those factors contributed to him not reaching his 3,000th strikeout until he was past 45 years old. That makes him four years older than Smoltz (the second oldest at almost 41 years old) when he collected his milestone strikeout.

There's another very interesting aspect to Niekro's career. For much of it, he pitched for a poorly performing Atlanta Braves team. This means that in addition to collecting a lot of strikeouts, he also collected a lot of losses. It's been said that you have to be a pretty good pitcher to lose 20 games. Niekro is the personification of that statement. Starting with the 1977 season he lost 20, 18, 20, and 18 games each year. Those Braves teams lost 101, 94, 93, and 80 games. Why mention this? Because Niekro did something in 1979 that only 11 pitchers since 1900 have accomplished.[1] That is, to win and lose at least 20 games in the same season. He went 21–20 in 1979, leading the league in both categories. Niekro is the only one of these 11 pitchers to lead the league in both wins and losses during the same year.

Another pitcher of the elite 19 is also a member of the group of 11 hurlers mentioned in the previous paragraph. That pitcher is Walter Johnson. Like Niekro, Johnson played on some very poor teams. Of course, with Johnson the team was the Washington Senators rather than the Braves, but only a great pitcher on a weak team will have the opportunity to get so many wins and losses in the same season. In

Part II—Analysis of Pitchers with 3,000 Strikeouts

Johnson's case, he went 25–20 with a 1.90 ERA in 1916. He lost 1–0 four times that year. This is another statistic that points to how great a pitcher Walter Johnson was. It's worth noting that Johnson was the ninth pitcher to accomplish the feat of winning and losing 20 games. In other words, nine of the 11 pitchers on the list did it before 1917. It wasn't accomplished again until 1973 when Wilbur Wood went 24–20 for the Chicago White Sox. In 1979, Niekro was the last of the 11, and the last pitcher period, to accomplish this feat.

The average number of games to reach 3,000 strikeouts is about 538. If we allow that roughly average is about 50 games above or below this figure (480–580 games) then there are six pitchers who reached 3,000 strikeouts in a below-average number of games. Those pitchers are Nolan Ryan, Justin Verlander, Max Scherzer, Pedro Martínez, Roger Clemens, and Randy Johnson. These six men are the most efficient pitchers in the elite group in terms of strikeouts. Not surprisingly, all six were below the average age of the group when they reached the milestone. Scherzer was the oldest of this subgroup at just over 37 years old when he collected his 3,000th strikeout.

Johnson reached 3,000 strikeouts in the fewest number of games, 362. Dividing 3,000 by 362 gives 8.3. In other words, from the beginning of his career until he attained the 3,000 milestone, Randy Johnson averaged 8.3 strikeouts per game. That's an impressive figure. With that in mind, why isn't Johnson's data point in the lower left corner (youngest and fewest games to 3,000) of the graph? Nolan Ryan occupies that position because he made his major league debut five years younger than Johnson. Ryan was 19 years old when he made his debut. Johnson was 24. That's why Ryan is in the far lower left of the graph.

The two pitchers at the other end of the games to 3,000 strikeouts scale are John Smoltz and Phil Niekro. They are the only two pitchers to take over 700 games to reach 3,000 strikeouts. It took 706 games for Smoltz and 757 games for Niekro. That's why both of their data points are in the upper right corner (oldest and most games to 3,000) on Graph 12. The reasons are the same as for why they were the oldest two pitchers to the milestone, so those will not be repeated here. There are four pitchers in a small group at roughly 600 games to the milestone. Those four hurlers are Don Sutton (605 games), Fergie Jenkins (607 games), Gaylord Perry (626 games), and Greg Maddux (630 games). The most interesting thing about this subgroup is that Sutton, Jenkins, and Perry are grouped with Maddux. It's doubtful that most fans think the first three men are the same caliber of pitcher as The Professor. However, all this

22. Age and Game Number at 3,000th Strikeout

grouping really says is that Maddux didn't collect strikeouts at the same rate as the great strikeout artists (like Randy Johnson) so it took him more games to reach 3,000 strikeouts. Setting aside the extreme outliers of Smoltz and Niekro, these four pitchers form an informal upper boundary of the number of games required to reach the milestone.

But wait, you say. What about Walter Johnson's data point in Graph 12? It lies above the previous four, since Johnson took 658 games to collect 3,000 strikeouts. That's correct, but Johnson was about 35½ years old when he reached the milestone, which is roughly 2½ years younger than Don Sutton, the youngest player in the other group of four. Johnson's data point is in the upper left portion of the graph, so he took the most games at the youngest age to reach the milestone.

What the location of Walter Johnson's data point really indicates is the tremendous workload that Johnson had during his career prior to reaching the milestone. Not counting his rookie year in 1907 when he didn't make his first appearance until August, over the 16 seasons from 1908 through 1923, Johnson averaged 33.7 starts per year, 28.4 complete games per year, and 308 innings pitched per year. To put the innings-pitched number in perspective, In 2023, Logan Webb of the S.F. Giants led the majors with 216 innings pitched. There were only five pitchers with more than 200 innings pitched in 2023. Of course, the game has changed significantly over the last century, so these recent numbers aren't too surprising. However, that doesn't diminish the fact that Walter Johnson pitched a lot, for a long time.

Similar observations can be made about Bert Blyleven. His data point in Graph 12 is below and to the left of W. Johnson's. So Blyleven took fewer games to reach 3,000 strikeouts (529 versus 658) and he did so at a younger age (35.3 versus 35.6 years old). But his data point is still above and to the left of many of the other pitchers. Once again, what this really says is that Blyleven also had a tremendous pitching load, from the start of his career in 1970, until he reached the milestone in 1986. Not including 1982, when he missed most of the year with an elbow injury, over 16 years Blyleven averaged 30.2 starts per year, 12.9 complete games per year, and almost 228 innings pitched per year. Although those numbers are not as impressive as the same numbers for Walter Johnson, Blyleven still pitched a lot, considering he finished his career in 1992, over 60 years after Johnson's career ended in 1927.

23

CLOSE, BUT NO CIGAR

As we did with the hitters, we can examine the pitchers who came closest to 3,000 strikeouts without reaching the milestone. The two most obvious candidates were mentioned earlier. At the conclusion of the 2023 season, Zach Greinke was just 21 strikeouts below 3,000 and Clayton Kershaw was 56 strikeouts short of the milestone. However, both are still active as of this writing, so by the time you read this, they both may have collected enough strikeouts to reach the 3,000 plateau. Therefore, the rest of the analysis in this section will focus on the pitchers who got within about 200 strikeouts of the milestone, but have no chance of increasing their career totals. The results are shown in Graph 13.

The award for the closest to the milestone without reaching it goes to Jim Bunning. Bunning finished just 145 strikeouts short of 3,000. Unlike other players whose career totals were impacted by events outside their control (wars, pandemics, labor work stoppages, etc.), it's likely that Bunning didn't quite get to the milestone because of a personal choice. Although he was drafted by the Detroit Tigers during his freshman year at college, he (and his parents) insisted he would finish school before becoming a full-time professional baseball player. As a result, he didn't make his debut until he was 23 years old. Had he started a few years earlier, he'd probably be one of the pitchers in this study. That said, it's also likely that his economics degree from Xavier University laid the foundation for his future in politics. After his baseball career ended, he served in the Kentucky State Senate, the U.S. House of Representatives, and the U.S. Senate.[1]

Bunning's baseball career spanned 17 years from 1955 to '71. His first year as a full-time starting pitcher, 1957, was one of the best of his career. He went 20–8 with a 2.69 ERA. Bunning started 30 games, had 14 complete games, led the American League with 267.1 innings

23. Close, but No Cigar

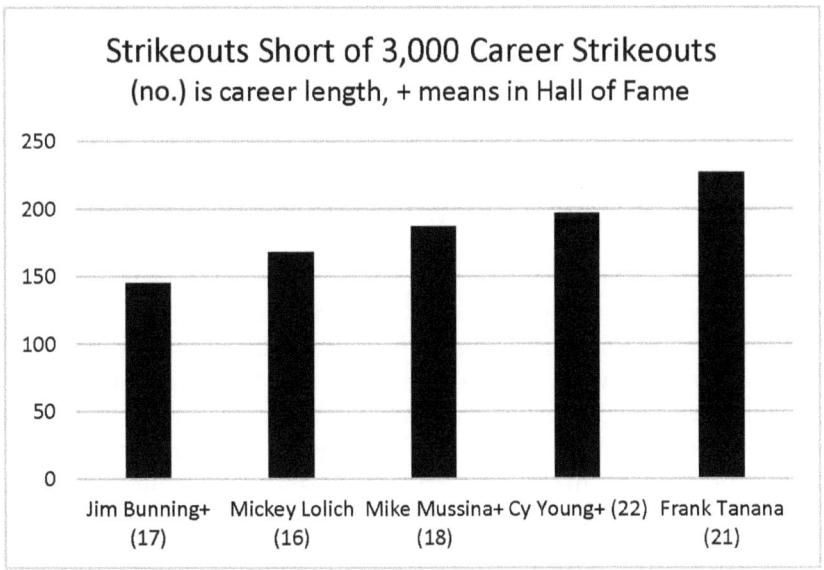

Graph 13: Pitchers Within About 200 Strikeouts of 3,000

pitched, and struck out 182 batters. To put those numbers in perspective, let's compare the same numbers for Cy Young Award winner Warren Spahn in 1957. There was only one Cy Young Award given each year from 1956 to 1966, so Spahn was the only winner. Spahn went 21–11 with a 2.69 ERA. He started 35 games, had 18 complete games, pitched 271 innings, and struck out 111 hitters. Comparing more recent sabermetric data for the same year, Bunning had an ERA+ of 144 and a WAR of 6.3, while Spahn's ERA+ was 130 with a WAR of 4.8. The point of this brief analysis is not to stir up controversy about the 1957 Cy Young Award, but rather to point out just how good a pitcher Jim Bunning was. At his best, he was comparable to one of the greats of all time.

Bunning was also a man of his time in the sense that he managed a heavy pitching workload. We noted that Bert Blyleven averaged 30.2 starts per year, 12.9 complete games per year, and almost 228 innings pitched per year for 16 years. Not including his first two years when he wasn't a full-time starter, Bunning averaged 31.9 starts per year, 9.2 complete games per year, and about 227 innings per year for the 15 years from 1957 to 1971. Those numbers are comparable to Blyleven's. But his career was just a little too short for him to get to 3,000 strikeouts, given the efficiency with which he rang batters up. This is best seen

Part II—Analysis of Pitchers with 3,000 Strikeouts

by comparing his strikeout numbers to those of Bob Gibson who, like Bunning, had a 17-year career. Gibson struck out more than 200 batters nine times and had a career strikeout rate per nine innings of 7.2. Bunning struck out more than 200 batters six times and had a career strikeout rate per nine innings of 6.8. There's enough of a difference in the number of 200 strikeout years and career strikeout rate to keep Bunning from reaching 3,000 strikeouts in the same number of seasons as Gibson.

However, round number bias has once again done an excellent player a disservice. Just like Sam Rice and Sam Crawford in the hitters' section, Bunning is in the Hall of Fame, but he would be much better known today if he had collected another 145 strikeouts because his name would come up every time another player reached the 3,000-strikeout milestone. That said, another reason for Bunning's relative anonymity is that he never played on a team that made it to the postseason. The next-closest player to 3,000 strikeouts without getting there, Mickey Lolich, is more well-known than Bunning largely because he had a postseason performance that led to a World Series victory.

Bunning pitched for the Tigers from 1955 to 1963. One of his rotation mates during his last season in Detroit was a 22-year-old rookie who'd spent the previous half-decade in the minors. After toiling for four years in the Detroit minor-league system, Mickey Lolich refused a demotion and declared he was done with baseball. But a 16-strikeout performance by Lolich for a semi-pro team caught the attention of the Portland Beavers. Lolich won 10 games for the Beavers in 1962, changed his mind about quitting baseball, and made his debut for the Tigers in May 1963.[2] Bunning and Lolich made 35 and 18 starts, respectively, for Detroit during the '63 campaign.

Although Lolich is most famous for his performance during the 1968 World Series (more on that shortly), his best seasons as a hurler came after "The Year of the Pitcher" in '68. In 1971, Lolich led all of baseball in wins (25), games started (45), and strikeouts (308). But more astounding than those figures are the numbers he put up in the complete game and innings pitched categories. Lolich threw 29 complete games and amassed an incredible 376 innings pitched in 1971. Those are the kinds of numbers that Walter Johnson put up 50 years earlier! In fact, Lolich's 376 innings pitched was the highest total since 1920 for any pitcher. That figure was exceeded the next year by Wilbur Wood, who threw 376.2 innings in 1972 (and went 24–20 for the White Sox in 1973), but those two figures (which are not likely to ever be exceeded

23. Close, but No Cigar

again) are still the highest innings-pitched totals since 1920. Lolich came in second to Vida Blue (who put up a 1.82 ERA against Lolich's 2.92 ERA, in 1971) in the voting for the Cy Young Award in the American League.

Of course, it's postseason performance (both good and bad) on the national stage that cements a player in the nation's consciousness. Lolich is best remembered for what he did in the 1968 World Series. In a season dominated by pitching, the teams that faced off in the '68 Series featured two of the most dominant pitchers of the year. The National League representative in the Series, the St. Louis Cardinals, featured the second pitcher to reach 3,000 strikeouts, Bob Gibson (who collected his 3,000th strikeout in 1974). The Tigers, who won the American League pennant, featured the last pitcher to win 30 games in a season, Denny McLain. McLain went 31–6 that year, and Gibson went 22–9. Lolich was 17–9.

It was Gibson versus McLain in Game One. The Cardinals came out on top, 4–0. Lolich evened the series in Game Two with a complete game 8–1 win. He helped his own cause in the game by hitting the only home run of his career. The Cardinals won the next game, so the Tigers were trailing two games to one when Gibson and McLain faced off again in Game Four. McLain lasted just 2.2 innings as Gibson and the Cardinals took a commanding 3–1 lead in the Series. Lolich stepped up again with another complete game as the Tigers won Game Five. But it didn't look good for the Tigers, as the Series was shifting back to St. Louis for the final two games and their ace had been beaten by Gibson twice.

Tiger manager Mayo Smith faced difficult pitching decisions for the games in St. Louis. He could go with his third starter in Game Six, and assuming they won, then have McLain face Gibson again in Game Seven. Those didn't seem like great options for either game. The alternative was also unattractive. He could pitch McLain in Game Six on two days' rest (after he had already started 43 games that season) and then have Lolich, also pitching on two days' rest, face Gibson in the final game, should the series get that far.[3] Smith settled on the latter course of action.

The Tigers put up 10 runs in the third inning of Game Six, and in spite of the short rest, McLain pitched a complete game, allowing just one run in the Tigers 13–1 victory. That set up the sixth World Series during the 1960s to go seven games. Lolich matched Gibson zero-for-zero for six innings, until the Tigers put up three runs in the seventh when Curt Flood lost his footing while chasing a long fly ball.

Part II—Analysis of Pitchers with 3,000 Strikeouts

In spite of pitching on very short rest, Lolich, like McLain in Game Six, went nine innings, allowing only one run as the Tigers won their first championship since 1945. Lolich is the last pitcher (as of 2023) to have three complete-game victories in the World Series.

Getting back to the subject at hand, however: why did Lolich finish 168 strikeouts shy of 3,000? The answer is that in spite of his tremendous workload, his career was just too short. Although he technically had a 16-year career, the last two years were not very productive, so he essentially had a 14-year career. Even though Lolich had seven seasons with more than 200 strikeouts, and a career-best 308 strikeouts in 1971, there weren't enough seasons for him to reach the milestone. None of the elite 19 got there in fewer than 17 seasons (Bob Gibson had a 17-year career) and Lolich didn't make it to that mark.

Modern fans who are more than 35 years old are likely to be most familiar with the next name in Graph 13. That's because Mike Mussina got lots of postseason exposure during the late 1990s and early 2000s. Pitching for Baltimore and the New York Yankees, Mussina appeared in 16 postseason series between 1996 and 2007. His 21 postseason starts are tied with Zach Greinke for the 13th-most all time.[4] Mussina was known as a big-game pitcher. He outdueled Randy Johnson twice in the 1997 American League Division Series, and with the Yankees facing elimination in Game Three of the Division Series in 2001, he threw seven shutout innings to keep the Bronx Bombers alive. That was the game where Derek Jeter made his memorable flip toss to home plate. Mussina pitched in two World Series with the Yankees (2001 and '03) but never won a title. Mussina became the answer to a trivia question when he was the winning pitcher in the contest where Cal Ripken, Jr., played in his 2,131st consecutive game.[5]

Moose (Mussina's nickname) had an 18-year career, but he came up 187 strikeouts short of 3,000. Although Mussina was not really thought of as a strikeout artist, he nonetheless collected a lot of strikeouts. He amassed more than 200 strikeouts four times, with a career-best 218 in 1997. But he didn't strike batters out at a rate that would allow him to reach 3,000 strikeouts in a relatively short career (compared to most of the elite 19). Mussina struck out 7.1 batters per nine innings over his career. That wasn't far below Gibson's 7.2 strikeouts per nine inning career figure, but the difference was enough to keep him off the list of pitchers with 3,000 career strikeouts. However, Mussina belongs to a more important club than the one being discussed in this tome: he was elected to the Hall of Fame in 2019.

23. Close, but No Cigar

Pitcher Frank Tanana's career is often summed up with the jaunty jingle, "Tanana and Ryan and two days of cryin'."[6] That's unfortunate because Tanana had a 21-year career and was good enough to place third in the Cy Young Award voting in 1976. The phrase alludes to the fact that Tanana and Nolan Ryan were the mainstays of the California Angels rotation from 1973 to 1979. There is an element of truth to the jingle. Ryan won 21 and 22 games in 1973 and '74, respectively, while Tanana won 19 games in 1976. The pair led the Angels to their first American League West Division title in 1979, but the team lost to the Orioles in the ALCS.

Tanana finished 227 strikeouts short of 3,000 for his career. He got that close because of his consistency over many years. Although he had three seasons with 200 or more strikeouts, he struck out over 100 batters during 18 campaigns. At his peak, when he was pitching with Ryan (was that a coincidence?), he was a very effective strikeout pitcher. In fact, Tanana led all of baseball in strikeouts with 269 in 1975. But like Mussina, the strikeout efficiency for his career, 6.0 strikeouts per nine innings, was not quite sufficient for Tanana to reach the milestone.

Almost every baseball fan is familiar with the name of the final hurler in Graph 13 who came up a little short of 3,000 strikeouts for his career. That would be Denton True Young. You've never heard of him? While Denton was pitching in the minor leagues, an errant fastball from the young pitcher tore up a fence, and one of the other players said it looked like a cyclone had hit it.[7] Denton was immediately nicknamed Cyclone, and sportswriters shortened that to Cy. Hence, the far more familiar Cy Young is the other pitcher who finished roughly 200 strikeouts short of 3,000.

We've already discussed some players who have their career totals surrounded by gold on the Baseball-Reference.com website. Ty Cobb, for instance, has one number that is highlighted in gold, his career .366 batting average. Rickey Henderson has three: career stolen bases (1,406), career caught stealing (335), and career runs scored (2,295). To have even one of these is a tremendous accomplishment, and having more than one means that you have achieved something that almost no other player in the history of the game has done.

With that in mind, Cy Young has *eight* career totals with gold around them. You read that right, eight! The most well-known of these eight numbers is 315. That's how many losses Young took in his career. No other pitcher lost as many games as Young did. Just kidding about 315 being Young's most famous career total. But that's something to

Part II—Analysis of Pitchers with 3,000 Strikeouts

Full length portrait of Cy Young delivering a pitch in 1908. Young holds the all-time career record in eight (!) pitching categories. The best pitcher award was named after him because he pitched in both leagues and had passed away shortly before the award was created in 1956 (Library of Congress).

keep in mind when we talk about the actual number that Young is most famous for. That would be 511. The other side of the win / loss ledger is that Young won 511 games. That's another number that is often cited as a career record that will never be broken (and not just by this scribe). Young has almost 100 more wins than Walter Johnson who is second with 417 victories.

But since we are discussing pitchers who came up short of 3,000 strikeouts, it's worth examining why Young didn't make it to the milestone. A big part of the reason is the time period when he pitched. Young's 22-year career spanned 1890–1911. There were simply far fewer strikeouts during that period. Team strikeouts in a season will make the point. The average team in the National League struck out 337 hitters for the whole season in 1900 (roughly the mid-point of Young's career). The average NL team in 2023 struck out 1,372 batters. All this says is

23. Close, but No Cigar

that it is a lot easier to strike hitters out now than it was when Young pitched. Another number that drives this point home is that Young's career strikeouts per nine innings was 3.4. That's very low compared to most of the pitchers who did reach the milestone. Young had two seasons with more than 200 strikeouts and a total of 18 seasons with more than 100 strikeouts, but that wasn't quite enough for him to attain the milestone.

However, Young would not be nearly as well known today as he is if his name only came up when pitching records are discussed. After all, he pitched over a century ago. But his moniker is bandied about every season as fans debate who the best pitcher is, and then comes up again after the season, when the Cy Young Award is given out.

The story behind why it is called the Cy Young Award is worth telling. The tale starts with the establishment of a formal Most Valuable Player Award in 1931, to be voted on annually by the Baseball Writers' Association of America (BBWAA). By the mid–1950s a mere five pitchers in each league had won an MVP award. The Commissioner of Baseball, Ford C. Frick (who had also been instrumental in the founding of the Hall of Fame in Cooperstown two decades earlier) believed that pitchers were being treated unfairly by the baseball writers, and pushed for the establishment of a similar award for the best hurler each season.[8] In a coincidence that has been very favorable to his legacy, Young passed away just three months before Frick brought his proposal to the owners in February 1956. The owners agreed to the establishment of the award, but who the award should be named after was contentiously debated. There were many partisans who thought Young (with his 511 wins) was the greatest pitcher ever, but other owners favored Walter Johnson or Christy Mathewson.[9]

However, Frick was insistent that there be just one award for both leagues. This requirement favored Young because he had spent about half his career in each league, over Johnson and Mathewson who had been in one league their whole careers. That, combined with Young's death being fresh in everyone's mind, tilted the vote in his favor. The BBWAA voted to name it the Cy Young Award at their summer meeting. It's interesting that the timing of his passing, and the simple fact he pitched in both leagues, was enough to swing the naming of the award after Young. Don Newcombe won the inaugural award after the 1956 season. It wasn't until 1967 (after Frick was no longer the Commissioner) that the best pitcher in each league would receive a Cy Young Award.

24

Who's Next to 3,000 Strikeouts?

In the last section, we examined the pitchers who nearly reached 3,000 strikeouts during their careers but came up a little short. We are going to do something similar in this section, except that the pitchers under examination are active (as of October 2023) and therefore still have a chance to get to the milestone. The question is, given the rarity of the accomplishment, are there any current pitchers who have a good chance to reach 3,000 strikeouts, and if so, how soon are they likely to get there? The two most likely candidates were mentioned earlier. Assuming neither hurler retires, Clayton Kershaw and Zach Greinke are close enough to the milestone that both should get there during the 2024 season. Since they are not there yet, as of this writing, it wasn't appropriate to discuss them in the section about the elite 19, but they deserve more extended treatment here.

At the end of the 2005 season, Zach Greinke was about as far from being thought of as an elite pitcher as it was possible to be. The once highly touted prospect had lost a league-leading 17 games and also had a 5.80 ERA. Given his obvious talent, the performance didn't make sense until Greike revealed that he'd been suffering from depression and an anxiety disorder for years, while trying to live up to the expectations of him.[1] He sought treatment during 2006, and missed all but the last week of the season. The rehabilitation alleviated his mental issues and by 2009 Greinke was fulfilling the earlier lofty expectations. He went 16–8 with a major league-leading 2.16 ERA and took home the American League Cy Young Award. The fact that he is now knocking on the door to 3,000 strikeouts is a testament to his resilience and hard work.

Six years after his Cy Young Award-winning season, Greinke put together one of the best seasons since baseball expanded in 1961. He

24. Who's Next to 3,000 Strikeouts?

won 19 games against only three losses, and had a major league best 1.66 ERA. Comparing that ERA to the league average, his ERA+ of 222 was the eighth best since expansion. The only pitchers with better seasons in terms of ERA+ since 1961 are Bob Gibson (1968), Dwight Gooden (1985), Greg Maddux (1994, '95), Pedro Martínez (1999, 2000), and Roger Clemens (2005).[2] But the Cy Young voters that year did not think Greinke's performance merited a second Cy Young Award. The award was given to Jake Arrieta, who went 22–6 with a 1.77 ERA (215 ERA+). Greinke didn't get cheated since both men had great seasons, but he certainly also deserved to win. Interestingly, the next pitcher we are going to talk about, Clayton Kershaw, was Greinke's teammate on the Dodgers in 2015, and came in third in the Cy Young voting. All Kershaw did that season was win 16 games, lose seven, and have a 2.13 ERA.

There are a couple of other interesting tidbits on Greinke's resume. He was traded from Milwaukee to the Angels in late July 2012, and he spent the last two months of the season in Anaheim. He made 13 starts for the Angels and struck out 78 batters during his time there. In one of those starts, he struck out 13 batters. That's a very good game for a pitcher, but doesn't appear particularly noteworthy in the context of a book which discusses the greatest strikeout pitchers of all time. However, Greinke struck those 13 batters out in just *five* innings that day. He's the only pitcher since 1920 to strike out 13 batters in five innings.[3] That caliber of strikeout talent helps to explain why he has six seasons with more than 200 strikeouts, and was only 21 strikeouts short of the 3,000-strikeout milestone after the 2023 season. If he hadn't missed almost all of the 2006 season, or if the 2020 season had not been truncated due to the pandemic, there would be 20 pitchers in the elite group with 3,000 strikeouts as this is being written, instead of 19. Finally, and just for fun, Greinke is also famous for a very slow pitch. In 2021 he tossed (which is the accurate word in this case) a 51-mph pitch for a strike. It's fun to watch. Just search the internet for, "Greinke 51 mph pitch."

What's the best way to quantify greatness in a pitcher? Is it wins, strikeouts, ERA, Cy Young Awards, or some other statistic? There are drawbacks to using any of these individually. And regardless of the measure, a related question is how long does the pitcher have to sustain it? Are one or two great seasons enough, or does longevity also have to be accounted for? One way to try and solve this problem is to look at a player's entire career and to also examine how good they were during their peak years. This is a common approach for Hall of Fame consideration.

Part II—Analysis of Pitchers with 3,000 Strikeouts

There are no easy answers to these questions, but ERA+, a modern analytics metric, compares a pitcher's seasonal ERA to the league average and adjusts for park effects. ERA+ reduces issues associated with pure ERA, such as the era a pitcher played in and strength of team effects. This makes it a good measure of pitcher effectiveness compared to his peers. Assuming longevity matters in the discussion of pitcher greatness, by this measure Clayton Kershaw is arguably the greatest pitcher ever.

Although Kershaw's pitching skills are widely respected, it's likely that most fans don't realize how great he truly is. The man has a career ERA of *2.48*. That's not just for one season, that's for his whole 16-year career! To put that in perspective, Sandy Koufax, the other Dodgers pitching great that Kershaw is often compared to (who spent much of his career in the pitcher friendly 1960s), had a career ERA of 2.76 over a 12-year career. Kershaw's 2.48 ERA translates into a career 157 ERA+. That's the highest ERA+ of any American or National League starting pitcher. It's better than Walter Johnson (147 ERA+), Christy Mathewson (136 ERA+), Greg Maddux (132 ERA+), Pedro Martínez (154 ERA+), and Roger Clemens (143 ERA+). His career ERA+ of 157 suggests that Kershaw is the greatest starting pitcher ever.

There are interesting parallels between the careers of Kershaw and Pedro Martínez. Kershaw and Martínez are two of three (Jacob deGrom is the third) AL or NL starting pitchers who have an ERA+ above 150. Both won three Cy Young Awards in four years, and the pattern of win, second place, win, win is the same for both. Kershaw won the Cy Young Award and the MVP Award in 2014, and there is a good argument to be made that Martínez, who came in second in the MVP voting in 1999, should similarly have won both awards that year.[4] Kershaw had one season with more than 300 strikeouts (301 in 2015) while Martínez had two (313 in 1999 and 305 in 1997). But Kershaw has one no-hitter to his credit and Martínez never did throw a no-hitter, although he got close four times.[5] Martínez finished his career with a 219–100 record, while to date, Kershaw is 210–92. And assuming Kershaw pitches in 2024, both will have more than 3,000 strikeouts to their credit. They both deserve to be in the conversation of greatest pitcher ever.

These tremendous career accomplishments make Kershaw's postseason travails surprising. As great as he's been during the regular season, he has struggled in the postseason. His postseason ERA is 4.49, compared to 2.48 during the regular season. His postseason win-loss percentage is .500 compared to .695 in the regular season. Although

24. Who's Next to 3,000 Strikeouts?

the list of Kershaw's poor games in the playoffs is long, what happened in the first game of the 2023 NLDS series against the Diamondbacks is the quintessential example of his postseason problems. In a late August 2023 start against Arizona, Kershaw threw five innings, allowing three hits and one earned run. Five weeks later against the same team in the NLDS, a fully rested Kershaw faced eight batters in the first inning. Six of them got hits, six of them scored, and Kershaw recorded just one out. His ERA for the game was 162. The Dodgers went on to lose the contest 11–2 and got swept in the series. It's hard to understand how these events have happened all through his career, but Kershaw isn't the only stellar pitcher that this has happened to in the postseason. Greg Maddux, Roger Clemens, and Dwight Gooden have also had postseason struggles.[6]

The obvious place to start the rest of the analysis is to look at the list of active pitchers with the most career strikeouts. This is easily done, since Baseball-Reference.com offers active players as one of the choices on the Leaders tab. The top four players on the list, Scherzer, Verlander, Greinke, and Kershaw, have already been discussed. Cole Hamels (2,560 strikeouts) and Adam Wainwright (2,202 strikeouts) are listed next, but both retired in 2023 so they will not be included in the analysis. However, the question of who might be the next pitcher to reach 3,000 strikeouts is not as simple as looking at the next pitcher on the list. That hurler is Chris Sale, with 2,189 career strikeouts. The issue is more complicated than simply looking at the number of strikeouts because the pitcher's age, and the rate at which he accumulates strikeouts, will have bearing on the possibility of him reaching the milestone.

These two variables are incorporated into the analysis as follows, but a couple of assumptions are necessary. In order to estimate how many years a player has left in his career, we have to assume a retirement age. Given that some of the elite pitchers we've discussed have pitched well into their 40s (Nolan Ryan to 46, Gaylord Perry to 44, Phil Niekro to 48) this is a difficult assumption to make accurately. But these three are clearly outliers, and since most pitchers don't make it much past 40 years old (if they even get that far) the retirement age assumption in this analysis is going to be 41 years old. The other assumption which will be made is that the average career strikeout rate per season, calculated as career strikeouts divided by years of career, will continue for the rest of the player's career. This is not likely to be correct, but it will provide some idea of how many strikeouts per season the pitcher can be expected to get going forward.

Table 15: Active Pitchers Most Likely to Reach 3,000 Strikeouts [As of October 2023]

Player	Years in Career	Age	Career Strikeouts (after 2023 season)	Required Strikeouts per year*	Average Strikeouts per year†	Average Minus Required	Years to 3,000 Ks	Projected Age at 3,000 Ks
Gerrit Cole	11	32	2152	94	196	101	4.3	36.3
Aaron Nola	9	30	1582	129	176	47	8.1	38.1
Madison Bumgarner	15	33	2070	116	138	22	6.7	39.7
Chris Sale	13	34	2189	160	168	8	4.8	38.8
Robbie Ray	10	31	1505	150	151	1	9.9	40.9
José Berríos	8	29	1190	151	149	-2	12.2	41.2
Luis Castillo	7	30	1156	168	165	-2	11.2	41.2
Blake Snell	8	30	1223	162	153	-9	11.6	41.6
Kevin Gausman	11	32	1603	155	146	-9	9.6	41.6
Lucas Giolito	8	28	1077	148	135	-13	14.3	42.3
Patrick Corbin	11	33	1590	176	145	-32	9.8	42.8
Eduardo Rodríguez	8	30	1107	172	138	-34	13.7	43.7
Yu Darvish	11	36	1929	214	175	-39	6.1	42.1
Zack Wheeler	9	33	1401	200	156	-44	10.3	43.3
Sonny Gray	11	33	1521	185	138	-47	10.7	43.7
Stephen Strasburg	13	34	1723	182	133	-50	9.6	43.6
Jacob deGrom	10	35	1652	225	165	-59	8.2	43.2
Lance Lynn	12	36	1906	219	159	-60	6.9	42.9

*Assuming career ends at 41 years old the calculation is (3,000-Career Strikeouts) / (41-Age)
†Average strikeouts per year through 2023. Calculation is Career Strikeouts / Years in Career

24. Who's Next to 3,000 Strikeouts?

With these two assumptions, we can do two separate calculations that each have bearing on the probability of the pitcher reaching 3,000 strikeouts. The first one is called Required Strikeouts per year. The idea behind this variable is to see how many strikeouts per year the player needs in order to reach 3,000 strikeouts if he is to retire at age 41. The calculation is (3,000-career strikeouts) divided by (41-age). The second variable is called Average Strikeouts per year. This is exactly what it sounds like. It's the average number of strikeouts the player has collected per season over his career. It's calculated as Career Strikeouts divided by Years in Career. These two variables can be combined to see if the pitcher is collecting enough strikeouts on average to reach 3,000 before turning 41 years old. The difference between these two numbers is referred to as Average minus Required. In order to reach the milestone, Average minus Required needs to be positive or the player probably won't get to the milestone. The results of this analysis are shown in Table 15. The pitchers are listed in order of decreasing Average minus Required, so the order in Table 15 doesn't exactly correspond to the list of active pitchers with the most career strikeouts.

The name at the top of the list in Table 15 isn't surprising. Gerrit Cole, born in a suburb of Los Angeles, has been on the national baseball radar since he was in high school, where he won several All-America team awards. Despite a potentially lucrative offer from the Yankees after he finished high school, Cole decided education came first, and he attended UCLA for three years before becoming the number one draft choice in the 2011 draft by the Pittsburgh Pirates.[7] He made his major league debut in 2013 and had his first 200 strikeout season (with 202) in 2015, when he went 19–8 with a 2.60 ERA.

Cole has been one of the best pitchers in baseball since then. He has collected strikeouts at a rate (career 10.4 strikeouts per nine innings) only exceeded by Max Scherzer (10.7 career) and Randy Johnson (10.6 career), of the elite pitchers in this study. His 326 strikeouts in 2019 led all of baseball and was the highest total during a season since Johnson struck out 334 in 2002. With the exception of the pandemic-shortened 2020 season, Cole has exceeded 200 strikeouts every year since 2018. He was the runner-up in the Cy Young Award voting in 2019 and 2021, but he finally broke through and won the award in 2023.

The data in Table 15 suggests that Gerrit Cole is the player who is most likely to be the next hurler to reach the milestone after Greinke and / or Kershaw. Cole is 848 strikeouts short of 3,000, but he will be a relatively youthful 33 years old during most of the 2024 season.

Part II—Analysis of Pitchers with 3,000 Strikeouts

He needs fewer than 100 strikeouts per year to reach 3,000 by the time he is 41, but he is averaging almost 200 strikeouts per year. Cole is the only pitcher on the list where Average minus Required is a three-digit number. If he can maintain his current strikeout rate he will reach the milestone in about five years during the 2028 season. But even if his strikeout rate declines as he ages, he should be able to reach the milestone if he can pitch to age 39 or 40.

The pitcher with the next best Average minus Required figure in Table 15 is Aaron Nola. His value of 47 is roughly half of Cole's, but it's still about twice as good as Madison Bumgarner, in third place. Nola was born in Baton Rouge, Louisiana, and went to Louisiana State University, where he was the National Pitcher of the Year in 2014. He was teammates with Alex Bregman on the Tigers squad in 2013 and '14.[8] There's an interesting aside about Bregman. He made his debut with Houston in late July 2016, but the Astros didn't reach the postseason that season. In every season to date (October 2023) since Bregman became the starting third baseman in 2017, the Astros went to the postseason and got at least as far as the ALCS. In four of those years the team reached the World Series, and they won the championship twice (2017 and 2022). In other words, Bregman has played in the ALCS every year of his eight-year career except for his rookie year. That's a pretty good run for anybody.

Getting back to Nola, he was drafted by the Phillies in 2014, and he spent just one full year in the minors before making his major league debut in 2015. After three years as a roughly .500 pitcher, Nola had a breakout season in 2018 when he went 17–6 with a 2.37 ERA. That was good enough for him to place third in the Cy Young voting. However, what's interesting about the voting that year is that Nola's Wins Above Replacement (WAR) in 2018 (9.7) was actually higher than the WAR of Jacob deGrom (9.5) who won the award. It's likely that deGrom's impressive 1.70 ERA put him over the top in terms of winning the award.

Aaron Nola has an older brother, Austin, who is also a major league player. The two were teammates at LSU and later made history in the 2022 National League Championship Series. Aaron, pitching Game Two of the series for the Phillies, faced his brother Austin, who was catching for the home San Diego Padres, twice during the game. Austin grounded out in the second inning and singled in the fifth off of his brother. Those at-bats were the first pitcher-versus-batter confrontation featuring brothers in the history of the MLB playoffs that started in 1903.[9]

24. Who's Next to 3,000 Strikeouts?

Like Cole, excepting the 2020 pandemic season, Aaron Nola has struck out 200 or more batters every season since 2018. That means his average strikeouts per year of 176 (in Table 15) may be a little low going forward. That, and his age, as he's two years younger than Cole, is in Nola's favor in terms of his chances of reaching the 3,000-strikeout milestone. Under the previous assumptions, Table 15 says he would reach the plateau in about eight years. However, at the end of the 2023 season, Nola is just over halfway to the milestone. That means he essentially needs to repeat what he's accomplished in terms of strikeouts during the first nine years of his career, again in the second nine or 10 years of his career. Although not impossible, that's a tall order, since a lot can happen in that long a time frame. This all means Cole is more likely to reach the milestone than Nola since he's a lot closer. Strengthening that argument is the fact that Nola is two seasons, but 570 strikeouts, behind Cole. He's very unlikely to have as many strikeouts 11 years into his career as Cole had at 11 years into his career. That makes it much more probable that Cole will reach the milestone than Nola.

The next two pitchers listed in Table 15, Madison Bumgarner and Chris Sale, have also averaged more strikeouts during their careers than they need to average in order to reach 3,000 by age 41. And both have over 2,000 strikeouts. Those facts make it seem like Bumgarner (Average minus Required of 22) and Sale (Average minus Required of 8) are more likely than Nola to reach the milestone since they were, respectively, 488 and 607 strikeouts ahead of Nola at the end of the 2023 season. However, Bumgarner is three years older than Nola, and Mad Bum got off to a terrible start in 2023, going 0–3 with a 10.26 ERA. He was released by the Diamondbacks after that start and didn't get picked up by another team. It seems unlikely he will get the chance to collect the next roughly 1,000 strikeouts he needs to reach the milestone. Sale is four years older than Nola and has had significant injuries the last few years. He missed all of the 2020 season and much of 2021 after Tommy John surgery. Sale missed almost all of 2022 with various injuries, and had a shoulder problem in 2023 that caused him to miss about two months of the season.[10] His age and injury history suggest he is unlikely to be able to collect the 811 strikeouts he needs to reach the milestone as he hasn't had a 200-strikeout season since 2019.

The only other pitcher with a positive Average minus Required in Table 15 is Robbie Ray. However, given the assumptions and uncertainties associated with both calculations, his value of +1 does not mean he will, or will not, reach the milestone. This is true for all the pitchers in

Part II—Analysis of Pitchers with 3,000 Strikeouts

the table, but is especially relevant to Ray. You can make an argument that his average strikeouts per year going forward is likely to be higher than the 151 shown in Table 15. Ray injured his flexor tendon in his first start of 2023 and missed the whole season. So the three strikeouts he got in 2023 lower his career average per year, but are not really representative of his pitching ability. Ray won the Cy Young Award in 2021 and collected a major league-leading 248 strikeouts along the way, but his 212 strikeouts in 2022 are probably a better indication of his near-term annual strikeout rate if he returns to form during the 2024 season. If that is the case, his situation is similar to Nola's. Ray is a year older and has a few less career strikeouts than Nola, but Ray could reach the milestone if he can put together a second half of his career similar to the first half.

All of the remaining pitchers in Table 15 have a negative value for Average minus Required. Given the caveats discussed in the previous paragraph, this does not guarantee that none of them will reach the milestone. But it does mean that there is a lower probability of any of them getting there. That is especially true of the pitchers with less than 1,500 career strikeouts, given how difficult it is to project pitcher longevity. Therefore, we are not going to discuss the rest of the pitchers in the table in detail. However, a few words about some of the names that stand out are in order.

Let's start with Yu Darvish. Darvish pitched for seven years in Japan before he began his U.S. career in 2012. He was the prototypical strikeout pitcher when he got here, striking out 221 and then a major league-leading 277 during his first two years with Texas. He's had two more 200 strikeout seasons since then, and has just under 2,000 strikeouts for his career. But the 1,250 strikeouts Darvish collected in Japan don't count toward his career total in the U.S., and he's now 36 years old because of his late start here. It's very unlikely he will reach the milestone. Lance Lynn doesn't have the strikeout pedigree that Darvish does (he has only one season with more than 200 strikeouts), but like Darvish, Lynn has more than 1,900 strikeouts. And also like Darvish, he is 36 years old. Lance Lynn isn't likely to reach 3,000 strikeouts, either.

Jacob deGrom is near the bottom of Table 15. But he's far from the bottom of any list of great pitchers. DeGrom won the Cy Young Award in 2018 with an ERA of 1.70. He bettered that ERA in 2021 when he put up an ERA of 1.08. There's no question he is a great pitcher, when he can pitch. As they say, the best ability is availability, and deGrom has been

24. Who's Next to 3,000 Strikeouts?

unavailable quite a bit over the course of his career. In spite of that, he has over 1,600 strikeouts. But he is 35 years old. He almost certainly won't make it to the 3,000 plateau. Finally, Stephen Strasburg has over 1,700 career strikeouts. Strasburg came into the league with great fanfare in 2010, and struck out 14 batters in his first start. He averaged 197 strikeouts per year from 2012 to 2019 and was the World Series MVP when Washington won the World Series in 2019. But he has a total of 28 strikeouts since then and his status for the 2024 season is uncertain. Three lost years in terms of career strikeouts means Strasburg is almost certainly not going to reach 3,000, even if he plays in 2024.

Chapter Notes

Chapter 1
1. John Romano, "3,000 Hits—A Milestone Among Milestones," *Tampa Bay Times*, August 8, 1999, 41.
2. David Fleitz, "Cap Anson," *Society for American Baseball Research: Biography Project*, accessed February 8, 2023, https://sabr.org/bioproj/person/cap-anson/.

Chapter 2
1. The Willie Mays Statistics Are Taken from Paul Casella, "Happy B-Day, Say Hey: 24 Amazing Willie Mays Stats," *MLB.com*, May 6, 2023, https://www.mlb.com/news/willie-mays-best-stats-and-accomplishments.
2. Will Leitch, "Most Valuable MVP: Ranking Every Winner," *MLB.com*, November 17, 2023, https://www.mlb.com/news/greatest-mvp-seasons-in-mlb-history-c300194658.
3. Andrew Harner, "Looking Back at the Novelty of Two All Star Games in MLB," *HowTheyPlay.com*, April 3, 2023, https://howtheyplay.com/team-sports/Remembering-when-Major-League-Baseball-hosted-two-All-Star-Games-each-season.
4. Dan Holmes, "For Kaline in the Outfield, Practice Made Perfect," *VintageDetroit.com*, April 18, 2013, https://www.vintagedetroit.com/for-kaline-in-the-outfield-practice-made-perfect/.

Chapter 3
1. John Klima, *The Game Must Go On: Hank Greenberg, Pete Gray, and the Great Days of Baseball on the Home Front in WWII* (New York: Thomas Dunne Books, 2015), 318.
2. Joseph Wancho, "Rod Carew," *Society for American Baseball Research: Biography Project*, accessed February 8, 2023, https://sabr.org/bioproj/person/rod-carew/.

Chapter 5
1. Josh Levitt, "Baseball Analysis: Why Lefties Rule," *Bleacher Report*, July 2, 2009, https://bleacherreport.com/articles/210701-lefties-rule.
2. Matthew Loftus, "Significance and Effect of Handedness in Baseball," *Valparaiso University*, accessed February 10, 2023, https://scholar.valpo.edu/cgi/viewcontent.cgi?article=1871&context=cus.
3. Jordan M. Young, "Safe! The Effect of Batting Hand on Making It to First Base," *Towards Data Science*, November 9, 2020, https://towardsdatascience.com/safe-the-effect-of-batting-hand-on-making-it-to-first-base-b89ac3a1888.
4. Steve Treder, "Bats Left, Throws Right (Part 1)," *Fangraphs* (blog), January 6, 2009, https://tht.fangraphs.com/bats-left-throws-right-part-1/.
5. Guy Molyneux and Phil Birnbaum, "The Southpaw Advantage," *Fangraphs* (blog), September 8, 2020, https://blogs.fangraphs.com/the-southpaw-advantage/.

Chapter 7
1. Dan Holmes, "Tigers Are the Only Team with Three 3,000 Hit Club Members," *Vintage Detroit Collection*, April

Chapter Notes

23, 2022, https://www.vintagedetroit.com/tigers-are-only-team-with-three-3000-hit-club-members/.

2. Steve West, "Wade Boggs," *Society for American Baseball Research: Biography Project*, last revised March 7, 2021, https://sabr.org/bioproj/person/wade-boggs/.

3. Fred Stein, "Mel Ott," *Society for American Baseball Research: Biography Project*, accessed February 2, 2023, https://sabr.org/bioproj/person/mel-ott/.

Chapter 8

1. "Major League Historical Totals (1876–present)," *Baseball-Reference*, accessed February 2, 2023, https://www.baseball-reference.com/leagues/.

2. James Jerpe, "Mayer Beats Pirates, but Wagner Gets Hit: Old Bismarck Reaches 3,000th Safety Mark After 17 Years of Wonderful Batting—Crowd Gives Mighty Cheer—Phillie Pitcher in Form," *Pittsburgh Gazette Times*, June 10, 1914, 10.

3. Major League Historical Totals (1876–present).

Chapter 9

1. C.Y. Chu, T. Chang, J. Chu, "Opposite Hand Advantage and the Overrepresentation of Left-Handed Players in Major League Baseball," *Academia Economic Papers*, June 2016, 171–205.

2. Robert Weintraub, *The Victory Season: The End of WWII and the Birth of Baseball's Golden Age* (New York: Back Bay Books, 2013), 207.

3. Gregory H. Wolf, "May 17, 1970: Hammerin' Hank Collects 3,000th Hit," *Society for American Baseball Research: Games Project*, accessed February 2, 2023, https://sabr.org/gamesproj/game/may-17-1970-hammerin-hank-aaron-collects-3000th-hit/#_edn6.

4. Douglas Jordan, "The Last Thousand-Hundred Man," *Baseball Research Journal*, Volume 49, No. 1, Spring 2020, 69–72.

Chapter 10

1. "The Fields of Major League Baseball," *ballparksofbaseball.com*, accessed February 2, 2023, https://www.ballparksofbaseball.com. All of the information about the different ballparks in this book is from this website.

2. Mark Bowman, "The Story Behind the Final Stop of Babe Ruth's Career," *MLB.com*, February 25, 2022, https://www.mlb.com/news/babe-ruth-ends-career-with-boston-braves.

3. "Boston Braves: History," *Baseball-Reference: Bullpen*, accessed February 2, 2023, https://www.baseball-reference.com/bullpen/Boston_Braves#:~:text=In%201912%2C%20journalists%20began%20to,last%20names%20of%20previous%20owners).

4. Audrey Stark, "What Can We Learn from the Worst Team in Baseball History?" *SBNation: Beyond the Box Score* (blog), February 4, 2019, https://www.beyondtheboxscore.com/2019/2/4/18140136/cleveland-spiders-the-worst-baseball-team-ever-ownership-collusion-tanking.

5. John Thorn, "World Series Centennial Review: 1920," *MLB.com: Our Game* (blog), October 20, 2020, https://ourgame.mlblogs.com/world-series-centennial-review-1920-cf6fe4fb11fc.

6. "Batting Helmet," *Baseball-Reference: Bullpen*, accessed February 2, 2023, https://www.baseball-reference.com/bullpen/Batting_helmet.

7. "Baseball History: Yankees Don't Want No Sissy Batting Helmets," *RIP Baseball*, accessed February 2, 2023, https://ripbaseball.com/2019/09/22/baseball-history-yankees-dont-want-no-sissy-batting-helmets/.

8. Paul Lucas, "Alex Torres and the History of Headgear in Baseball," *ESPN.com*, April 22, 2015, https://www.espn.com/mlb/story/_/id/12741917/uni-watch-history-headgear-mlb-alex-torres.

9. Matt Snyder, "Al Michaels Says Twins Used Artificial Noise in 1987 World Series," *CBSSports.com*, February 5, 2015, https://www.cbssports.com/mlb/news/al-michaels-says-twins-used-artificial-noise-in-1987-world-series/.

Chapter Notes

10. Gregory H. Wolf, "May 13, 1958: Stan Musial Delivers in the Pinch for His 3,000th Hit," *Society for American Baseball Research: Games Project*, accessed February 5, 2023, https://sabr.org/gamesproj/game/may-13-1958-stan-musial-delivers-in-the-pinch-for-his-3000th-hit/.
11. Robert Dorin, "September 12, 1979: Carl Yastrzemski's 3,000th Hit," *Society for American Baseball Research: Games Project*, accessed February 5, 2023, https://sabr.org/gamesproj/game/september-12-1979-carl-yastrzemskis-3000th-hit/.

Chapter 11

1. Douglas Jordan, "September 22, 1993: Nolan Ryan Throws Final Pitch for Rangers in Decorated 27-Year Career," *Society for American Baseball Research: Games Project*, accessed February 5, 2023, https://sabr.org/gamesproj/game/september-22-1993-sad-moment-ends-nolan-ryans-career/.
2. Robert Weintraub, *The Victory Season: The End of WWII and the Birth of Baseball's Golden Age* (New York: Back Bay Books, 2013), 423.
3. Francis Kinlaw, "The Trials, Tribulations, and Challenges of Al Kaline," *Baseball Research Journal*, Volume 50, No. 2, Fall 2021, 32–42.
4. Andy Sturgill, "Pete Rose," *Society for American Baseball Research: Biography Project*, accessed February 5, 2023, https://sabr.org/bioproj/person/pete-rose/#sdendnote4sym.
5. Joseph Wancho, "Rod Carew."
6. Joel Badzinski, "St. Paul Style of Winfield, Molitor Took Them a Long Way," *Twin Cities Pioneer Press*, August 11, 2016, https://www.twincities.com/2016/08/11/st-paul-style-of-winfield-molitor-took-them-a-long-way/#:~:text=Winfield%20and%20Molitor%2C%20who%20were,1990s%20but%20never%20played%20together.
7. "Book Excerpt: Rickey, On the Life of Baseball Legend Rickey Henderson," *CBSNews*, July 10, 2022, https://www.cbsnews.com/news/book-excerpt-rickey-on-the-life-of-baseball-legend-rickey-henderson-by-howard-bryant/, in *Rickey: The Life and Legend of an American Original*, by Howard Bryant, Mariner Books, 2022.
8. Joseph Wancho, "Rickey Henderson," *Society for American Baseball Research: Biography Project*, accessed February 5, 2023, https://sabr.org/bioproj/person/rickey-henderson/.

Chapter 12

1. Aastha Thapa, "Top 89 Pete Rose Quotes for Success," *PlayersBio*, June 29, 2022, https://playersbio.com/pete-rose-quotes/.
2. Moss Klein, "A's Lead the League in Plugging Holes," *The Sporting News*, Baseball: AL Report, May 13, 1991, 39.
3. "Rickey Henderson Quotes and Sayings," *Inspiringquotes.us*, accessed February 6, 2023, https://www.inspiringquotes.us/author/5581-rickey-henderson.
4. Doug Skipper, "Dave Winfield," *Society for American Baseball Research: Biography Project*, accessed February 6, 2023, https://sabr.org/bioproj/person/dave-winfield/.
5. "Eddie Collins Quotes," *Baseball Almanac*, accessed February 6, 2023, https://www.baseball-almanac.com/quotes/quoclls.shtml.
6. Fred McMane and Stuart Shea, *The 3,000 Hit Club: Stories of Baseball's Greatest Hitters* (New York: Skyhorse Publishing, 2012), 77.

Chapter 13

1. "The 3,000-Hit Club," *National Baseball Hall of Fame*, accessed February 6, 2023, http://exhibits.baseballhalloffame.org/3000_hit_club/index.htm.
2. Maxwell Kates, "Frank Robinson," *Society for American Baseball Research: Biography Project*, accessed February 6, 2023, https://sabr.org/bioproj/person/frank-robinson/#sdendnote19sym.
3. Doug Skipper, "Willie Keeler," *Society for American Baseball Research:*

Chapter Notes

Biography Project, accessed February 6, 2023, https://sabr.org/bioproj/person/willie-keeler/.

4. Fred Stein, "Al Simmons," *Society for American Baseball Research: Biography Project*, accessed February 6, 2023, https://sabr.org/bioproj/person/al-simmons/.

5. Joe Posnanski, "The Baseball 100: No. 17, Rogers Hornsby," *The Athletic*, March 10, 2020, https://theathletic.com/1664621/2020/03/10/the-baseball-100-no-17-rogers-hornsby/.

6. JRB, "What Happened to Hornsby in 1930?" *Baseball Fever*: Forums, October 10, 2007, https://www.baseball-fever.com/forum/general-baseball/history-of-the-game/33464-what-happened-to-hornsby-in-1930. The information in this post by JRB is corroborated in Hornsby's SABR biography.

Chapter 14

1. Dan Szymborski, "The 3,000-Hit Club Is Closed for Maintenance," *Fangraphs* (blog), September 23, 2021, https://blogs.fangraphs.com/the-3000-hit-club-is-closed-for-maintenance/.

2. A.J. Cassavell, "At 29, Machado Joins MLB Royalty with 1,500 Hits, 250 HR," *MLB.com*, June 15, 2022, https://www.mlb.com/news/manny-machado-records-career-hit-1-500.

3. John Denton, "Why Arenado Has a Specific Age in Mind for Retirement," *MLB.com*, March 5, 2023, https://www.mlb.com/news/nolan-arenado-ponders-end-of-career-retirement?partnerId=zh-20230306-844210-mlb-1-A&qid=1026&utm_id=zh-20230306-844210-mlb-1-A&bt_ee=Rk7H3cylY8oe2i1dOQSeTgUyq9tQUHZWq64g01rjiV38comsU%2B72pCK4hfXXlLNT&bt_ts=1678118614793.

Chapter 15

1. Paul W. Eaton, "Griffmen Do Best When Injured Most," *The Sporting News*, August 2, 1923, 2.

2. E-mail correspondence with David W. Smith on August 30, 2023.

3. Joshua Schulman, "Former Phillies Ace Curt Schilling Falls Short of Hall of Fame Yet Again," *Thatballsouttahere.com*, December 6, 2022, https://thatballsouttahere.com/2022/12/06/phillies-curt-schilling-hall-fame-2/.

Chapter 16

1. "Before Radar Guns Bob Feller," *YouTube*, https://www.youtube.com/watch?v=IhZ7t_DNi9w (last accessed August 31, 2023).

2. C. Paul Rogers III, "Bob Feller," *Society for American Baseball Research: Biography Project*, accessed August 31, 2023, https://sabr.org/bioproj/person/bob-feller/.

3. J. Conrad Guest, "Ty Cobb Talks About the Greatest Pitcher He Ever Faced," *VintageDetroit.com*, January 2, 2013, https://www.vintagedetroit.com/ty-cobb-talks-about-the-greatest-pitcher-he-ever-faced/.

4. Mike Mashon, "Film of the Washington Senators Winning the 1924 World Series Found!" *Library of Congress Blogs*, October 2, 2014, https://blogs.loc.gov/now-see-hear/2014/10/film-of-the-washington-senators-winning-the-1924-world-series-found/.

5. John Thorn, "Pitching: Evolution and Revolution," *OurGameMLBlogs.com*, August 6, 2014, https://ourgame.mlblogs.com/pitching-evolution-and-revolution-efd3a5ebaa83.

6. Terry Sloope, "Bob Gibson," *Society for American Baseball Research: Biography Project*, accessed August 31, 2023, https://sabr.org/bioproj/person/bob-gibson/.

7. Bob Gibson and Reggie Jackson with Lonnie Wheeler, *Sixty Feet, Six Inches* (New York: Anchor Books, 2009), 8.

8. Bill James, "Big Game Pitchers, Part VII," *Bill James Online*, January 26, 2014, https://www.billjamesonline.com/big_game_pitchers_part_vii/.

9. Those five pitchers are Cy Young, Pud Galvin, Walter Johnson, Phil Niekro, and Nolan Ryan.

10. Douglas Jordan, "September 22,

Chapter Notes

1993: Nolan Ryan Throws Final Pitch for Rangers in Decorated 27-Year Career," *Society for American Baseball Research: Games Project*, accessed September 3, 2023, https://sabr.org/gamesproj/game/september-22-1993-sad-moment-ends-nolan-ryans-career/

11. Chris Haft, "The Top Ten Moments of Carlton's Career," *MLB.com*, December 21, 2021, https://www.mlb.com/news/steve-carlton-top-moments-of-career.

12. Stathead Baseball analysis conducted on September 4, 2023, https://stathead.com/tiny/gObO2.

13. Daniel Marks, "The Best Players of the Last 50 Years—Part XI—Starting Pitchers (1–10)," *Bill James Online*, August 8, 2021, https://www.billjamesonline.com/the_best_players_of_the_last_50_years_-_part_xi_-_starting_pitchers_1-10/.

14. Tom Seaver, "Consistency Quotes," *BrainyQuote.com*, accessed September 6, 2023, https://www.brainyquote.com/topics/consistency-quotes.

15. Gregory H. Wolf, "Don Sutton," *Society for American Baseball Research: Biography Project*, accessed September 6, 2023, https://sabr.org/bioproj/person/don-sutton/#_ednref1.

16. Stathead Baseball analysis conducted on September 6, 2023, https://stathead.com/tiny/nYJG6.

17. Phil Niekro, "Phil Niekro Quotes," *BrainyQuote.com*, accessed September 7, 2023, https://www.brainyquote.com/authors/phil-niekro-quotes#:~:text=I%20never%20knew%20how%20to,whatever%20they're%20throwing%20nowadays.

18. Gregory H. Wolf, "Bert Blyleven," *Society for American Baseball Research: Biography Project*, accessed September 30, 2023, https://sabr.org/bioproj/person/bert-blyleven/.

19. Quotes About Greg Maddux, *Baseball-Almanac.com*, accessed September 23, 2023, https://www.baseball-almanac.com/quotes/greg_maddux_quotes.shtml.

20. Bill Nowlin, "October 19, 2004: Curt Schilling Keeps Red Sox Alive in 'Bloody Sock Game,'" *Society for American Baseball Research: Games Project*, accessed September 11, 2023, https://sabr.org/gamesproj/game/october-19-2004-curt-schilling-keeps-red-sox-alive-in-bloody-sock-game/#_ednref3.

21. Stathead Baseball analysis conducted on September 12, 2023, https://stathead.com/tiny/M4Uom.

22. Baseball-Reference Career ERA+ Leaders search on September 12, 2023, https://www.baseball-reference.com/leaders/earned_run_avg_plus_career.shtml.

23. Stathead Baseball analysis conducted on September 12, 2023, https://stathead.com/tiny/izTQh.

24. Bill James, "Big Game Pitchers, Part VII."

Chapter 18

1. Tom Hufford, "September 27, 1987: Phil Niekro Returns to the Braves for Final Start," *Society for American Baseball Research: Games Project*, accessed September 20, 2023, https://sabr.org/gamesproj/game/september-27-1987-phil-niekro-returns-to-braves-for-final-start/.

2. Mike Kelly, "Nolan Ryan Becomes Baseball's First Million Dollar Man," *National Baseball Hall of Fame*, accessed September 21, 2023, https://baseballhall.org/discover-more/stories/inside-pitch/nolan-ryan-million-dollar-man#:~:text=On%20Nov.,dollar%2Da%2Dyear%20contract.

Chapter 19

1. Daniel R. Levitt, "Stan Coveleski," *Society for American Baseball Research: Biography Project*, accessed September 22, 2023, https://sabr.org/bioproj/person/stan-coveleski/.

Chapter 20

1. Jesse Kratz, "Ceremonial First Pitches," *U.S. National Archives Blog*, March 28, 2023, https://prologue.blogs.archives.gov/2023/03/28/ceremonial-first-pitches/.

Chapter Notes

2. Jim Gates, "Clicking Turnstiles," *National Baseball Hall of Fame*, accessed September 26, 2023, https://baseballhall.org/clicking-turnstiles.

3. William Leggett, "The Heavenly Home of the Anaheim Angels," *Sports Illustrated Vault*, July 4, 1966, https://vault.si.com/vault/1966/07/04/the-heavenly-home-of-the-anaheim-angels.

4. "The Greatest Non-Baseball Related Events in Dodger Stadium History," *Discover Los Angeles*, March 14, 2019, https://www.discoverlosangeles.com/the-greatest-non-baseball-events-in-dodger-stadium-history.

5. Curt Smith, "Jack Murphy Stadium, San Diego," *Society for American Baseball Research: Biography Project, Ballparks*, accessed September 29, 2023, https://sabr.org/bioproj/park/jack-murphy-stadium-san-diego/.

6. Cliff Christl, "Part I: How Milwaukee Became the Packers' Second Home," *Packers.com*, June 22, 2023, https://www.packers.com/news/part-i-how-milwaukee-became-the-packers-second-home.

Chapter 21

1. Bill Nowlin, "Curt Schilling," *Society for American Baseball Research: Biography Project*, accessed September 30, 2023, https://sabr.org/bioproj/person/curt-schilling/.

2. Cindy Thomson, "Fergie Jenkins," *Society for American Baseball Research: Biography Project*, accessed September 30, 2023, https://sabr.org/bioproj/person/fergie-jenkins/.

Chapter 22

1. Stathead Baseball analysis conducted on October 3, 2023, https://stathead.com/tiny/uzZAq.

Chapter 23

1. Ralph Berger, "Jim Bunning," *Society for American Baseball Research: Biography Project*, accessed October 9, 2023, https://sabr.org/bioproj/person/jim-bunning/.

2. Dan Holmes, "Mickey Lolich," *Society for American Baseball Research: Biography Project*, accessed October 10, 2023, https://sabr.org/bioproj/person/mickey-lolich/.

3. Mark Armour, "The Unexpected Hero (1968 World Series)," *Mark Armour Blog*, accessed October 11, 2023, https://marklaurencearmour.wordpress.com/2018/06/06/the-unexpected-hero-1968-world-series/.

4. Stathead Baseball analysis conducted on October 12, 2023, https://stathead.com/tiny/mAX62.

5. Mark Feinsand, "11 Moments That Got Moose to Cooperstown," *MLB.com*, December 7, 2022, https://www.mlb.com/news/mike-mussina-s-top-moments-c303002702.

6. "Frank Tanana Career Highlights," *This Day in Baseball*, December 28, 2018, https://thisdayinbaseball.com/frank-tanana-career-highlights/.

7. Vince Guerrieri, "The Ohio Town That Baseball Legend Cy Young Called Home," *OhioMagazine.com*, May 2022, https://www.ohiomagazine.com/ohio-life/article/the-ohio-town-baseball-legend-cy-young-called-home.

8. Elizabeth Muratore, "Why the Cy Young Award Was Named After Cy Young," *MLB.com*, February 2, 2023, https://www.mlb.com/news/cy-young-award-history.

9. Marty Appel, "National Pastime Museum: Birth of the Cy Young Award," *Byline Marty Appel*, accessed October 14, 2023, http://www.appelpr.com/?page_id=3365.

Chapter 24

1. Nick Poust, "Three Years After Considering Quitting, Greinke's a Cy Young Favorite," *BleacherReport.com*, September 27, 2009, https://bleacherreport.com/articles/262567-three-years-after-considering-quitting-greinkes-a-cy-young-favorite.

2. Stathead Baseball analysis conducted on October 19, 2023, https://stathead.com/tiny/R0Ocg.

Chapter Notes

3. Anne Rogers, "Top Ten Moments of Zack Greinke's Career, *MLB.com*, March 26, 2022, https://www.mlb.com/news/zack-greinke-top-10-career-moments#:~:text=13%20strikeouts%20in%20five%20innings&text=According%20to%20ESPN%20Stats%2C%20Greinke,leading%20to%20his%20shorter%20start.

4. Chris Haft, "Pedro Martínez's Top Ten Moments," *MLB.com*, September 17, 2023, https://www.mlb.com/news/pedro-martinez-top-10-moments.

5. Haft, "Pedro Martínez's Top Ten Moments."

6. Craig Calcaterra, "Clayton Kershaw Is Not Alone in His Postseason Struggles," *NBC.com*, October 10, 2019, https://www.nbcsports.com/mlb/news/clayton-kershaw-is-not-alone-in-his-postseason-struggles.

7. David Gaston, "Pittsburgh Pirates: Prospect Profile on Young Number One Pick Gerrit Cole," *BleacherReport.com*, September 13, 2011, https://bleacherreport.com/articles/844503-mlb-pittsburgh-pirates-prospect-profile-gerrit-cole-everything-you-need-to-kn.

8. "#10 Aaron Nola," LSU Baseball, *LSUsports.net*, accessed October 17, 2023, https://lsusports.net/sports/bsb/roster/season/2013/player/aaron-nola/.

9. Glenn Gilbeau, "Aaron Nola Versus Austin Nola Just Made History in MLB Postseason, but Mom and Dad Had Mixed Emotions," *OutKick.com*, October 21, 2022, https://www.outkick.com/aaron-nola-vs-austin-nola-just-made-history-in-mlb-postseason-but-mom-and-dad-had-mixed-emotions/.

10. Molly Burkhardt, "Sale Resumes Throwing After MRI Reveals Good News," *MLB.com*, June 29, 2023, https://www.mlb.com/news/chris-sale-second-mri-resumes-throwing.

Bibliography

Players with 3,000 Hits

Baggot, Andy. *Robin Yount: The Legend Lives On.* Milwaukee: Milwaukee Brewers Publications, 1995.
Boggs, Wade. *Boggs!* New York: McGraw-Hill, 1986.
Brett, George. *George Brett: From Here to Cooperstown.* Lenexa, KS: Addax Publishing Group, 1999.
Brock, Lou, and Franz Schulze. *Stealing Is My Game.* Hoboken: Prentice Hall, 1976.
Broomer, Stuart. *Paul Molitor: Good Timing.* Toronto: ECW Press, 1994.
Bryant, Howard. *Rickey: The Life and Legend of an American Original.* Boston: Mariner Books, 2022.
Carew, Rod, and Jaime Aron. *One Tough Out: Fighting Off Life's Curveballs.* Chicago: Triumph Books, 2020.
Gay, Timothy. *Tris Speaker: The Rough-and-Tumble Life of a Baseball Legend.* San Jose: Lyons Press, 2007.
Geoffreys, Clayton. *Mike Trout: The Inspiring Story of One of Baseball's All-Stars.* Winter Park, FL: Calvintir Books, 2020.
Hawkins, Jim, and Ernie Harwell. *Al Kaline: The Biography of a Tigers Icon.* Chicago: Triumph Books, 2013.
Hittner, Arthur D. *Honus Wagner: The Life of Baseball's "Flying Dutchman."* Jefferson, NC: McFarland, 2003.
Huhn, Rick. *Eddie Collins: A Baseball Biography.* Jefferson, NC: McFarland, 2008.
Komatsu, Narumi, translated by Philip Gabriel. *Ichiro on Ichiro.* Seattle: Sasquatch Books, 2004.
Leerhsen, Charles. *Ty Cobb: A Terrible Beauty.* New York: Simon & Schuster, 2015.
Lucas, Greg. *Houston to Cooperstown: The Houston Astros' Biggio and Bagwell Years.* Indianapolis: Blue River Press, 2017.
Maraniss, David. *Clemente: The Passion and Grace of Baseball's Last Hero.* New York: Simon & Schuster, 2007.
Mays, Willie, and John Shea. *24: Life Stories and Lessons from the Say Hey Kid.* New York: St. Martin's Press, 2020.
McMane, Fred, and Stuart Shea. *The 3,000 Hit Club: Stories of Baseball's Greatest Hitters.* New York: Skyhorse Publishing, 2012.
Moore, Terence. *The Real Hank Aaron: An Intimate Look at the Life and Legacy of the Home Run King.* Chicago: Triumph Books, 2022.
O'Connor, Ian. *The Captain: The Journey of Derek Jeter.* Boston: Houghton Mifflin Harcourt, 2011.
Parker, Clifton Blue. *Big and Little Poison: Paul and Lloyd Waner, Baseball Brothers.* Jefferson, NC: McFarland, 2002.
Rains, Rob, and John Rooney. *Albert Pujols: Simply the Best.* Chicago: Triumph Books, 2009.

Bibliography

Ripken, Cal, Jr., and Donald T. Phillips. *Get in the Game: 8 Elements of Perseverance That Make the Difference.* New York: Gotham Books, 2007.
Ritter, Lawrence S. *The Glory of Their Times: The Story of the Early Days of Baseball Told by the Men Who Played It.* New York: William Morrow, 1992.
Roberts, Selena. *A-Rod: The Many Lives of Álex Rodríguez.* New York: Harper, 2009.
Rose, Pete, and Rick Hill. *My Prison Without Bars.* Emmaus, PA: Rodale Books, 2004.
Rosenberg, Howard W. *Cap Anson 1: When Captaining a Team Meant Something, Leadership in Baseball's Early Years.* Tile Books, 2003.
Rubano, Gregory. *In Ty Cobb's Shadow: The Story of Napoleon Lajoie, Baseball's First Superstar.* Glocester, RI: Stillwater River Publications, 2016.
Vecsey, George. *Stan Musial: An American Life.* New York: Ballantine Books, 2011.
Winfield, Dave, and Tom Parker. *Winfield: A Player's Life.* New York: W.W. Norton, 1988.
Wolf, Rich. *Tony Gwynn: He Left His Heart in San Diego.* Portland, ME: Lone Wolf Press, 2014.
Yastrzemski, Carl. *Yaz: Baseball, the Wall, and Me.* New York: Doubleday, 1990.

Pitchers with 3,000 Strikeouts

Fallon, Michael. *Dodgerland: Decadent Los Angeles and the 1977–78 Dodgers.* Lincoln: University of Nebraska Press, 2016.
Gibson, Bob, with Lonnie Wheeler. *Stranger to the Game: The Autobiography of Bob Gibson.* New York: Penguin Group, 1996.
Jenkins, Fergie, with Lew Freedman. *Fergie: My Life from the Cubs to Cooperstown.* Chicago: Triumph Books, 2009.
Johnson, Randy, and Jim Rosenthal. *Randy Johnson's Power Pitching: The Big Unit's Secrets to Domination, Intimidation, and Winning.* New York: Three Rivers Press, 2003.
Kashatus, William C. *Lefty and Tim: How Steve Carlton and Tim McCarver Became Baseball's Best Battery.* Lincoln: University of Nebraska Press, 2022.
Madden, Bill. *Tom Seaver: A Terrific Life.* New York: Simon & Schuster, 2020.
Martínez, Pedro, and Michael Silverman. *Pedro.* Boston: Mariner Books, 2016.
Niekro, Phil, and Tom Bird. *Knuckle Balls.* Freundlich Books, 1986.
Pearlman, Jeff. *The Rocket That Fell to Earth: Roger Clemens and the Rage for Baseball Immortality.* New York: Harper Perennial, 2010.
Perry, Gaylord, with Bob Sudyk. *Me and the Spitter: An Autobiographical Confession.* New York: Saturday Review Press, 1974.
Posnanski, Joe. *The Baseball 100.* New York: Avid Reader Press / Simon & Schuster, 2023.
Ryan, Nolan, and Harvey Frommer. *Throwing Heat: The Autobiography of Nolan Ryan.* New York: Doubleday, 1988.
Sabathia, CC, and Chris Smith. *Till the End.* New York: Roc Lit 101 / Random House, 2021.
Smoltz, John, and Don Yaeger. *Starting and Closing: Perseverance, Faith, and One More Year.* New York: William Morrow Paperbacks, 2013.
Thomas, Henry W. *Walter Johnson: Baseball's Big Train.* Lincoln: University of Nebraska Press, Bison Books, 1998.
Thornley, Stew. *Baseball in Minnesota: The Definitive History.* St. Paul: Minnesota Historical Society Press, 2006.

Index

Aaron, Henry 9, 13, 16, 18–21, 26, 30, 32, 37, 39, 46, 50, 61, 64–66, 76, 78, 86, 88–89, 93, 95, 101, 113, 173, 175, 181
Aberdeen, Maryland 84
Acuña, Ronald 34. 108
Alabama 77–78, 176, 181
Alexander, Grover 125
All-Star Game 16, 59, 61, 174
Alomar, Sandy 62
Altuve, Jose 107, 110–112
American League 18, 36, 40, 43, 68, 101, 103, 125–126, 136, 140, 142, 148, 152, 158, 164, 188, 191, 198
American League Championship Series (ALCS): (1979) 193; (1987) 139; (2004) 147; (2009) 150; (2017–2023) 202; (2023) 152
American League Division Series (ALDS): (1995) 2; (1997) 192; (2001) 50, 192; (2004) 146
Anaheim, California 132, 172, 178, 197
Anchorage, Alaska 179
Andrus, Elvis 33, 107, 110–111
Anheuser-Busch 72, 81
Anson, Cap 8, 10–11, 13, 25, 31, 37, 40–41, 49, 64, 77, 117, 131
Arenado, Nolan 110, 112–114
Arizona Diamondbacks 44, 48, 143, 146, 156, 158, 160, 199, 203
Arkansas 80
Arlington, Texas 64, 168
Arráez, Luis 108
Arrieta, Jake 197
Atlanta, Georgia 39, 67, 173–175
Atlanta Braves 37, 39, 61, 67, 138–139, 149–150, 156–158, 160, 174, 185
awards: All-Star selections 8–10, 16, 22–23, 35, 61, 137, 165; Cy Young 52, 62–63, 119, 128, 130, 133–134, 136–138, 140–141, 143–144, 146, 149–152, 158, 165–167, 173–174, 189, 191, 193, 195–198, 201, 204; Gold Glove 8–10, 13, 16–17, 35, 113, 129, 144, 163–165; Most Valuable Player 8–10, 13–15, 22, 35–36, 62, 103, 105–107, 113, 128, 140, 152, 195, 198;

Rookie of the Year 8–10, 13, 22, 50, 62, 103, 133–134; Silver Slugger 23
Aybar, Erick 36

Bagby, Jim 69
ballparks *see* stadiums
ballparksofbaseball.com website 170
Baltimore, Maryland 42, 47, 65, 78, 80, 84, 182
Baltimore Orioles 17, 37, 39, 43, 46–47, 73, 84, 103–104, 134, 175, 192–193
Bannister, Alan 118
Baseball-Reference.com 6, 14, 28, 49–50, 65, 96, 103–104, 117, 125, 132, 193, 199
Baseball Research Journal 2
Baseball Writers' Association of America 14, 195
Baton Rouge, Louisiana 202
batting helmet history 69
The Beatles 171
Beattie, Jim 26, 60, 73
Beaver Falls, Pennsylvania 78
Beckley, Jake 100, 104
Belanger, Mark 17
Beltré, Adrian 9, 19, 23–24, 27, 32, 35–36, 38, 46–47, 54, 64, 76, 83, 86, 93–94, 96, 98, 109–112, 179, 181
Berra, Yogi 14, 107
Berríos, José 200
The Big Red Machine 163
Biggio, Craig 9, 19, 26, 32, 37, 46–47, 54, 64, 76, 83, 86, 91, 93–94, 96, 109–110, 112
Blaine, Ohio 178
Blue, Vida 191
Blyleven, Bert 117–118, 120–121, 127, 138–140, 149, 153–154, 156–157, 159, 163, 168, 172, 177, 179, 184, 187, 189
Boggs, Wade 9, 19–20, 22–23, 26, 32, 34–35, 38, 41, 46–47, 49–50, 53, 57–58, 64, 76, 82–84, 86, 88, 93, 95, 101, 127, 143, 182
Bonds, Barry 91, 100, 104–105
Boston Braves 48, 67
Boston, Massachusetts 64, 67, 71, 73, 174
Boston Globe 73

217

Index

Boston Red Sox 2, 37, 41–42, 46, 48, 54, 69, 73, 81, 134, 145, 147, 156
Branca, Ralph 82
Bregman, Alex 202
Brett, George 9, 19, 22–23, 26, 32, 38, 46, 57–58, 64, 76, 82, 86, 91, 93, 95, 133, 172
Brock, Lou 9, 17, 19, 26, 32–33, 38, 43, 46, 64, 76, 80–81, 86, 89–92, 95, 172, 174
Brooklyn, New York 69, 171
Brooklyn Dodgers 38, 43–44, 48
Brooklyn Robins 68, 164
Brooklyn Superbas 48
Buckner, Bill 62, 145
Buffett, Warren 127
Buhner, Jay 2
Bumgarner, Madison 146, 200, 202–203
Bunning, Jim 188–190

Cabrera, Miguel 6, 10, 17–19, 23, 27, 32, 37–38, 46–47, 64, 76, 83, 86, 91–93, 95, 101, 113
Calhoun, Kole 118, 163
California 77, 82, 133, 165, 174, 176, 178–179, 181
California Angels 22, 39, 46, 48, 132–133, 159, 170, 193
Callison, Johnny 36
Cambria, Joe 21
Campanella, Roy 44
Canada 135, 139, 179
Canseco, José 130
Carew, Rod 9, 17, 19, 21–22, 26, 32, 37, 39, 46–48, 57–58, 63–64, 76, 81–83, 86, 88, 93, 95, 172
Caribbean 21, 77
Carlton, Steve 118, 120–121, 133–136, 140–141, 144, 150, 154–156, 160, 165–167, 169, 176–177, 180, 184
Carrasco, Hector 26, 60, 70
Carter, Gary 45
Cartwright, Alexander 75
Castillo, Luis 200
Cepeda, Orlando 113
Chapman, Aroldis 63
Chapman, Ray 68, 165
Chartiers, Pennsylvania 78, 84, 178
Chávez, Eric 36
Chicago, Illinois 16, 40, 53, 65, 71–72, 82, 101
Chicago Colts 37
Chicago Cubs 40, 46–48, 71, 106, 134, 136, 156–157, 160, 173–174
Chicago White Sox 37, 48, 92, 134–135, 161, 170, 186, 190
Christmas 82
Cincinnati, Ohio 64–65, 80–81, 159, 172–173, 181
Cincinnati Reds 37, 42, 46, 48, 61, 65–66, 81, 101, 103, 133–134, 156, 160, 165, 170, 173
Civil War 75, 77
Clemens, Roger 63, 117–121, 137, 139–144, 146, 148, 150, 152, 154, 156, 164, 166–167, 169, 176, 178, 180–181, 184–186, 197–199
Clemente, Roberto 9, 16, 19, 20–21, 26, 32, 38, 46, 59, 65, 76, 78, 86, 93, 95, 99
Cleveland, Ohio 39, 65, 67–69
Cleveland Blues 68
Cleveland Bronchos 68
Cleveland Indians 36–39, 40–41, 46–48, 68–69, 104, 123, 130, 135, 151, 164–165, 169
Cleveland Naps 68
Cleveland Spiders 68
Clio, Alabama 181
Cobb, Ty 8, 14, 16, 19, 23, 25, 30–33, 35, 37, 42, 45–46, 51, 59, 65–67, 76–77, 81, 86–90, 92–96, 98, 101, 106, 124, 155, 193
Cochrane, Mickey 69
Cole, Gerrit 142, 152, 200–203
College World Series 127
Collins, Eddie 8, 19–20, 25, 30, 32–33, 37, 46–47, 58–59, 65–67, 76–78, 86, 91–93, 95, 100, 121, 161
Collins, Rip 25, 58, 60
Colorado 47, 113
Colorado Rockies 6, 44–47, 53, 114, 160
Cook, Aaron 26, 60
Coolidge, Calvin 124
Cooperstown, New York 6, 8, 10, 75, 119, 164, 195
Corbin, Patrick 200
Cordero, Will 36
Coveleski, Stan 118, 164–165, 169
COVID-19 pandemic 108, 112, 116, 188, 197, 201, 203
Crawford, Brandon 177
Crawford, Sam 101, 103–104, 190
Cuba 21, 77, 83
Curry, Stephen 1

Dark, Al 13
Darvish, Yu 200, 204
Davis, Mike 118, 163
Dayton, Ohio 178, 181
dead-ball era 101, 120, 128, 147
deGrom, Jacob 45, 148, 198, 200, 202, 204
Denver, Colorado 47, 54, 64
Detroit, Michigan 14, 39–40, 45, 64–66, 190–191
Detroit Tigers 33, 36–39, 46–48, 51–52, 101, 129, 139–140, 152, 173, 188, 190–192
DiMaggio, Joe 34, 41–42, 74
Dominican Republic 24, 77, 83, 179, 181
Donora, Pennsylvania 78

Index

Doubleday, Abner 75
Doyle, Larry 43
Drabowsky, Moe 26, 60, 71–72
Dropo, Walt 14
Drysdale, Don 44

Eckersley, Dennis 26, 60, 62–63, 70
eephus pitch 59, 197
Erstad, Darin 34
Evans, Dwight 73

Feller, Bob 122–124
Fingers, Rollie 130
Flood, Curt 129, 191
Florida 133, 176
Fort Worth, Texas 2
Fortugno, Tim 26, 60
Foxx, Jimmie 113
Freeman, Freddie 107–108, 110–112
Freese, David 146
Fresno, California 165, 176
Frick, Ford C. 195
Frisch, Frankie 43

Gaffney, James 67
Gagné, Eric 135
Galvin, Pud 138
Garvey, Steve 44, 173
Gatun, Panama 81
Gausman, Kevin 200
Gehrig, Lou 20, 41, 74, 92, 113
Gentry, Gary 170
Georgia 77
Gerónimo, César 118, 131, 163, 168, 175
Giambi, Jason 50
Giannoulas, Ted 173
Gibson, Bob 80, 118, 120–122, 124, 126–130, 139, 148, 154, 156, 159, 163, 168, 172, 174–179, 182, 184, 190–192, 197
Gibson, Kirk 62, 145, 171
Giolito, Lucas 200
Glavine, Tom 149
Goldschmidt, Paul 109–111
Gonzalez, Luis 143
Gooden, Dwight 45, 197, 199
Gordon, Joe 36
Gowdy, Hank 125
Gray, Sonny 200
Green Bay Packers 174
Greinke, Zach 116, 188, 192, 196–197, 199, 201
Griffey, Ken, Jr. 2, 45, 78, 113, 179
Griffey, Ken, Sr. 78, 179
Griffith, Clark 100
Grove, Lefty 120
Gwynn, Tony 9, 19–20, 22–23, 26, 32, 35, 38, 46–47, 65, 76, 82–83, 86, 88–89, 93, 95, 101, 174, 181

Hamels, Cole 199
Haney, Chris 26, 41, 60
Harang, Aaron 118
Havre de Grace, Maryland 182
Heilmann, Harry 103
Helton, Todd 45
Henderson, Dave 130
Henderson, Rickey 9, 17, 19, 23, 26, 32–35, 38, 43–44, 46–47, 49, 59, 65, 76, 82–83, 86, 89–91, 93, 95, 119, 130, 161, 172, 174, 193
Henrich, Tommy 69
Hernandez, Keith 45, 118, 133, 164–165
Hershiser, Orel 44
Hodges, Gil 44
Hornsby, Roger 100, 104–106
Hosmer, Eric 110, 112, 118, 164
Houston, Texas 65, 159
Houston Astros 37, 48, 134, 142, 152, 156–157, 159, 161, 170, 202
Houston Colt .45s 159
Howard, Elston 14
Howitt, Dan 131
Hubbard, Texas 181
Humbolt, Kansas 178
Hunter, Catfish 22, 136
Hutchinson, Fred 72

Illinois 77, 82
Irvin, Monte 43

Jackson, Reggie 74
The Jacksons 171
Jacobs, Bucky 122
James, Bill 92, 129, 135, 139, 150, 161; Bill James Online 135; black ink test 139–141; *The New Bill James Historical Baseball Abstract* 135
Japan 13, 35, 77, 83, 97, 131, 204
Jenkins, Ferguson 118, 121, 135–136, 145, 154, 156, 169, 172–173, 177, 179–180, 184, 186
Jeter, Derek 9, 14–15, 19, 23, 27, 30, 32, 38, 41, 46, 49–50, 52–53, 63, 65, 70, 74, 76, 80, 83, 86–89, 92–93, 95, 98, 141, 192
John, Elton 171
Johnson, Randy 2, 117–118, 121, 132, 140–144, 146, 148, 152, 154, 156, 158–160, 163, 169, 176–177, 180–181, 184, 186–187, 192, 201
Johnson, Walter 101, 117–126, 129, 135, 138–139, 141–142, 149, 153–154, 157, 159, 164, 168–169, 176–179, 183–187, 190, 194–195, 198
Jones, Andrew 113
Jones, Randy 173
Jones, Sam 72

219

Index

Kaline, Al 9, 14–17, 19, 26, 32, 37, 46–47, 49–50, 65, 70, 76, 78–80, 86, 93, 95, 113, 181
Kansas 176
Kansas City, Missouri 65, 71
Kansas City Athletics 43–44, 160–161
Kansas City Royals 38, 46, 48, 134, 158, 160
Keeler, Willie 22, 42, 96, 100, 104–105
Kennedy, John F. 169
Kentucky 188
Kershaw, Clayton 44, 116, 132, 148, 171, 188, 196–199, 201
Klein, Chuck 35, 96
knuckleball 138
Koosman, Jerry 45, 170
Korean War 20
Koufax, Sandy 44, 132–133, 147, 149, 171, 198
Kroc, Ray 173

Lajoie, Nap 8, 18–19, 25, 32, 35, 37, 39–40, 46, 49–50, 54, 65, 67–68, 76–77, 86, 88, 93, 95–96
Lamp, Dennis 26, 60
Lansford, Carney 130
Leake, Mike 27, 59–60
Lee, Cliff 151
Leonard, Dutch 128
Lincoln, Abraham 81
Lolich, Mickey 189–192
Long Island, New York 77, 80, 83
Longoria, Evan 109–111
Lopez, Felipe 118
Los Angeles, California 43–44, 76, 82, 168, 170–171, 181, 201
Los Angeles Angels 37, 39–40, 151, 158–159, 171, 197
Los Angeles Dodgers 38, 44, 48, 137, 145, 156, 160–161, 171
Los Angeles Times 145
Louisiana State University 202
Lowell, Mike 118, 142, 163
Lynn, Fred 13
Lynn, Lance 200, 204

Machado, Manny 110, 112–114
Mack, Connie 33
Macmillan Baseball Encyclopedia 50
Maddux, Greg 118, 121, 136–137, 143–145, 148–150, 154, 156–157, 167, 169, 171–172, 176–178, 180–181, 184, 186–187, 197–199
Madonna 171
Manakin Sabot, Virginia 178
Mantle, Mickey 41, 74, 79, 113
Marshalltown, Iowa 77
Martínez, Edgar 45
Martínez, Pedro 118, 121, 136, 144,
147–149, 151, 153–154, 156, 159–160, 168, 177, 179–181, 184, 186, 197–198
Maryland 77, 83
Mathews, Eddie 113
Mathewson, Christy 120, 195, 198
Matlack, Jon 26, 59–60
Mattingly, Don 41, 54
Mayer, Erskine 25, 51, 60
Mays, Carl 68, 165
Mays, Willie 2, 9, 15–16, 18–21, 26, 32, 38, 43, 46–48, 50, 59, 61, 64, 76, 78, 83, 86–87, 91–93, 95, 100, 113, 181
McCarthy, Joe 69
McCarver, Tim 128
McCovey, Willie 78, 181
McCutchen, Andrew 107, 110–111
McGraw, John 43
McGwire, Mark 130
McHale, Marty 25, 60
McKeon, Jack 6
McLain, Denny 128, 191–192
McNally, Dave 26, 60
memory palace technique 1
Merkle, Fred 145
Mesa, José 26, 60, 63
Miami Marlins 38, 48, 53–54
Michaels, Al 70
Michigan 176
Miley, Wade 27, 60
Milwaukee, Wisconsin 39, 64, 67, 151, 168, 172, 174–175
Milwaukee Brewers 38, 48, 151, 156, 158, 161, 175
Minneapolis, Minnesota 39, 64, 80, 157–159
Minnesota 43, 47, 71, 77
Minnesota Twins 21, 38–39, 43, 46–48, 61–62, 70–71, 132, 135, 139, 150, 156, 158–159, 172
"Miracle Mets" 170
Missouri 176
Molitor, Paul 9, 17, 19, 26, 30, 32, 38, 43, 46, 49, 53, 61, 65, 70–71, 76, 82–83, 86, 93–95, 101, 109–110, 112, 181
Montgomery, Bob 69
Montréal, Canada 47, 65
Montréal Expos 39, 42, 44–47, 158, 165–166
Morneau, Justin 15, 135
Morris, Jack 139, 146, 150, 173
Munson, Thurman 22
Murphy, John Ryan 118
Murray, Eddie 9, 19, 26, 32, 37, 39, 46–48, 56, 59, 64, 70, 76, 82–83, 86, 89, 93, 95, 113, 172, 181
Musial, Stan 9, 16, 19–20, 26, 30, 32, 38, 46, 49–50, 54, 65, 71–73, 76, 78, 86–87, 89, 92–93, 95, 107, 171–172, 179

220

Index

Mussina, Mike 189, 192–193
Myers, Elmer 25, 33, 60

Nagoya, Japan, 83
Namath, Joe 78, 179
National Association 10–11
National Baseball Hall of Fame and Museum 8, 10, 21–22, 36, 45, 50, 62, 65, 78, 100–105, 119, 135, 139, 164–165, 190, 192, 195, 197; *see also* Cooperstown, New York
National League 11, 14, 23, 40, 44, 48–49, 65, 68, 82, 96, 103, 126–127, 142, 146, 148–149, 151, 158–159, 173–174, 191, 194, 198, 202
National League Championship Series (NLCS): (1969) 138; (1971) 130; (1980) 134; (1982) 138; (1984) 173; (1991) 150; (1992) 150; (2009) 151; (2022) 202
National League Division Series (NLDS): (1995) 2; (1997) 192; (2001) 192; (2004) 146; (2008) 150, 151; (2023) 199
Nebraska 41, 82, 84, 127, 176
Netherlands 139, 179
New York 75, 77
New York, New York 14, 48, 65, 75, 80, 101, 170
New York Giants 26, 42–43, 48, 82, 125, 145
New York Knickerbocker Club 75
New York Mets 44–46, 104, 133–135, 152, 156, 159–160, 165, 170
New York Times 6, 145
New York Yankees 2, 10, 14, 23, 33, 38–39, 41, 43, 46–48, 50, 52, 67, 69, 73–74, 103, 125, 140, 143, 147, 150–151, 156–157, 160, 165, 174, 192, 201
Newcombe, Don 195
Nicaragua 20
Niekro, Joe 138
Niekro, Phil 117–118, 121, 137–139, 153–157, 168, 176–181, 184–187, 199
Nine: A Journal of Baseball History and Culture 1
Nippon Professional Baseball 35, 83
no-hitter 130, 139, 152, 171, 198
Nola, Aaron 200, 202–204
Nola, Austin 202
North Carolina 176
Northrup, Jim 129

Oakland, California 82, 161
Oakland Athletics 26, 43, 46–47, 62, 118, 130, 136, 160–161, 168, 171
Ohio 81, 176, 178, 181
Oklahoma 78
Oliva, Tony 21
Omaha, Nebraska 41, 127, 178, 182

O'Malley, Walter 171
Ortiz, David 54
Oswalt, Roy 129
Ott, Mel 43, 113

Paige, Satchel 78, 181
Palmeiro, Rafael 9–10, 19, 26, 32, 37, 43, 46, 49, 65, 76, 83, 86–87, 93, 96, 119
Palmer, Jim 175
Panama 22, 77, 81
pandemic 188, 197, 201; *see also* COVID-19 pandemic
Parrish, Larry 118
Pederson, Joc 177
pennant (American League): 1907–9, Tigers 101; 1920, Indians 164; 1924–25, 1933, Senators 101, 169; 1929–31, Philadelphia Athletics 105; 1965, Twins 21; 1968, Tigers 191; 1969, Orioles 104; 1995, Mariners 2
pennant (National League): 1908, N.Y. Giants 145; 1951, N.Y. Giants 82; 1957–58, Braves 174; 1961, Reds 103; 1967–68, Cardinals 174
Pennsylvania 77–78, 181
Pequannock, New Jersey 80
Perry, Gaylord 63, 118, 121, 129–130, 137–140, 153–154, 156, 158, 169, 172–173, 176–179, 184–186, 199
Perry, Jim 138
Philadelphia, Pennsylvania 43–44, 64, 66, 80, 165, 169
Philadelphia Athletics 32–33, 40, 43–45, 47, 59, 105–106, 160–161
Philadelphia Phillies 42, 44, 46, 66–67, 134–136, 146, 151, 156, 160, 165, 179, 202
Philadelphia Quakers 44
Phoenix, Arizona 168, 179
Piñeiro, Joel 26, 60
Pittsburgh, Pennsylvania 25, 65, 67, 78, 80, 179
Pittsburgh Pirates 25–26, 38–39, 46, 48, 51, 67, 84, 130, 139, 150, 169–170, 201
Plank, Eddie 162
Pope John Paul II 171
Posnanski, Joe 105
Presley, Elvis 171
Price, David 27, 52, 63
Puerto Rico, 20, 77–78
Pujols, Albert 10, 14, 19, 23–24, 27, 30, 32, 37, 39–40, 46, 49, 54, 59, 65, 76, 83, 86, 91, 93, 95, 104, 113–114, 141, 179, 181

Raines, Tim 69
Randolph, Willie 73
Ray, Robbie 200, 203–204
Reese, Pee Wee 44
Refugio, Texas 159, 178

Index

Rentería, Edgar 141
Retrosheet 50, 65, 117
Reyes, Jose 45
Rhode Island 77
Rice, Sam 99–105, 190
Richmond, Virginia 178
Ripken, Cal, Jr. 9, 19, 26, 32, 37, 43, 46–48, 64, 70, 76, 82–84, 86, 93, 95, 172, 182, 192
Rivera, Mariano 143, 148
Robinson, Frank 100, 103–104, 106, 113
Robinson, Jackie 13, 44
Rodríguez, Álex 9–10, 19, 23, 27, 32, 38, 46–47, 49, 52–53, 62, 65, 70, 74, 76, 80, 83, 86, 91, 93, 95, 113, 119, 163
Rodríguez, Eduardo 200
Rogers, Steve 26, 60
Rollins, Jimmy 34, 177
Rosado, José 26, 60–62
Rosario, Amed 103
Rose, Pete 9–10, 19, 26, 30, 32–33, 37, 42, 45–47, 49, 54, 56, 65–66, 76, 80–81, 83–84, 86–89, 92–93, 95, 103, 172–173, 181
round number bias 5, 99, 101, 137, 164, 190
Ruel, Muddy 125–126
Rusin, Chris 27, 60
Ruth, Babe 16, 20, 41, 61, 66–67, 74, 140, 173
Ryan, Nolan 2, 10, 77, 117–118, 120–121, 125, 130–134, 137, 140, 142, 145, 148, 150, 153–156, 159, 163, 169–170, 172–173, 175–178, 180–181, 184, 186, 193, 199

Sabathia, CC 118–121, 150–151, 154, 156, 164, 168, 176–177, 180–181, 184
St. Louis, Missouri 64, 71–72, 89, 114, 174, 168, 172, 174, 178, 191
St. Louis Browns 42, 47, 68, 115
St. Louis Cardinals 14, 26, 38–39, 48, 71–72, 80, 128–129, 133–134, 156, 160, 165, 174–175, 191
St. Paul, Minnesota 39, 70–71, 80, 82, 181
St. Petersburg, Florida 41
Sale, Chris 199–200, 203
San Angelo, Texas 178, 181
San Diego, California 35, 65, 169, 172–173, 178
San Diego Chicken 173; *see also* Giannoulas, Ted
San Diego Padres 23, 26, 35, 38–39, 44, 48, 130, 156, 158, 161, 173–174, 202
San Francisco, California 43, 64, 130, 165, 176
San Francisco Giants 38, 43, 48, 130, 135, 187
Santo, Ron 113
Scherzer, Max 118–121, 136, 151–152, 154, 156, 160, 164, 168, 171, 176–178, 180, 184, 186, 199, 201

Schilling, Curt 118–119, 121, 136, 143, 145–147, 149, 154, 156, 164, 168, 177, 179–180, 184–185; "Bloody sock" starts 146–147
Schmidt, Mike 44
Schulte, Frank 14
Scully, Vin 62
Seattle, Washington 2, 45, 65, 131
Seattle Mariners 2, 34, 44–47, 97, 140, 142, 158, 160, 174
Seattle Pilots 174
Seaver, Tom 22, 45, 117–118, 121, 133–138, 141, 151, 154, 156, 165, 169–170, 172–173, 176–177, 180–181, 184
Senzatela, Antonio 27, 60
Sewell, Rip 25, 58, 60, 67
Shocker, Urban 115
"Shot Heard 'Round the World" 82
Shur, Gus 36
Simmons, Al 100, 104–105
Simpson, Joe 118
Simpson, Wayne 26, 60–61
Sisler, George 34
Smith, Dan 26, 60
Smith, David W. 117
Smith, Elmer 69
Smith, Mayo 191
Smith, Red 36
Smoltz, John 118, 120–121, 139, 149–150, 153–154, 156–157, 169, 176–177, 180, 184–187
Snell, Blake 200
Snider, Duke 44
Society for American Baseball Research (SABR) 2–3, 77, 147; Biography Project 2; Games Project 2
Soriano, Alphonso 143
Spahn, Warren 122–123, 158, 160, 189
Spalding Guide 49–50
Speaker, Tris 8, 18–19, 25, 30, 32, 37, 39, 46, 48, 57–59, 65, 68, 76–77, 86–88, 93, 95, 103, 181
spitball 129, 137, 164
stadiums: Anaheim Stadium 64, 168, 171–172; Arlington Stadium 168; Baker Bowl 64–67; Braves Field 64, 67; Briggs Stadium 67; Busch Memorial Stadium 64; Busch Stadium I 72; Busch Stadium II 168, 172, 174; Candlestick Park 43, 64; Chase Field 168; Comerica Park 6, 64; Comiskey Park 16; Coors Field 64, 145; County Stadium 64, 168, 172, 174–175; Crosley Field 64–66; Dodger Stadium 168, 170–171, 174; Ebbets Field 69; Fenway Park 54, 64, 67, 71, 73, 171; Globe Life Park 64; Great American Ballpark 168; Griffith Stadium 124, 126, 168–169; Hubert H. Humphrey Metrodome 47,

Index

64, 70, 168, 172; Jack Murphy Stadium 168–169, 172–173; Kauffman Stadium 65, 71; League Park 65, 67–70; Los Angeles Memorial Coliseum 170–171; McAfee Coliseum 168; Memorial Stadium 65, 80; Minute Maid Park 65; Navin Field 65–67; Olympic Stadium 65; Pro Player Stadium 168; Qualcomm Stadium 65, 174; Redland Field 65; Riverfront Stadium 65–66, 168–170, 172–174; Safeco Field 65; San Diego Stadium 169, 173; Shea Stadium 74; Skydome 169; Sportsman's Park 72; Three Rivers Stadium 65; Tiger Stadium 67; Tropicana Field 41; Turner Field 169; Veterans Stadium 169; Wrigley Field 65, 71–72, 169, 171–172, 174; Yankee Stadium 23, 52, 65, 70, 74, 80, 163
Strasburg, Stephen 200, 205
strike zone changes 126
strikeout rate (historic) 126–127
Sutton, Don 117–118, 121, 137–140, 149–150, 154, 156, 158, 160–161, 168, 172, 175–177, 180–181, 184, 186–187
Suzuki, Ichiro 9–10, 13–14, 16, 19, 23, 27, 32–35, 38, 45–47, 49, 53–54, 57–58, 64, 76, 83, 86, 88–89, 92–97, 109–110, 131
Swisher, Nick 118

Taft, Howard 169
Tammany Hall 67
Tampa, Florida 41, 65, 84, 182
Tampa Bay Rays 26–27, 38, 41, 46, 48, 52, 118, 158
Tanana, Frank 189, 193
Temple Cup 68
Templeton, Garry 118
Terry, Bill 43
Texas 77, 130, 159, 168, 176, 178, 181
Texas Rangers 2, 27, 38, 48, 52, 131, 136, 139, 152, 158–159, 204
Thomson, Bobby 82
Thomson, John 26, 59–60
The 3,000 Hit Club: Stories of Baseball's Greatest Hitters 3, 12
The Three Tenors 171
RMS *Titanic* 81
Tommy John surgery 149, 203
Toronto, Canada 146, 169
Toronto Blue Jays 44, 48, 156, 160
Torre, Joe 10
Trammell, Alan 36
triple crown: batting 15, 40, 103, 105; pitching 141, 151
Triple Play 69–70
Trombley, Mike 26, 59–60, 70
Trout, Mike 110, 112–114
Tulowitski, Troy 177

University of California–Los Angeles 201

Valenzuela, Fernando 44, 171
Vallejo, California 176
Venezuela, 77, 83
Verlander, Justin 27, 52, 60, 62–63, 118–121, 136, 141, 151–152, 154, 156, 163–164, 168, 172, 176–178, 180, 184, 186, 199
Versalles, Zoilo 21
Victoria, British Colombia 135
Viola, Frank 26, 60, 63, 81
Virginia 176, 178
Vizquel, Omar 118, 144, 164, 166–167
Votto, Joey 107, 109–111, 135

Waddell, Rube 123
Wagner, Honus 8, 16, 18–19, 23, 25, 30, 32, 38, 46, 49–51, 54, 64–66, 76–78, 80, 84–86, 88, 93, 95, 179
Wainwright, Adam 114, 199
Walker, Larry 135
Wallach, Tim 118, 165–166
Walnut Creek, California 176
Wambsganss, Bill 69–70
Waner, Paul 8, 16, 19–20, 25, 32, 37, 39, 46, 58, 64, 67, 76, 78, 86, 88–89, 92–93, 95, 100, 121
Washington, D.C. 21, 39, 124, 126, 157, 168–169
Washington Nationals 39, 44, 126, 152, 160, 205
Washington Senators 21, 38–39, 42–43, 46, 48, 100–101, 124–126, 157–159, 169–170, 185
"We Are Family" Pittsburgh Pirates 139
Webb, Earl 1
Webb, Logan 187
Wegener, Mike 26, 59–60
West Virgina 82
Westfield, Alabama 181
Wheeler, Zack 200
Williams, Ted 20, 34, 42, 59, 100
Williamston, North Carolina 178
Winfield, Dave 9, 19, 26, 32, 38, 43, 46–47, 62, 64, 70–71, 76, 80, 82–84, 86, 91, 93–94, 96, 109–112, 172, 181
Winn, Early 63
Winn, Randy 118, 166
Wood, Wilber 186, 190
Woods, Kerry 152
World Series 1, 36, 62, 69–70, 101, 107, 146–147, 171, 174, 192; (1903) 41; (1909) 51; (1919) 92, 161; (1920) 68–69, 164; (1924) 101, 125, 169; (1925) 169, (1929) 105–106; (1930) 105; (1931) 105; (1957) 67, 174; (1958) 174; (1959) 170; (1961) 103; (1963) 171; (1964) 129; (1966) 103; (1967) 80, 129, 174; (1968) 129, 174, 190–191;

Index

(1969) 104, 134, 170; (1970) 173; (1972) 173; (1974) 137; (1975) 173; (1976) 173; (1977) 137; (1978) 137; (1979) 139; (1980) 134; (1982) 137, 175; (1984) 173; (1986) 62, 135, 145; (1987) 70, 139; (1988) 62, 146, 171; (1991) 70, 146, 150; (1992) 150; (1993) 146; (1996) 50; (1998) 174; (2001) 50, 143, 146 192; (2003) 192; (2004) 147; (2009) 151; (2011) 146; (2013) 2; (2014) 146; (2017) 202; (2019) 126, 152, 205; (2022) 202; (2023) 152
World Series MVP 80, 129, 139, 141, 146, 205
World War I 100
World War II 20–21, 122–123, 126, 158, 179, 181
Wright, David 45

Xavier University 188

Yastrzemski, Carl 9, 15, 19, 22, 26, 30, 32, 37, 42, 46, 64, 73, 76, 80–81, 86, 89, 93, 95, 171
"The Year of the Pitcher" 128, 190
Young, Cy 68, 120, 124, 138, 189, 193–195
Yount, Robin 9, 19, 22–23, 26, 32, 38, 46–47, 63–64, 76, 82, 86, 88–89, 91–93, 96, 133, 172, 175

Zachary, Tom 25, 60
Zeist, Netherlands 139

www.ingramcontent.com/pod-product-compliance
Ingram Content Group UK Ltd.
Pitfield, Milton Keynes, MK11 3LW, UK
UKHW032036070125
453275UK00004BA/185